UNTOLD COMIC TALES FROM THE HIT TV SERIES ON THE CW

RIVERDALE®

ALL-NEW STORIES

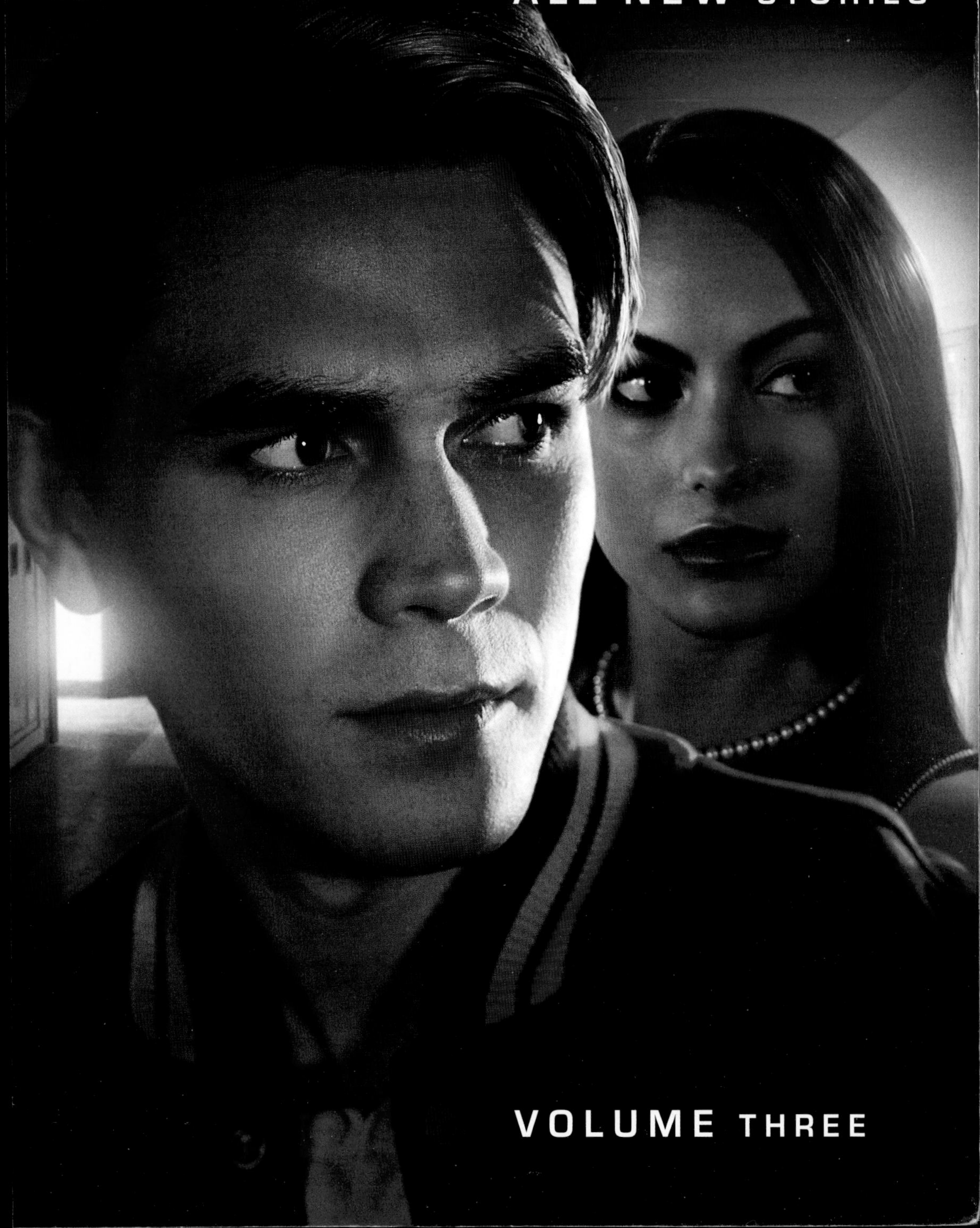

VOLUME THREE

UNTOLD COMIC TALES FROM THE HIT TV SERIES ON THE CW

RIVERDALE®

WRITTEN BY:
GREG MURRAY & AARON ALLEN

WITH ART BY:
THOMAS PITILLI, ANDRE SZYMANOWICZ,
JANICE CHIANG & JOHN WORKMAN

CHIEF EXECUTIVE OFFICER/PUBLISHER:
JON GOLDWATER

CHIEF CREATIVE OFFICER:
ROBERTO AGUIRRE-SACASA

EDITOR-IN-CHIEF:
VICTOR GORELICK

LEAD DESIGNER:
KARI MCLACHLAN

All photos courtesy of The CW/Warner Bros.

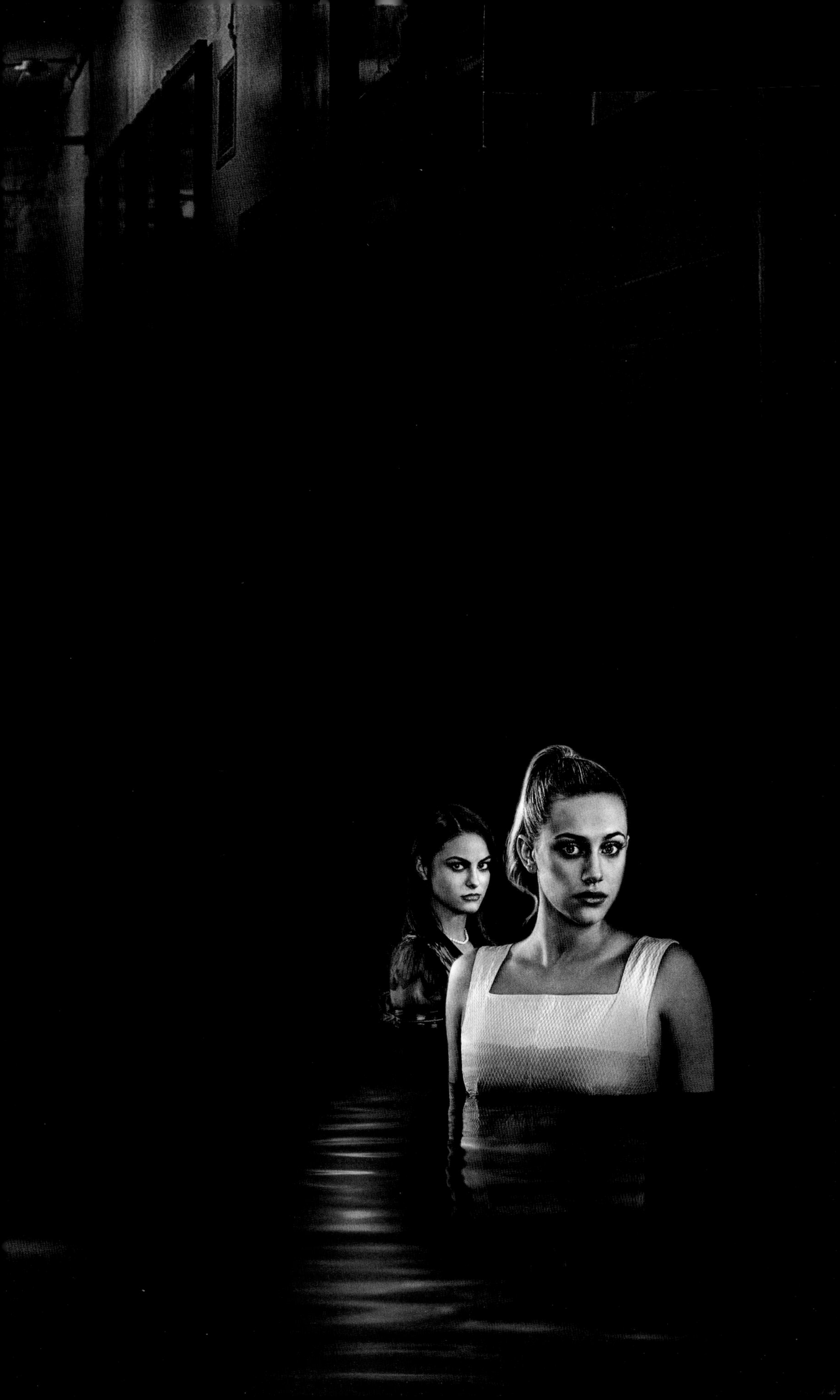

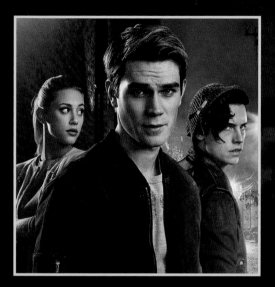

HANDS ON A
HARD BODY

WRITER:
GREG MURRAY

ART:
THOMAS PITILLI

COLORS:
ANDRE SZYMANOWICZ

LETTERS:
JANICE CHIANG

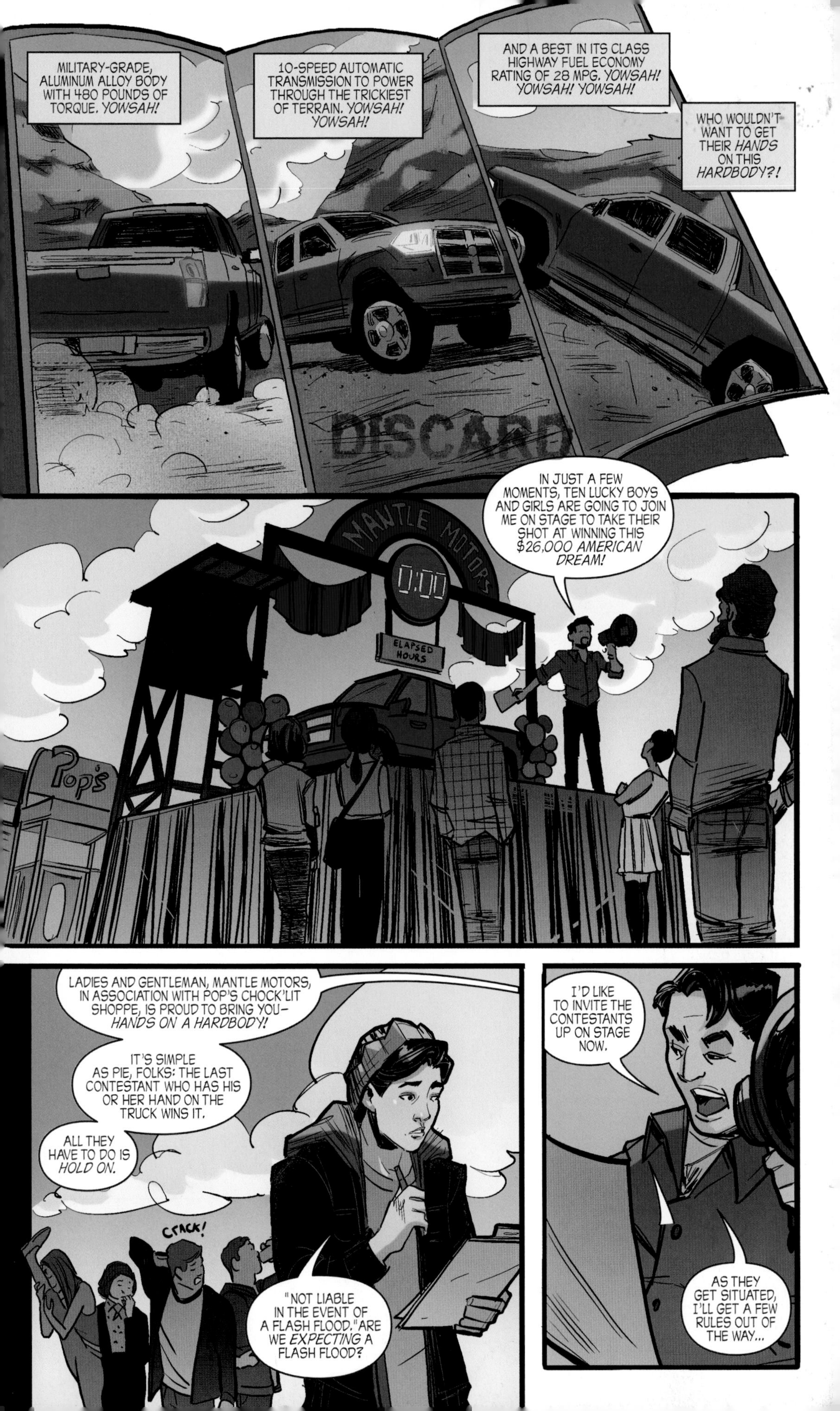
MILITARY-GRADE, ALUMINUM ALLOY BODY WITH 480 POUNDS OF TORQUE. YOWSAH!
10-SPEED AUTOMATIC TRANSMISSION TO POWER THROUGH THE TRICKIEST OF TERRAIN. YOWSAH! YOWSAH!
AND A BEST IN ITS CLASS HIGHWAY FUEL ECONOMY RATING OF 28 MPG. YOWSAH! YOWSAH! YOWSAH!
WHO WOULDN'T WANT TO GET THEIR HANDS ON THIS HARDBODY?!
DISCARD
IN JUST A FEW MOMENTS, TEN LUCKY BOYS AND GIRLS ARE GOING TO JOIN ME ON STAGE TO TAKE THEIR SHOT AT WINNING THIS $26,000 AMERICAN DREAM!
MANTLE MOTORS
0:00
ELAPSED HOURS
Pop's
LADIES AND GENTLEMAN, MANTLE MOTORS, IN ASSOCIATION WITH POP'S CHOCK'LIT SHOPPE, IS PROUD TO BRING YOU—HANDS ON A HARDBODY!
IT'S SIMPLE AS PIE, FOLKS: THE LAST CONTESTANT WHO HAS HIS OR HER HAND ON THE TRUCK WINS IT.
ALL THEY HAVE TO DO IS HOLD ON.
CRACK!
"NOT LIABLE IN THE EVENT OF A FLASH FLOOD." ARE WE EXPECTING A FLASH FLOOD?
I'D LIKE TO INVITE THE CONTESTANTS UP ON STAGE NOW.
AS THEY GET SITUATED, I'LL GET A FEW RULES OUT OF THE WAY...

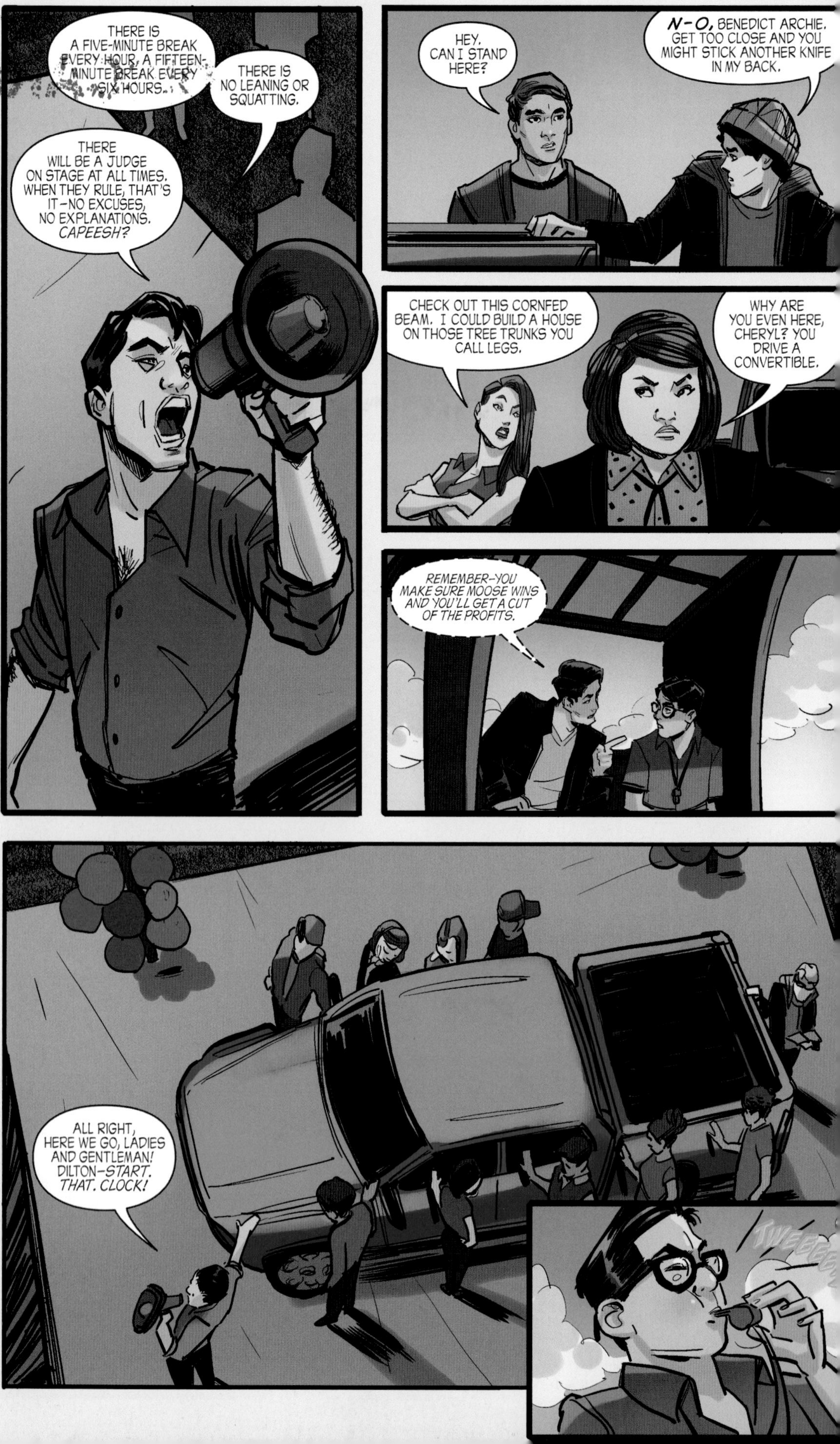
THERE IS A FIVE-MINUTE BREAK EVERY HOUR, A FIFTEEN-MINUTE BREAK EVERY SIX HOURS.
THERE IS NO LEANING OR SQUATTING.
THERE WILL BE A JUDGE ON STAGE AT ALL TIMES. WHEN THEY RULE, THAT'S IT–NO EXCUSES, NO EXPLANATIONS. CAPEESH?
HEY. CAN I STAND HERE?
N–O, BENEDICT ARCHIE. GET TOO CLOSE AND YOU MIGHT STICK ANOTHER KNIFE IN MY BACK.
CHECK OUT THIS CORNFED BEAM. I COULD BUILD A HOUSE ON THOSE TREE TRUNKS YOU CALL LEGS.
WHY ARE YOU EVEN HERE, CHERYL? YOU DRIVE A CONVERTIBLE.
REMEMBER–YOU MAKE SURE MOOSE WINS AND YOU'LL GET A CUT OF THE PROFITS.
ALL RIGHT, HERE WE GO, LADIES AND GENTLEMAN! DILTON–START. THAT. CLOCK!

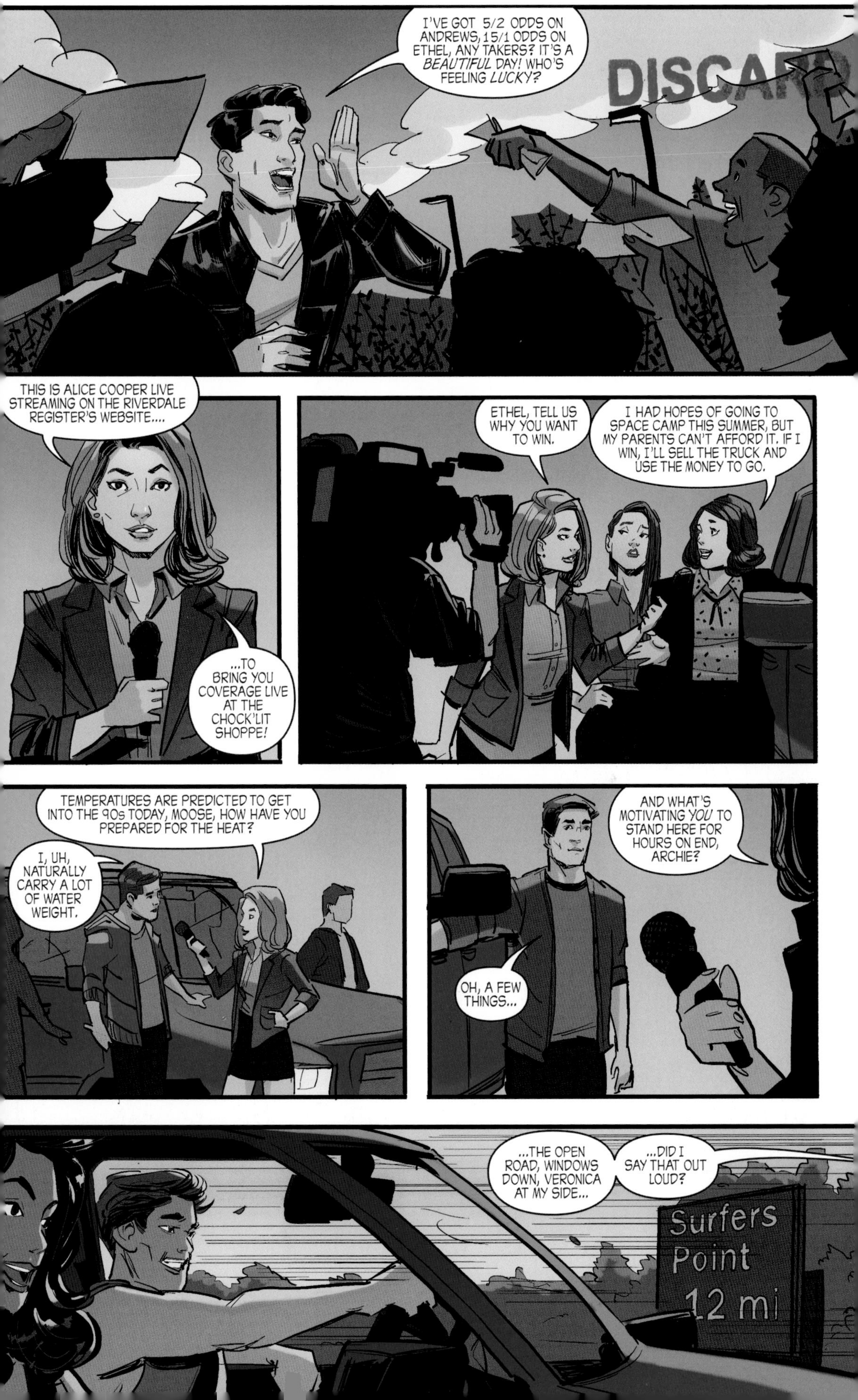

I'VE GOT 5/2 ODDS ON ANDREWS, 15/1 ODDS ON ETHEL, ANY TAKERS? IT'S A *BEAUTIFUL* DAY! WHO'S FEELING *LUCKY*?
DISCA
THIS IS ALICE COOPER LIVE STREAMING ON THE RIVERDALE REGISTER'S WEBSITE....
...TO BRING YOU COVERAGE LIVE AT THE CHOCK'LIT SHOPPE!
ETHEL, TELL US WHY YOU WANT TO WIN.
I HAD HOPES OF GOING TO SPACE CAMP THIS SUMMER, BUT MY PARENTS CAN'T AFFORD IT. IF I WIN, I'LL SELL THE TRUCK AND USE THE MONEY TO GO.
TEMPERATURES ARE PREDICTED TO GET INTO THE 90s TODAY, MOOSE, HOW HAVE YOU PREPARED FOR THE HEAT?
I, UH, NATURALLY CARRY A LOT OF WATER WEIGHT.
AND WHAT'S MOTIVATING *YOU* TO STAND HERE FOR HOURS ON END, ARCHIE?
OH, A FEW THINGS...
...THE OPEN ROAD, WINDOWS DOWN, VERONICA AT MY SIDE...
...DID I SAY THAT OUT LOUD?
Surfers Point 12 mi

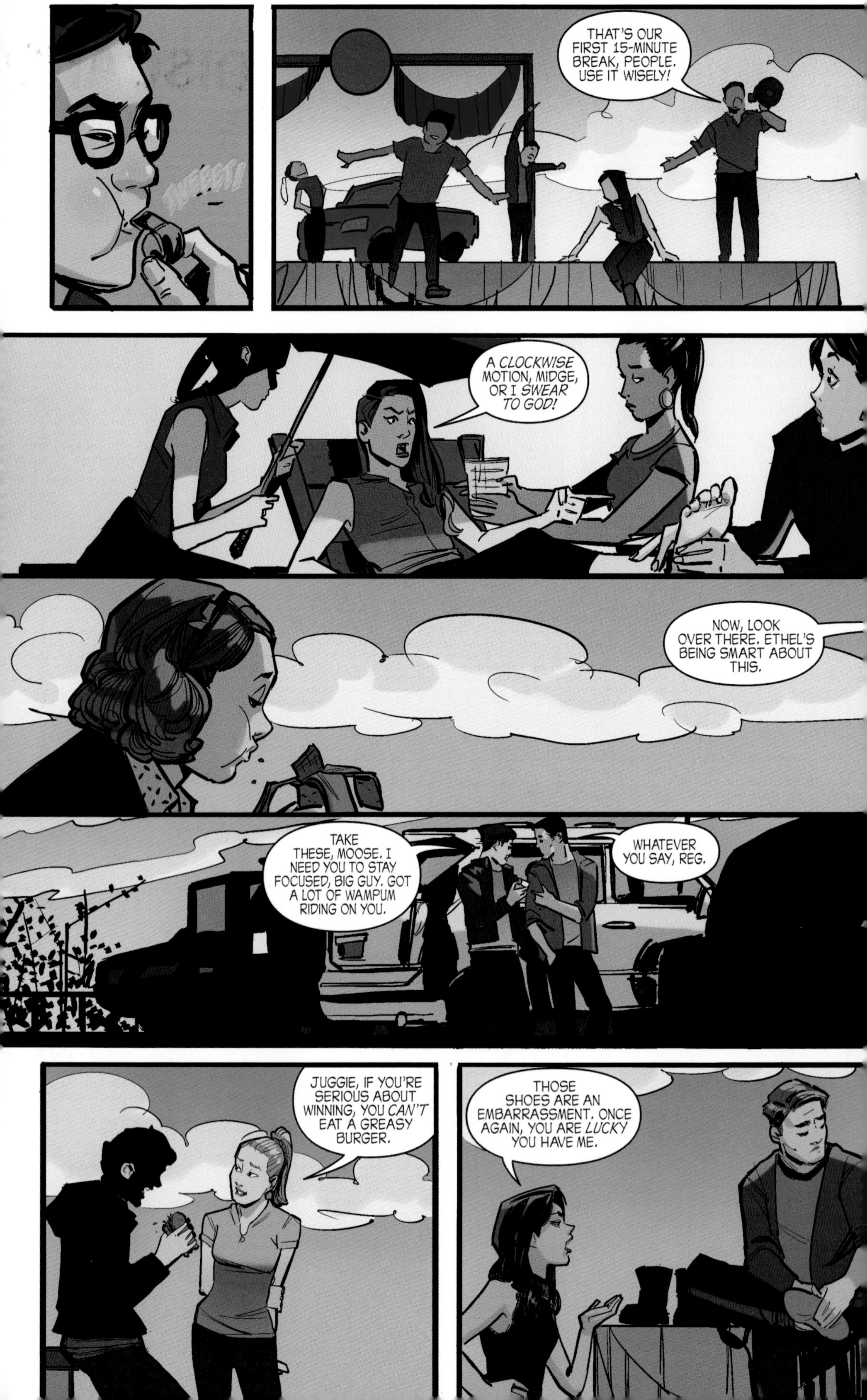
TWEEET!!
THAT'S OUR FIRST 15-MINUTE BREAK, PEOPLE. USE IT WISELY!
A CLOCKWISE MOTION, MIDGE, OR I SWEAR TO GOD!
NOW, LOOK OVER THERE. ETHEL'S BEING SMART ABOUT THIS.
TAKE THESE, MOOSE. I NEED YOU TO STAY FOCUSED, BIG GUY. GOT A LOT OF WAMPUM RIDING ON YOU.
WHATEVER YOU SAY, REG.
JUGGIE, IF YOU'RE SERIOUS ABOUT WINNING, YOU CAN'T EAT A GREASY BURGER.
THOSE SHOES ARE AN EMBARRASSMENT. ONCE AGAIN, YOU ARE LUCKY YOU HAVE ME.

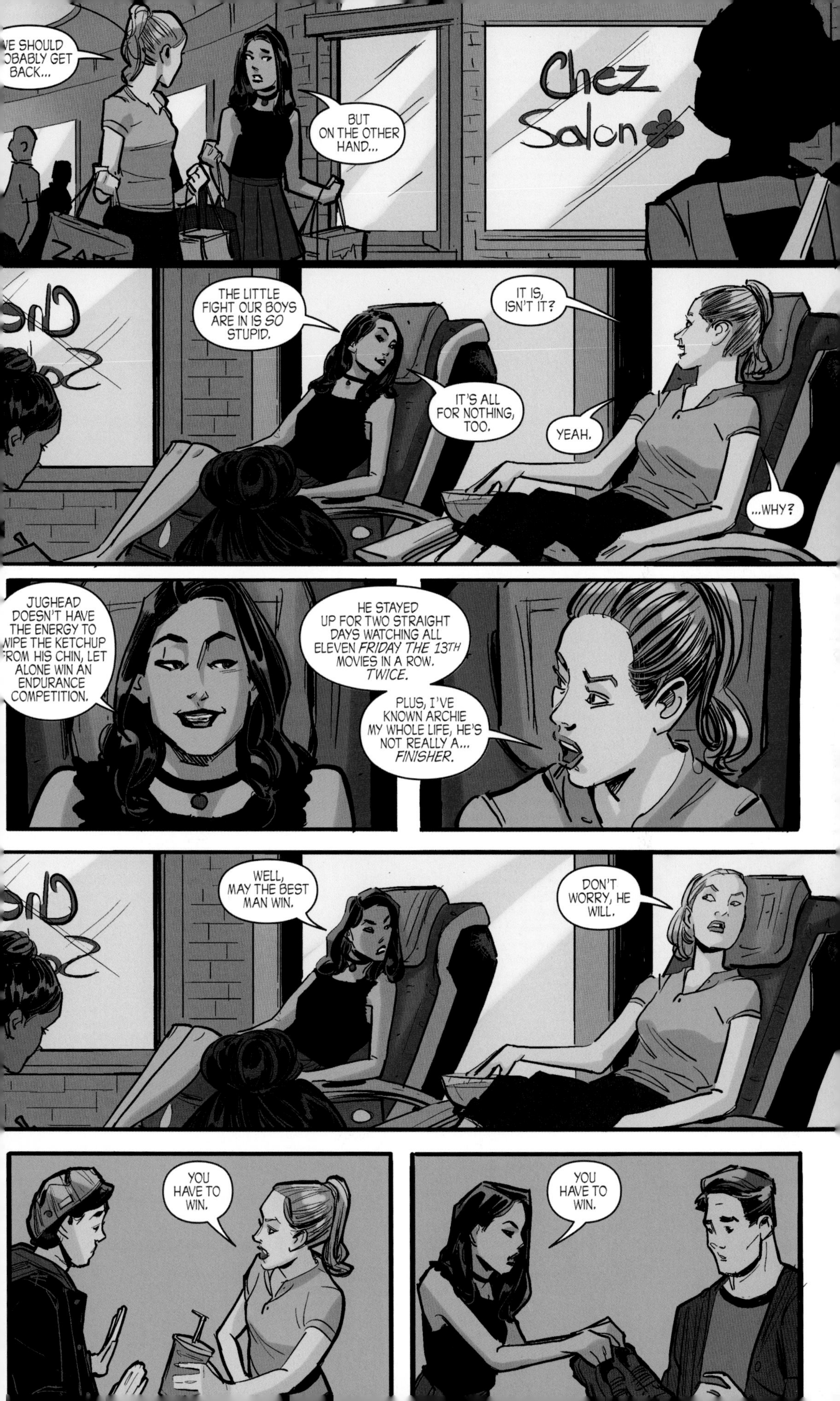

WE SHOULD PROBABLY GET BACK...
BUT ON THE OTHER HAND...
Chez Salon
THE LITTLE FIGHT OUR BOYS ARE IN IS *SO* STUPID.
IT IS, ISN'T IT?
IT'S ALL FOR NOTHING, TOO.
YEAH.
...WHY?
JUGHEAD DOESN'T HAVE THE ENERGY TO WIPE THE KETCHUP FROM HIS CHIN, LET ALONE WIN AN ENDURANCE COMPETITION.
HE STAYED UP FOR TWO STRAIGHT DAYS WATCHING ALL ELEVEN *FRIDAY THE 13TH* MOVIES IN A ROW. *TWICE.*
PLUS, I'VE KNOWN ARCHIE MY WHOLE LIFE, HE'S NOT REALLY A... *FINISHER.*
WELL, MAY THE BEST MAN WIN.
DON'T WORRY, HE WILL.
YOU HAVE TO WIN.
YOU HAVE TO WIN.

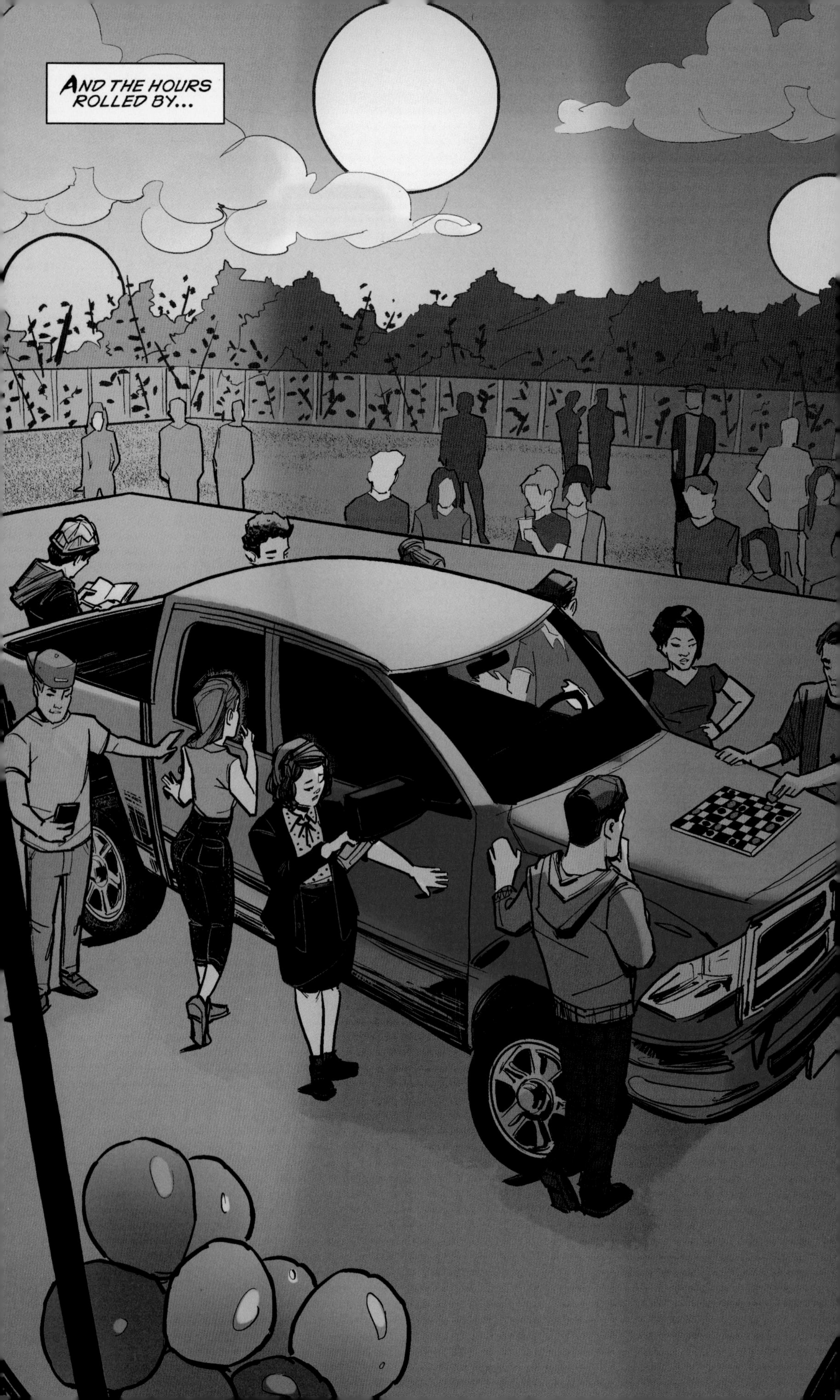
AND THE HOURS ROLLED BY...

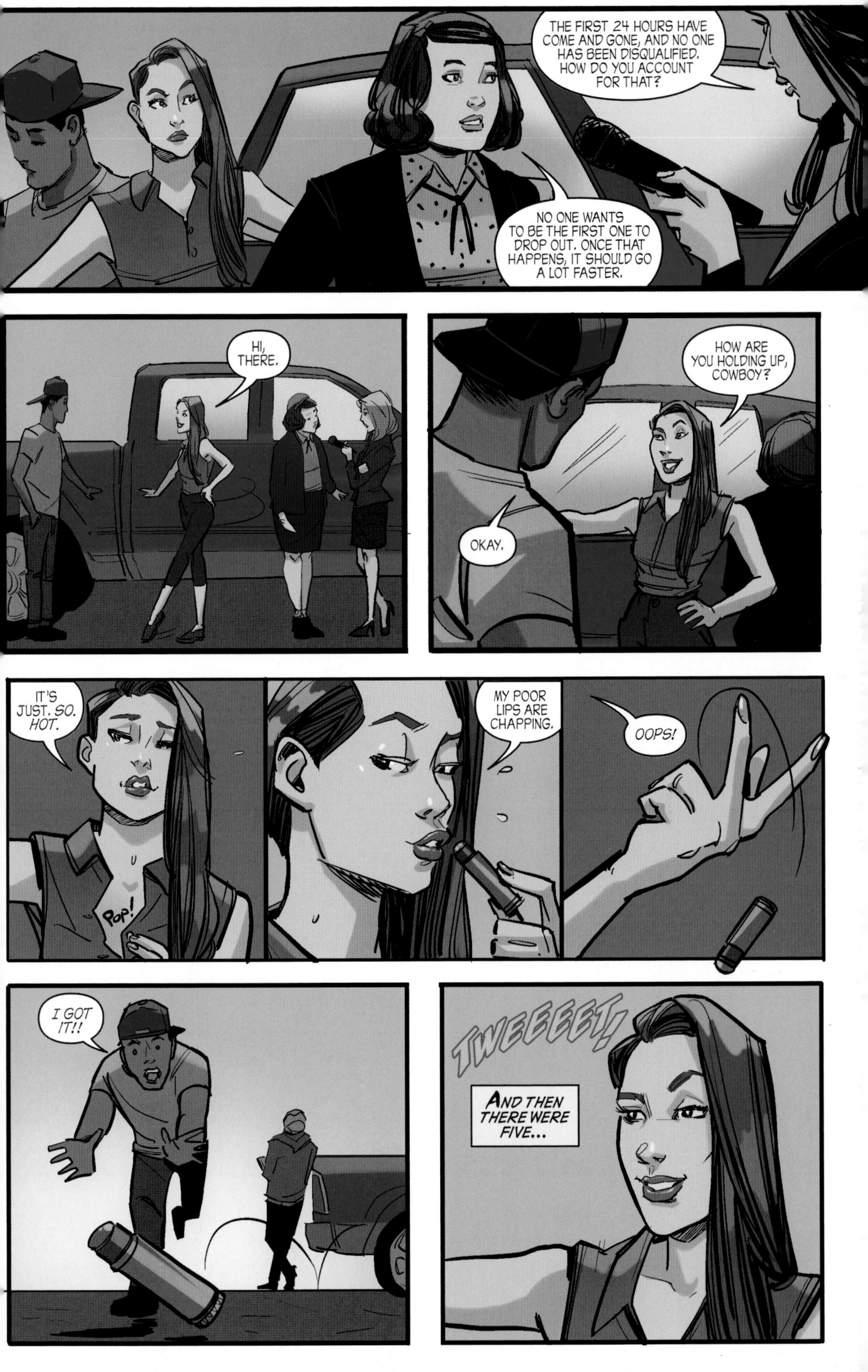
THE FIRST 24 HOURS HAVE COME AND GONE, AND NO ONE HAS BEEN DISQUALIFIED. HOW DO YOU ACCOUNT FOR THAT?
NO ONE WANTS TO BE THE FIRST ONE TO DROP OUT. ONCE THAT HAPPENS, IT SHOULD GO A LOT FASTER.
HI, THERE.
HOW ARE YOU HOLDING UP, COWBOY?
OKAY.
IT'S JUST. SO. HOT.
POP!
MY POOR LIPS ARE CHAPPING.
OOPS!
I GOT IT!!
TWEEEET!
AND THEN THERE WERE FIVE...

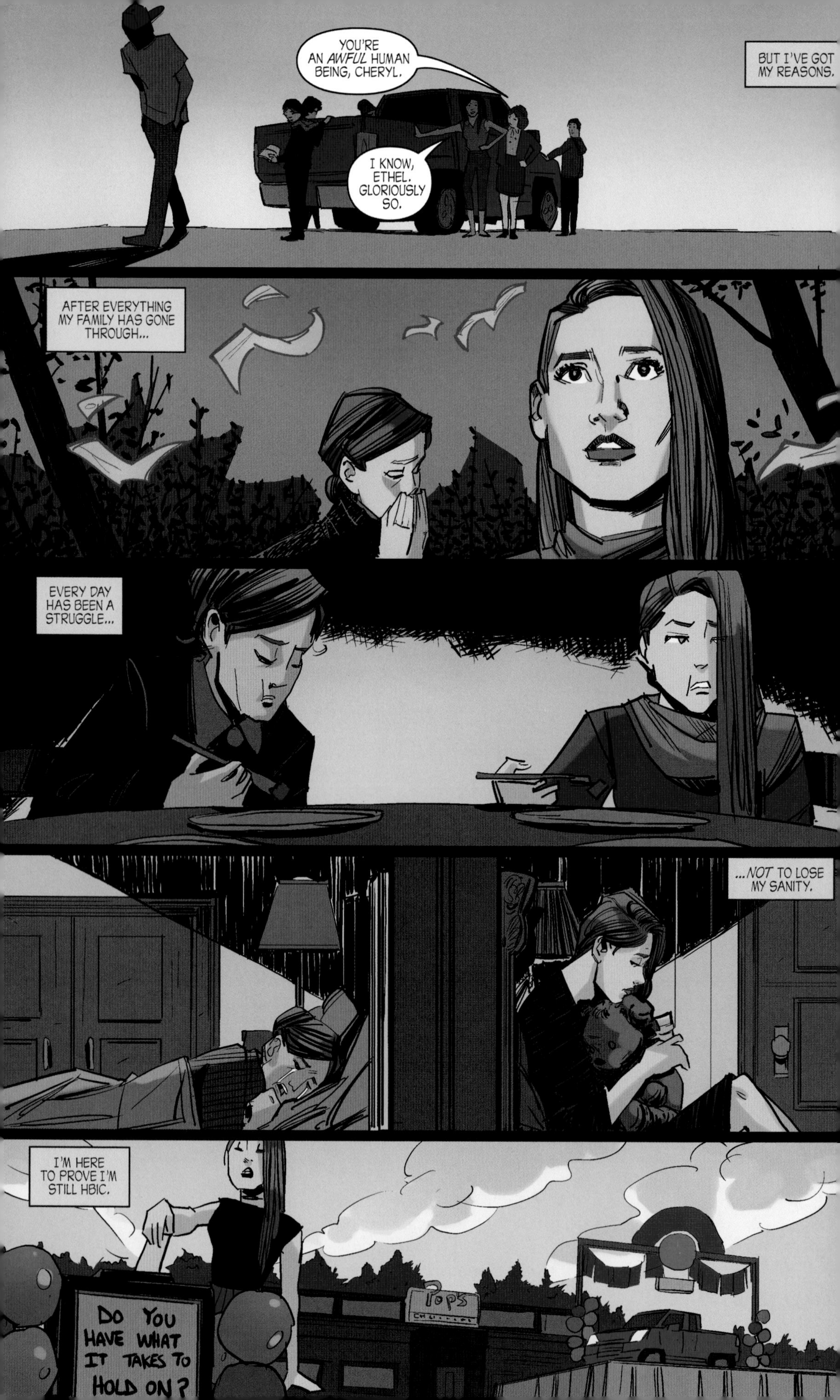
YOU'RE AN *AWFUL* HUMAN BEING, CHERYL.
I KNOW, ETHEL. GLORIOUSLY SO.
BUT I'VE GOT MY REASONS.
AFTER EVERYTHING MY FAMILY HAS GONE THROUGH...
EVERY DAY HAS BEEN A STRUGGLE...
...*NOT* TO LOSE MY SANITY.
I'M HERE TO PROVE I'M STILL HBIC.
DO YOU HAVE WHAT IT TAKES TO HOLD ON?
POP'S

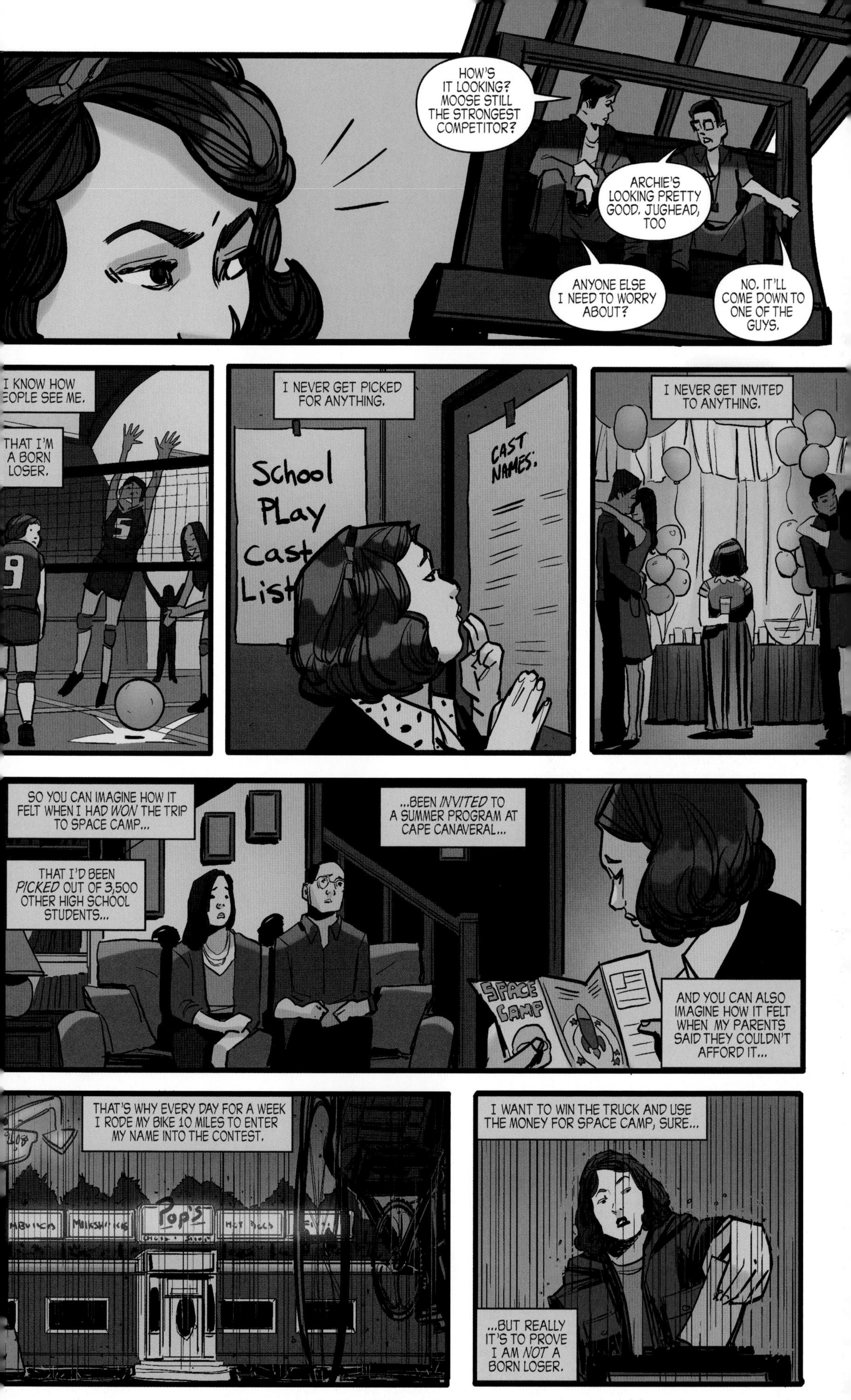
HOW'S IT LOOKING? MOOSE STILL THE STRONGEST COMPETITOR?
ARCHIE'S LOOKING PRETTY GOOD. JUGHEAD, TOO
ANYONE ELSE I NEED TO WORRY ABOUT?
NO. IT'LL COME DOWN TO ONE OF THE GUYS.
I KNOW HOW PEOPLE SEE ME.
THAT I'M A BORN LOSER.
I NEVER GET PICKED FOR ANYTHING.
School Play Cast List
CAST NAMES:
I NEVER GET INVITED TO ANYTHING.
SO YOU CAN IMAGINE HOW IT FELT WHEN I HAD *WON* THE TRIP TO SPACE CAMP...
THAT I'D BEEN *PICKED* OUT OF 3,500 OTHER HIGH SCHOOL STUDENTS...
...BEEN *INVITED* TO A SUMMER PROGRAM AT CAPE CANAVERAL...
SPACE CAMP
AND YOU CAN ALSO IMAGINE HOW IT FELT WHEN MY PARENTS SAID THEY COULDN'T AFFORD IT...
THAT'S WHY EVERY DAY FOR A WEEK I RODE MY BIKE 10 MILES TO ENTER MY NAME INTO THE CONTEST.
Pop's
I WANT TO WIN THE TRUCK AND USE THE MONEY FOR SPACE CAMP, SURE...
...BUT REALLY IT'S TO PROVE I AM *NOT* A BORN LOSER.

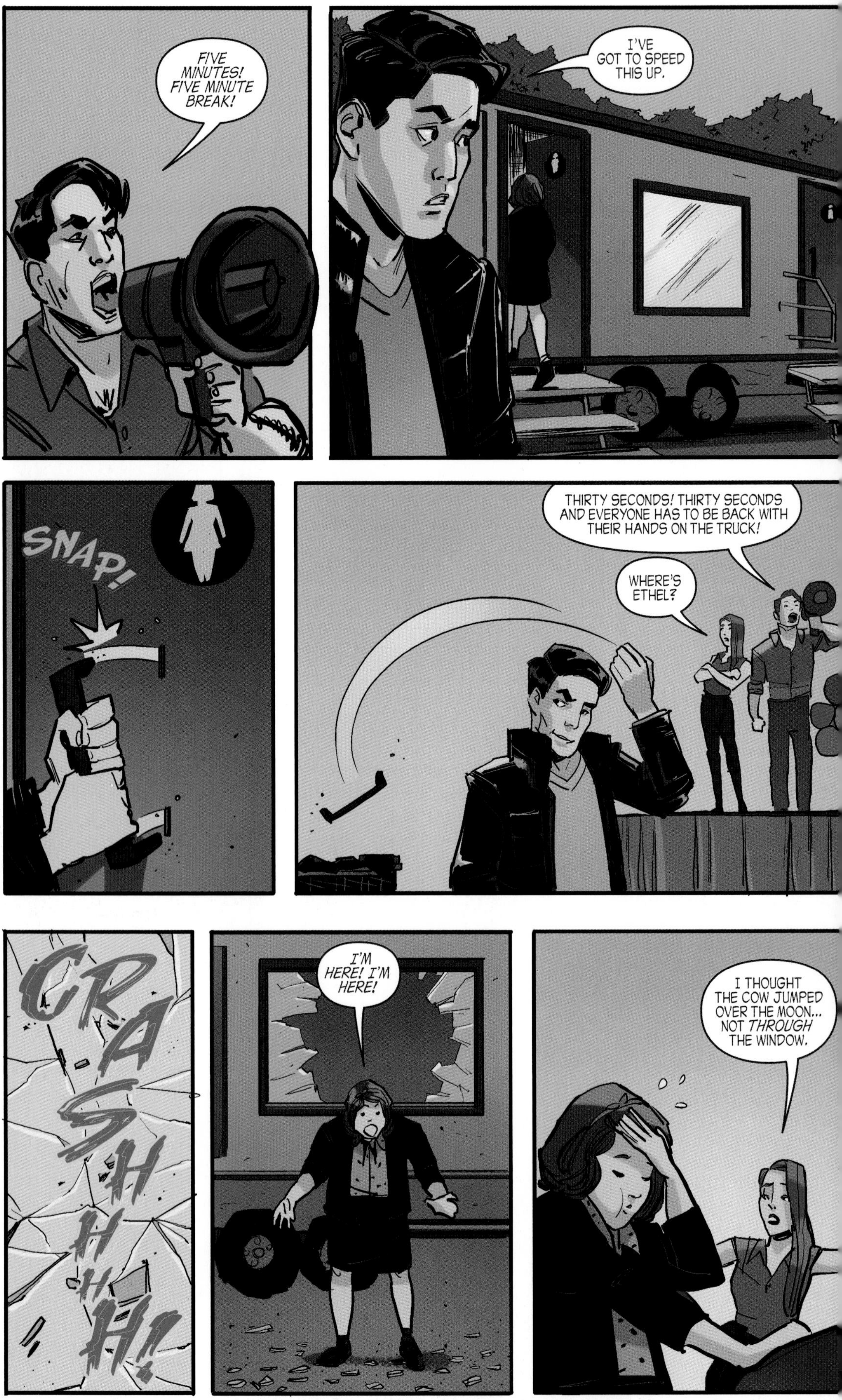

FIVE MINUTES! FIVE MINUTE BREAK!
I'VE GOT TO SPEED THIS UP.
SNAP!
THIRTY SECONDS! THIRTY SECONDS AND EVERYONE HAS TO BE BACK WITH THEIR HANDS ON THE TRUCK!
WHERE'S ETHEL?
CRASHHHH!
I'M HERE! I'M HERE!
I THOUGHT THE COW JUMPED OVER THE MOON... NOT *THROUGH* THE WINDOW.

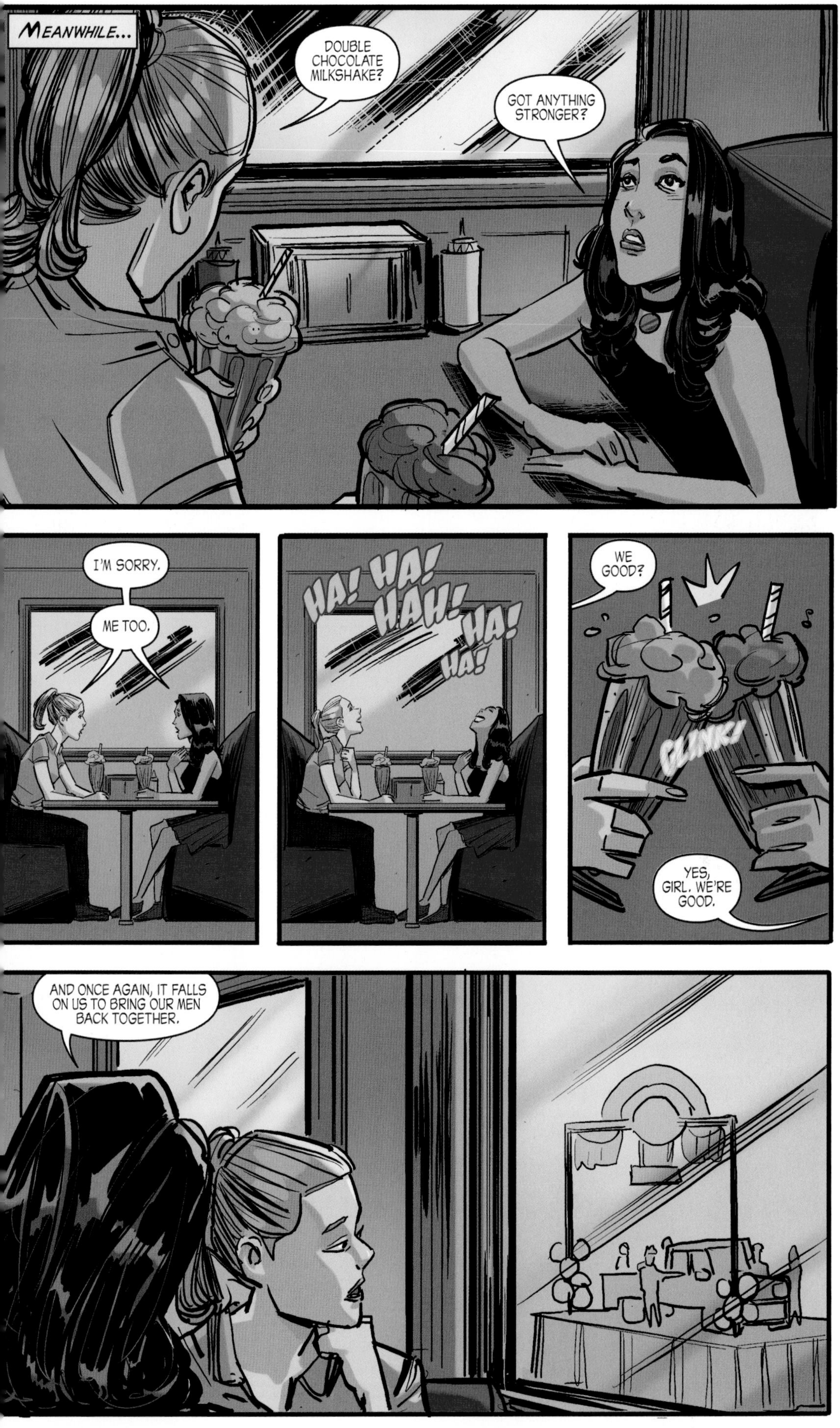
MEANWHILE...
DOUBLE CHOCOLATE MILKSHAKE?
GOT ANYTHING STRONGER?
I'M SORRY.
ME TOO.
HA! HA! HAH! HA! HA!
WE GOOD?
CLINK!
YES, GIRL. WE'RE GOOD.
AND ONCE AGAIN, IT FALLS ON US TO BRING OUR MEN BACK TOGETHER.

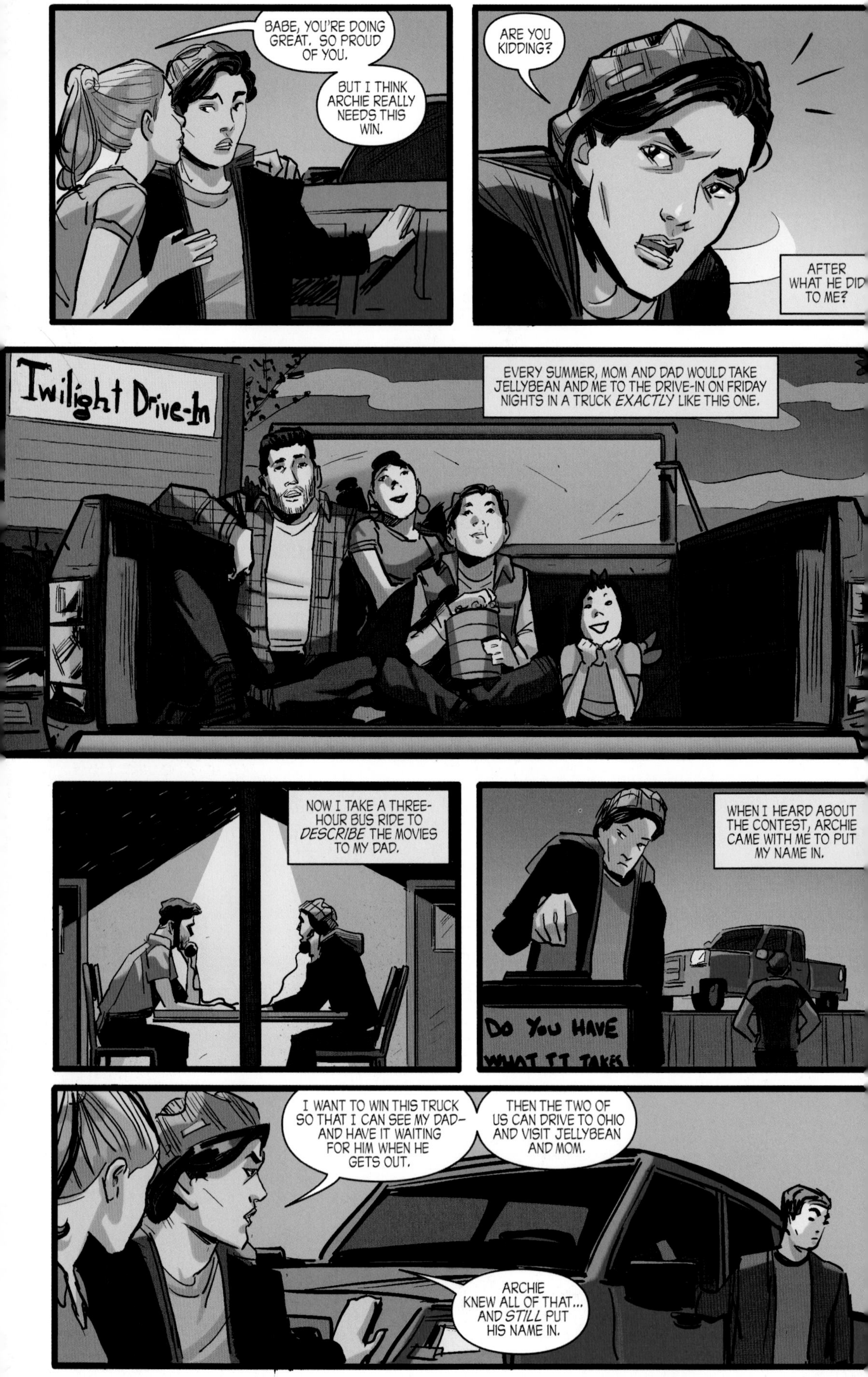
BABE, YOU'RE DOING GREAT. SO PROUD OF YOU.
BUT I THINK ARCHIE REALLY NEEDS THIS WIN.
ARE YOU KIDDING?
AFTER WHAT HE DID TO ME?
Twilight Drive-In
EVERY SUMMER, MOM AND DAD WOULD TAKE JELLYBEAN AND ME TO THE DRIVE-IN ON FRIDAY NIGHTS IN A TRUCK EXACTLY LIKE THIS ONE.
NOW I TAKE A THREE-HOUR BUS RIDE TO DESCRIBE THE MOVIES TO MY DAD.
WHEN I HEARD ABOUT THE CONTEST, ARCHIE CAME WITH ME TO PUT MY NAME IN.
DO YOU HAVE
I WANT TO WIN THIS TRUCK SO THAT I CAN SEE MY DAD– AND HAVE IT WAITING FOR HIM WHEN HE GETS OUT.
THEN THE TWO OF US CAN DRIVE TO OHIO AND VISIT JELLYBEAN AND MOM.
ARCHIE KNEW ALL OF THAT... AND STILL PUT HIS NAME IN.

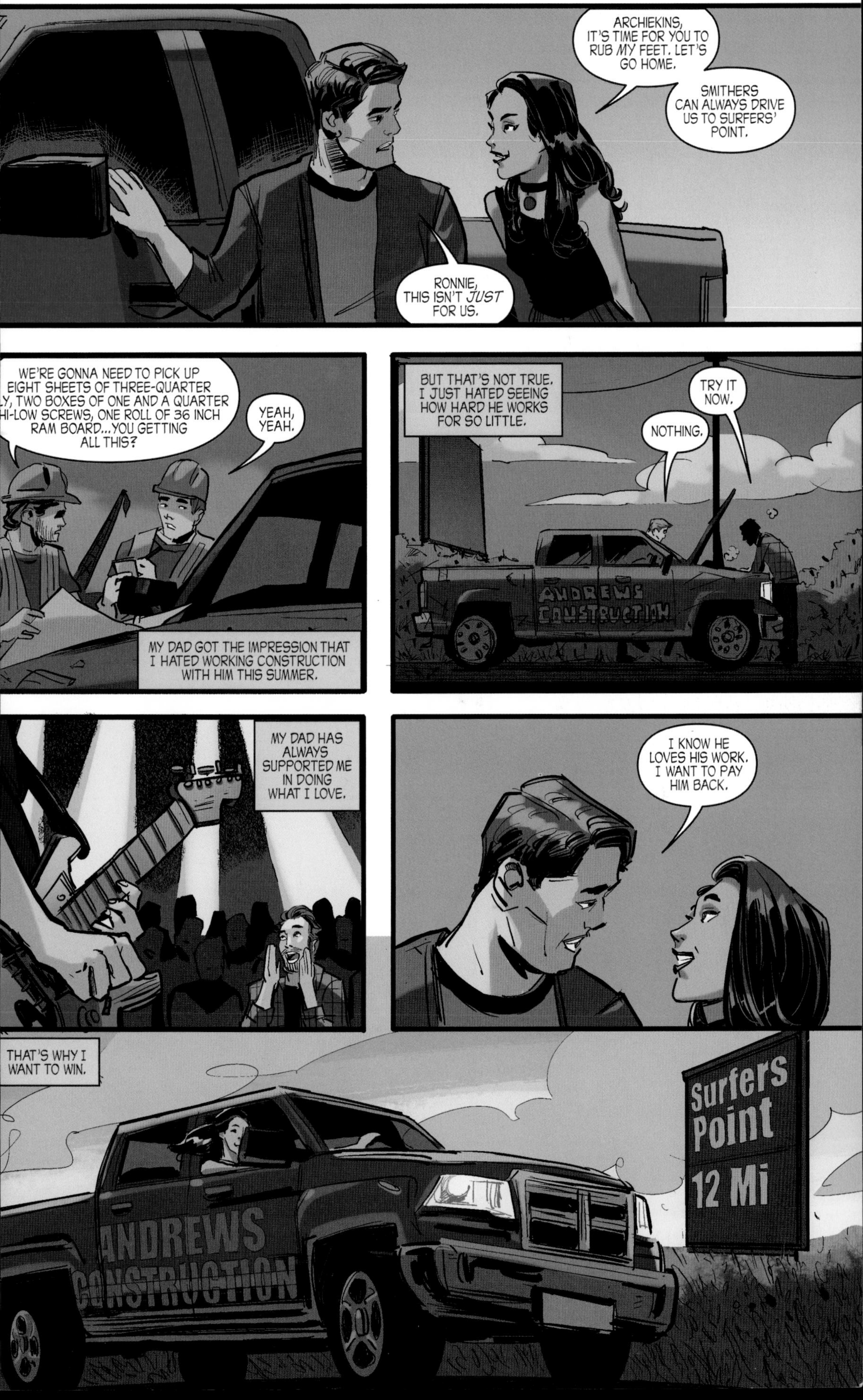

ARCHIEKINS, IT'S TIME FOR YOU TO RUB MY FEET. LET'S GO HOME.
SMITHERS CAN ALWAYS DRIVE US TO SURFERS' POINT.
RONNIE, THIS ISN'T JUST FOR US.
WE'RE GONNA NEED TO PICK UP EIGHT SHEETS OF THREE-QUARTER PLY, TWO BOXES OF ONE AND A QUARTER HI-LOW SCREWS, ONE ROLL OF 36 INCH RAM BOARD...YOU GETTING ALL THIS?
YEAH, YEAH.
MY DAD GOT THE IMPRESSION THAT I HATED WORKING CONSTRUCTION WITH HIM THIS SUMMER.
BUT THAT'S NOT TRUE. I JUST HATED SEEING HOW HARD HE WORKS FOR SO LITTLE.
TRY IT NOW.
NOTHING.
ANDREWS CONSTRUCTION
MY DAD HAS ALWAYS SUPPORTED ME IN DOING WHAT I LOVE.
I KNOW HE LOVES HIS WORK. I WANT TO PAY HIM BACK.
THAT'S WHY I WANT TO WIN.
ANDREWS CONSTRUCTION
Surfers Point
12 Mi

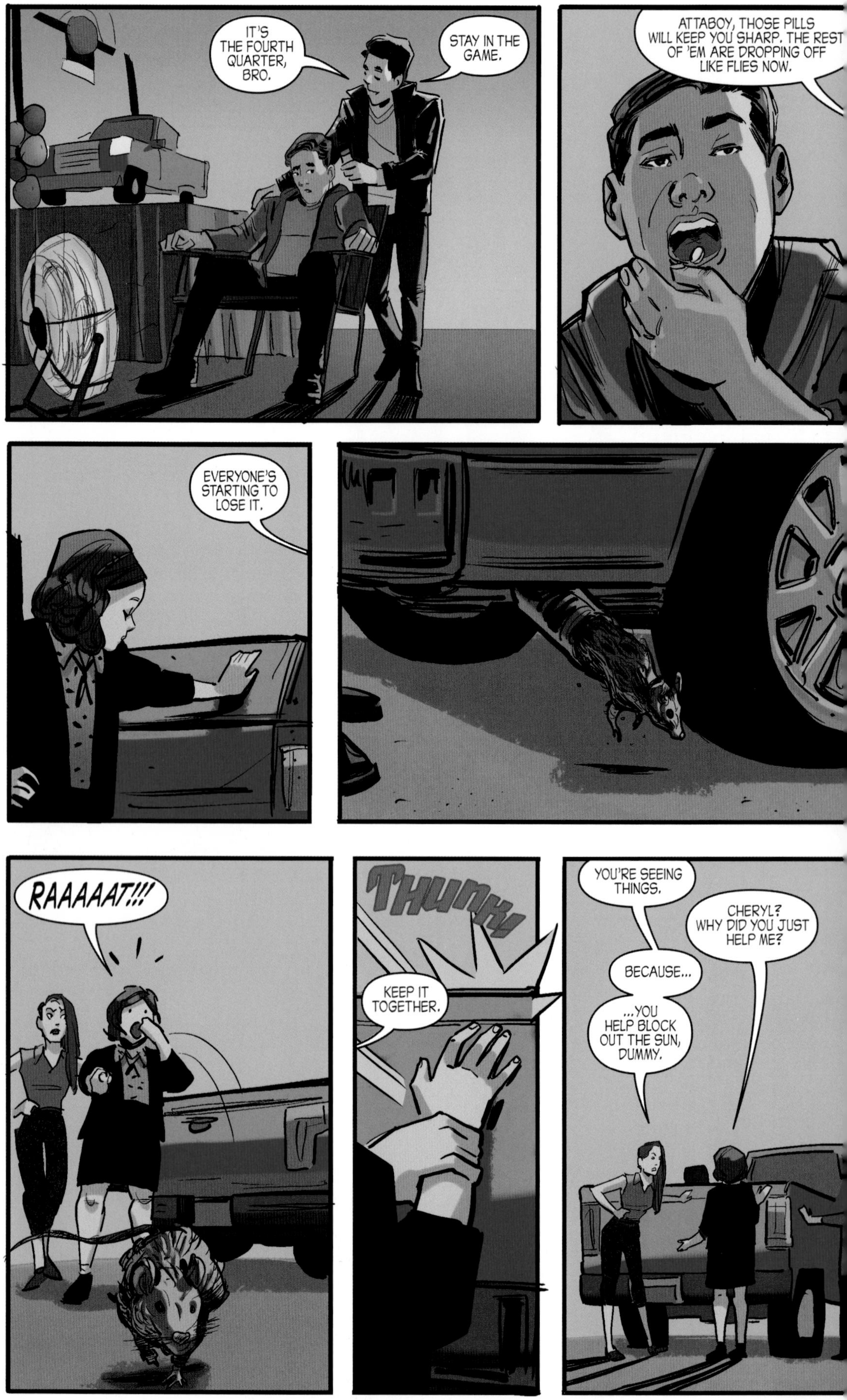
IT'S THE FOURTH QUARTER, BRO.
STAY IN THE GAME.
ATTABOY, THOSE PILLS WILL KEEP YOU SHARP. THE REST OF 'EM ARE DROPPING OFF LIKE FLIES NOW.
EVERYONE'S STARTING TO LOSE IT.
RAAAAAT!!!
THUNK!
KEEP IT TOGETHER.
YOU'RE SEEING THINGS.
CHERYL? WHY DID YOU JUST HELP ME?
BECAUSE...
...YOU HELP BLOCK OUT THE SUN, DUMMY.

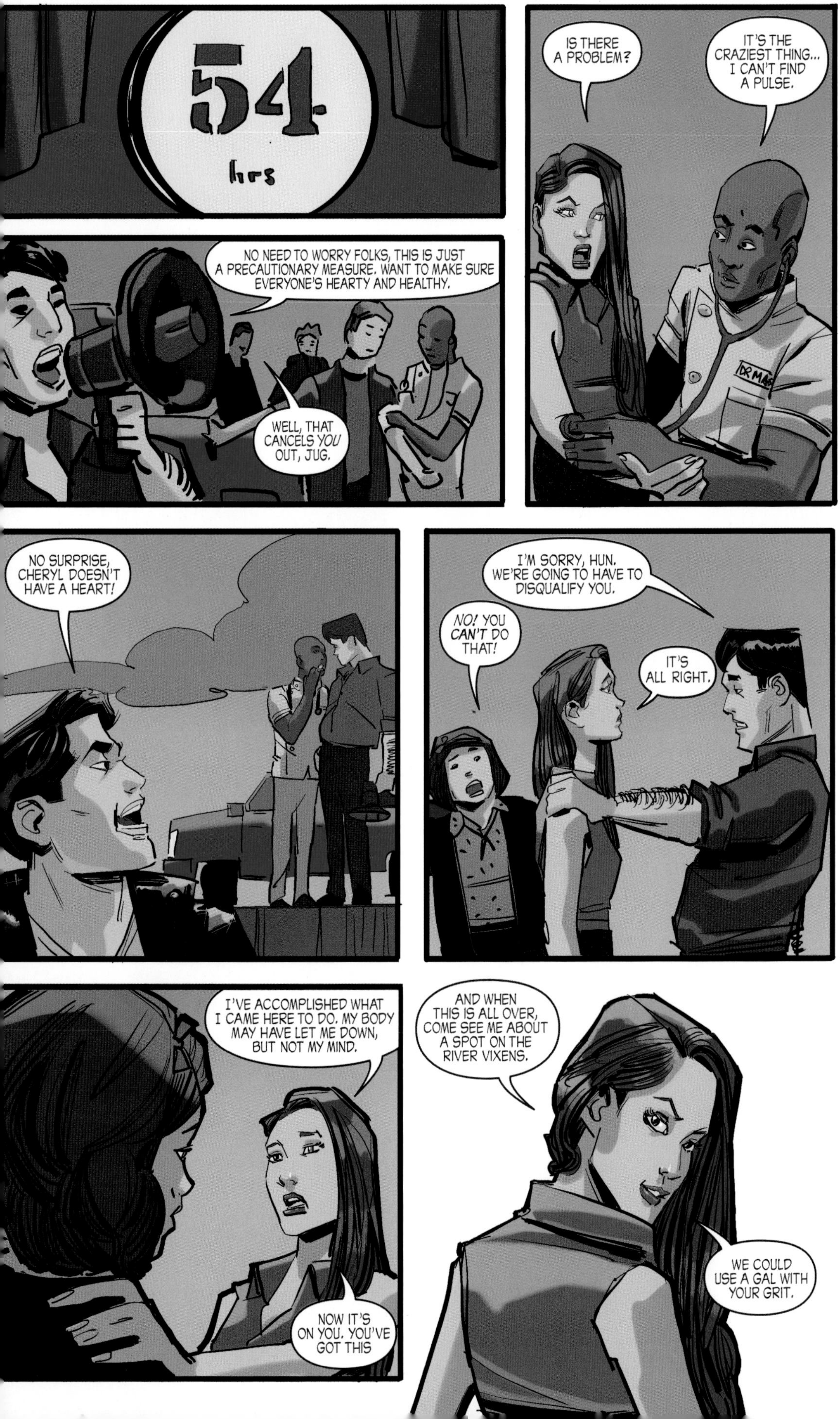
54
hrs
IS THERE A PROBLEM?
IT'S THE CRAZIEST THING... I CAN'T FIND A PULSE.
NO NEED TO WORRY FOLKS, THIS IS JUST A PRECAUTIONARY MEASURE. WANT TO MAKE SURE EVERYONE'S HEARTY AND HEALTHY.
WELL, THAT CANCELS YOU OUT, JUG.
DR MA
NO SURPRISE, CHERYL DOESN'T HAVE A HEART!
I'M SORRY, HUN. WE'RE GOING TO HAVE TO DISQUALIFY YOU.
NO! YOU CAN'T DO THAT!
IT'S ALL RIGHT.
I'VE ACCOMPLISHED WHAT I CAME HERE TO DO. MY BODY MAY HAVE LET ME DOWN, BUT NOT MY MIND.
NOW IT'S ON YOU. YOU'VE GOT THIS
AND WHEN THIS IS ALL OVER, COME SEE ME ABOUT A SPOT ON THE RIVER VIXENS.
WE COULD USE A GAL WITH YOUR GRIT.

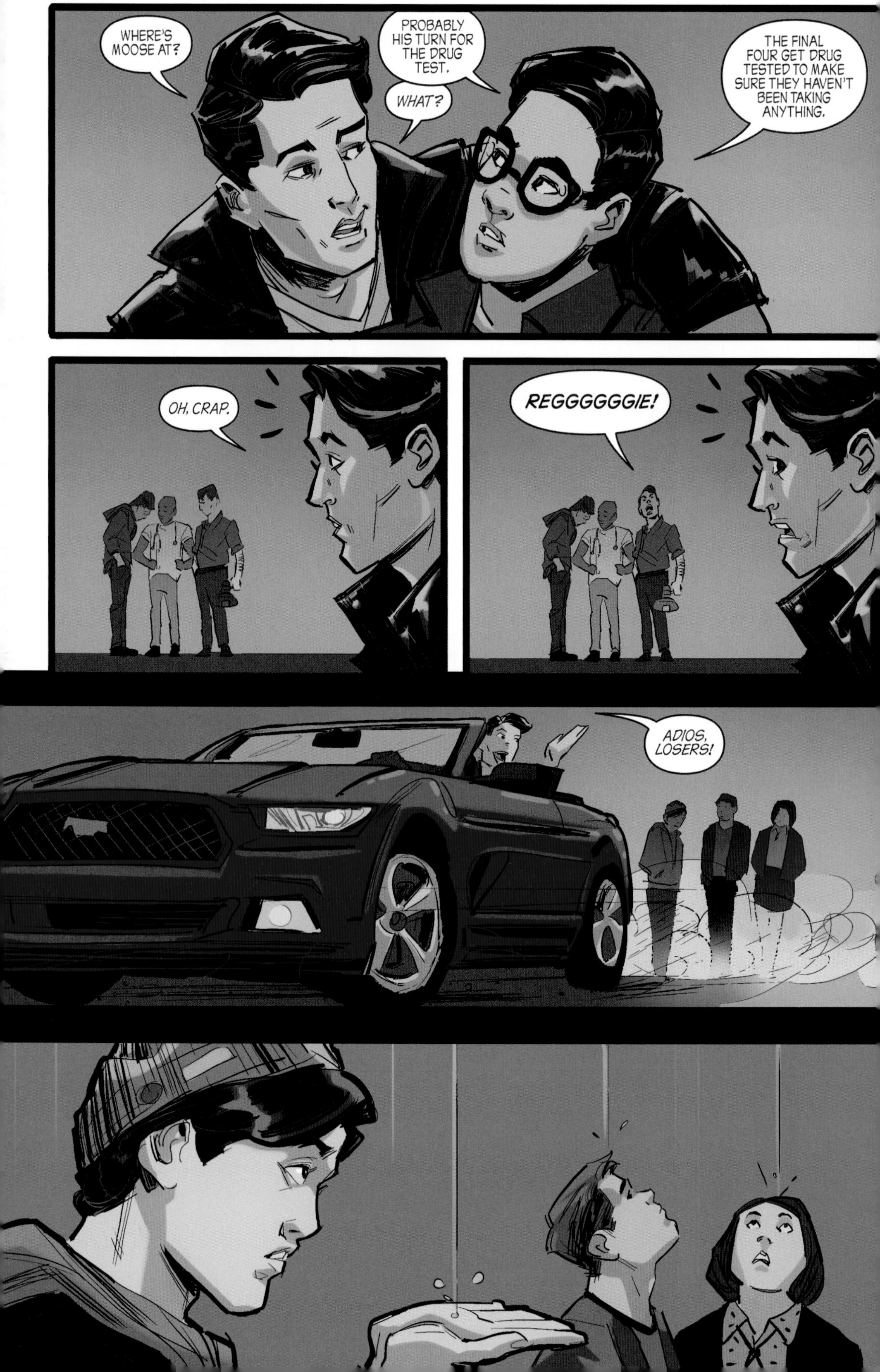
WHERE'S MOOSE AT?
PROBABLY HIS TURN FOR THE DRUG TEST.
WHAT?
THE FINAL FOUR GET DRUG TESTED TO MAKE SURE THEY HAVEN'T BEEN TAKING ANYTHING.
OH, CRAP.
REGGGGGGIE!
ADIOS, LOSERS!

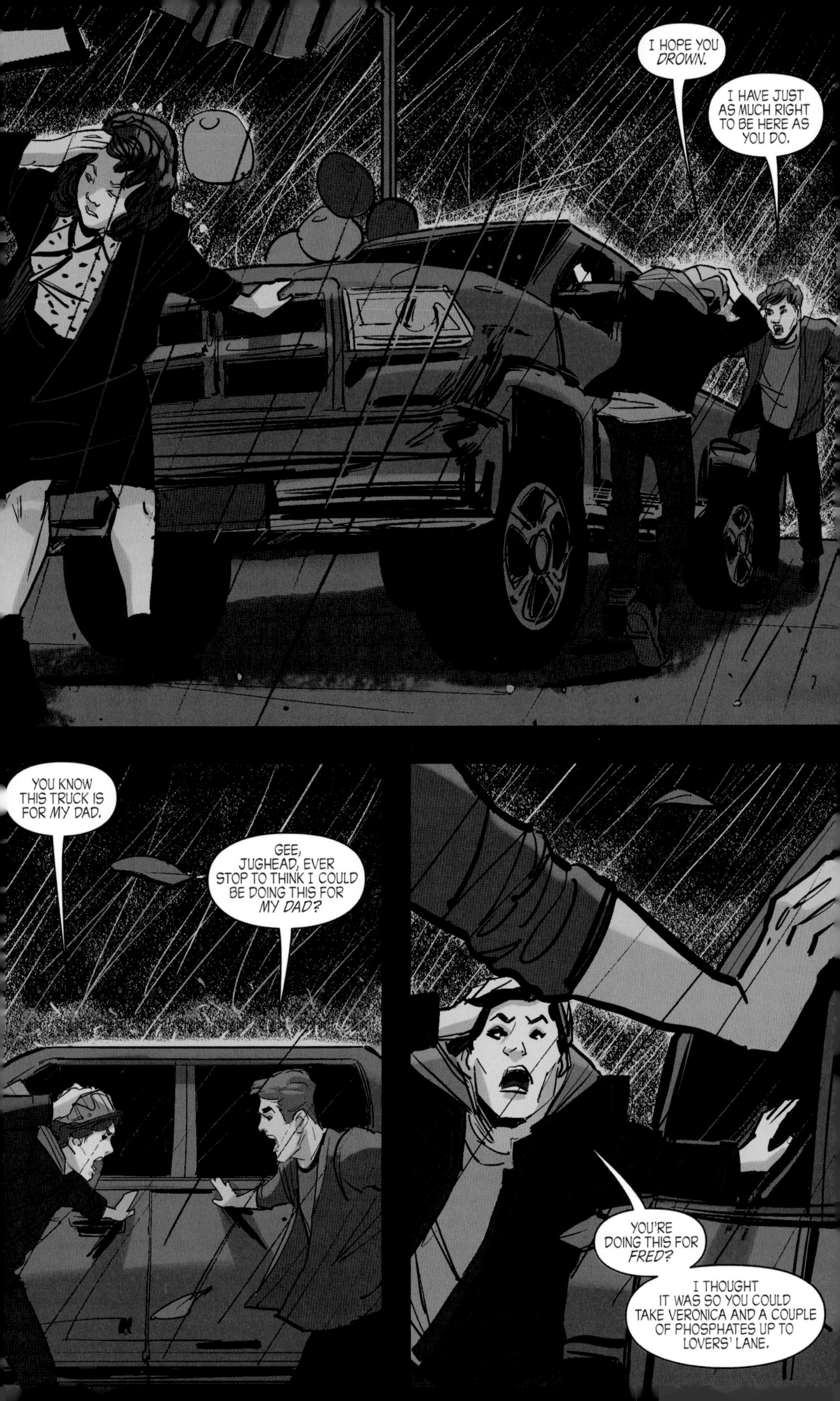
I HOPE YOU DROWN.
I HAVE JUST AS MUCH RIGHT TO BE HERE AS YOU DO.
YOU KNOW THIS TRUCK IS FOR MY DAD.
GEE, JUGHEAD, EVER STOP TO THINK I COULD BE DOING THIS FOR MY DAD?
YOU'RE DOING THIS FOR FRED?
I THOUGHT IT WAS SO YOU COULD TAKE VERONICA AND A COUPLE OF PHOSPHATES UP TO LOVERS' LANE.

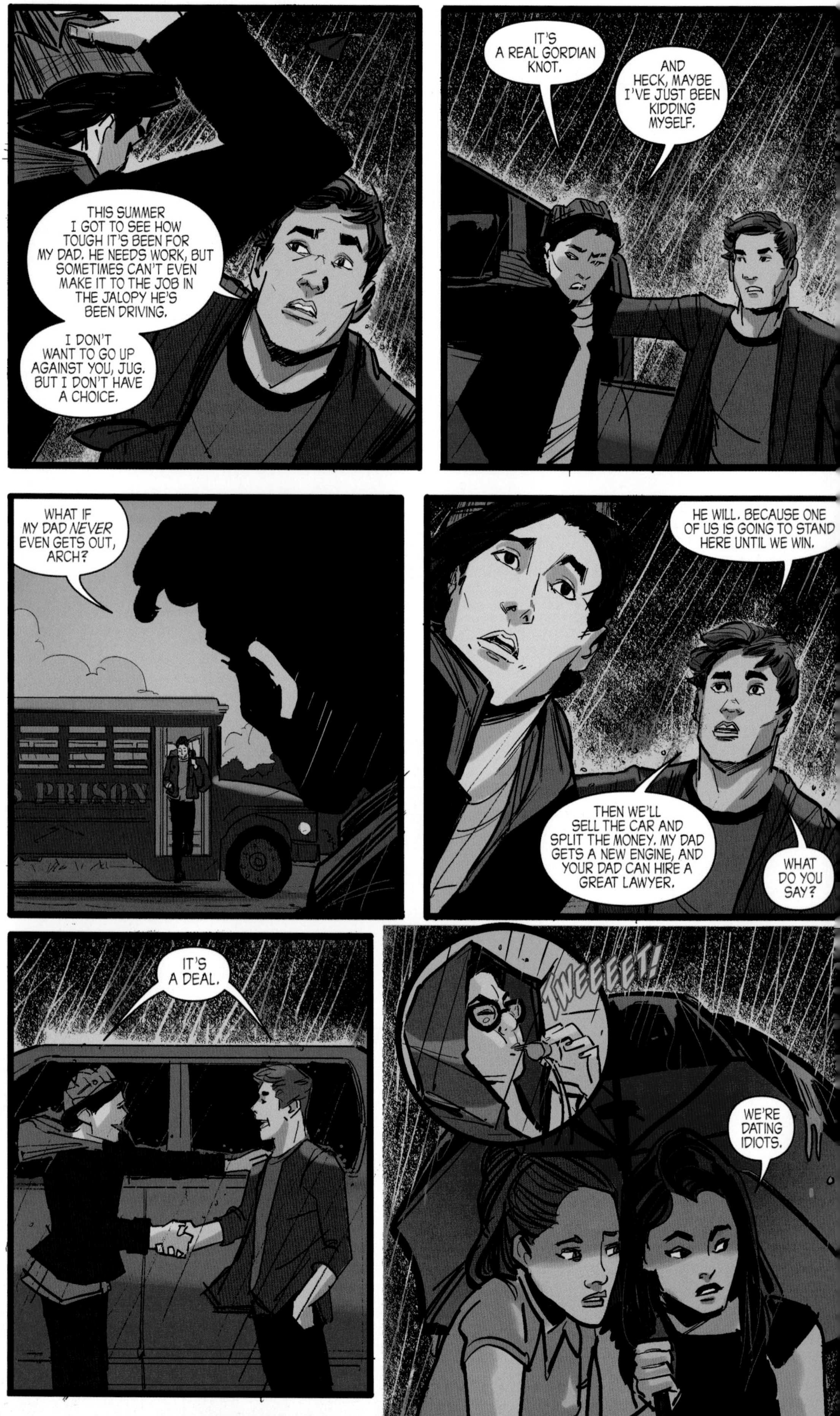
THIS SUMMER I GOT TO SEE HOW TOUGH IT'S BEEN FOR MY DAD. HE NEEDS WORK, BUT SOMETIMES CAN'T EVEN MAKE IT TO THE JOB IN THE JALOPY HE'S BEEN DRIVING.
I DON'T WANT TO GO UP AGAINST YOU, JUG. BUT I DON'T HAVE A CHOICE.
IT'S A REAL GORDIAN KNOT.
AND HECK, MAYBE I'VE JUST BEEN KIDDING MYSELF.
WHAT IF MY DAD *NEVER* EVEN GETS OUT, ARCH?
PRISON
HE WILL. BECAUSE ONE OF US IS GOING TO STAND HERE UNTIL WE WIN.
THEN WE'LL SELL THE CAR AND SPLIT THE MONEY. MY DAD GETS A NEW ENGINE, AND YOUR DAD CAN HIRE A GREAT LAWYER.
WHAT DO YOU SAY?
IT'S A DEAL.
TWEEEET!
WE'RE DATING IDIOTS.

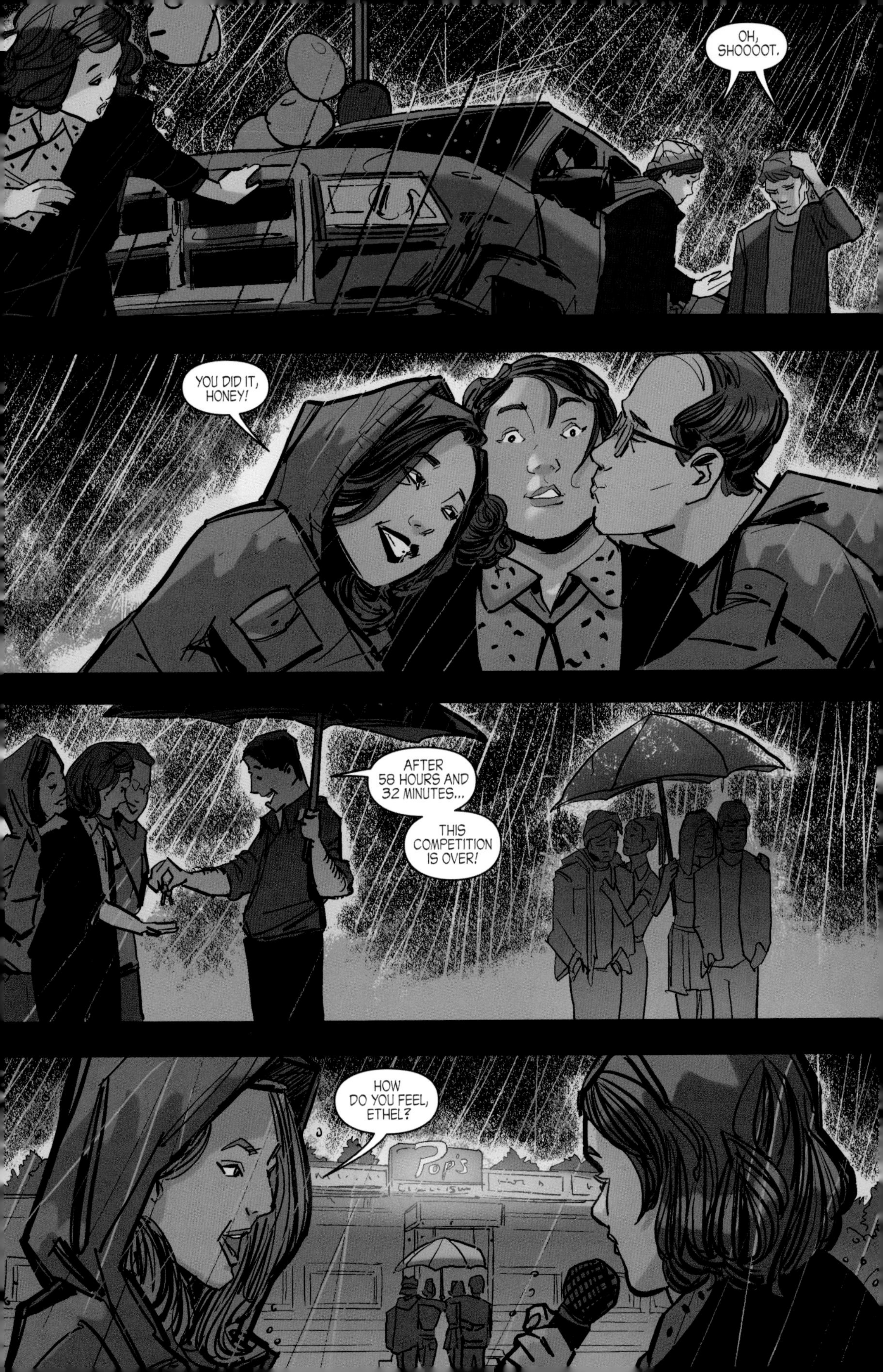
OH, SHOOOOT.
YOU DID IT, HONEY!
AFTER 58 HOURS AND 32 MINUTES...
THIS COMPETITION IS OVER!
HOW DO YOU FEEL, ETHEL?
Pop's

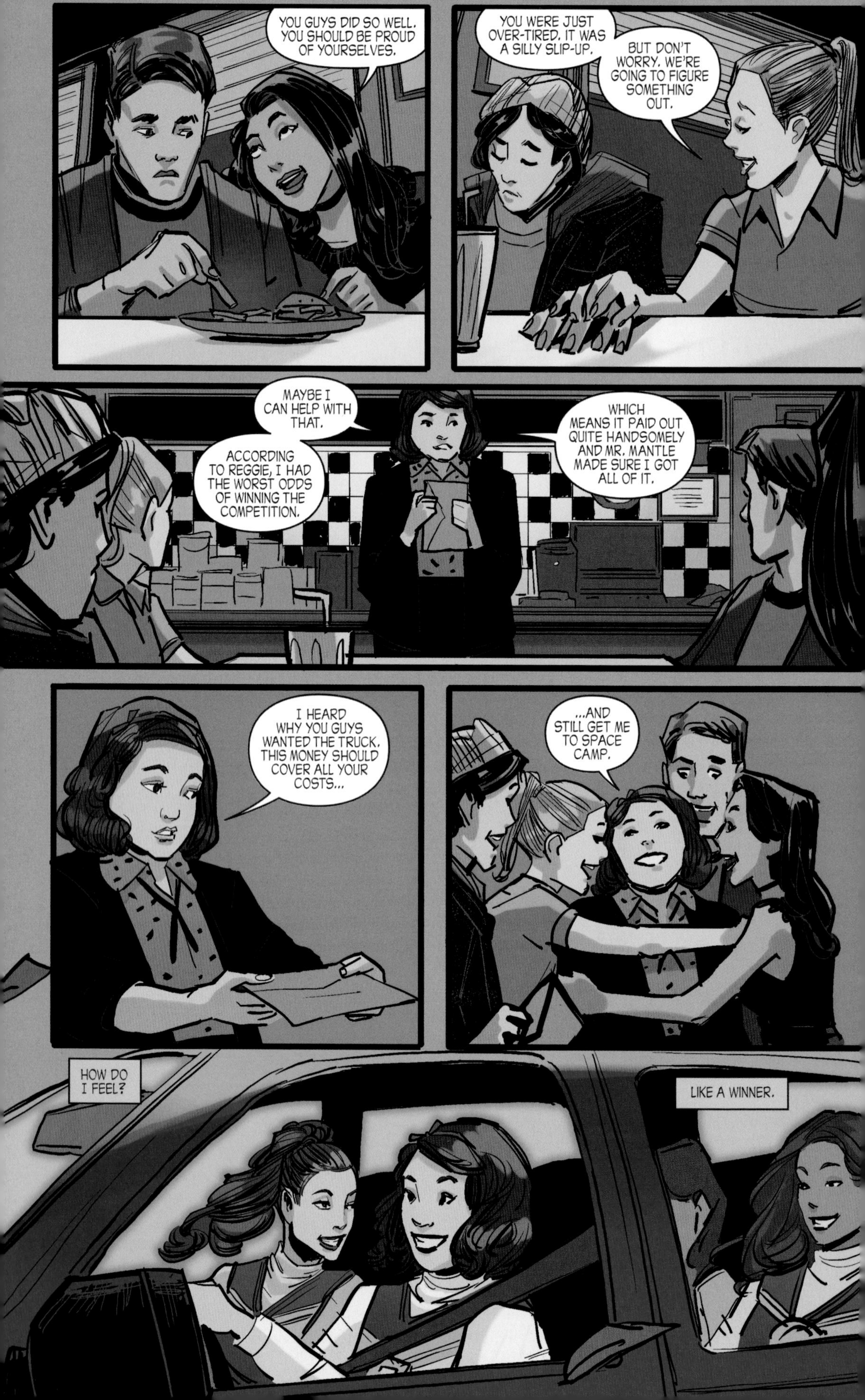
YOU GUYS DID SO WELL. YOU SHOULD BE PROUD OF YOURSELVES.
YOU WERE JUST OVER-TIRED. IT WAS A SILLY SLIP-UP.
BUT DON'T WORRY. WE'RE GOING TO FIGURE SOMETHING OUT.
MAYBE I CAN HELP WITH THAT.
ACCORDING TO REGGIE, I HAD THE WORST ODDS OF WINNING THE COMPETITION.
WHICH MEANS IT PAID OUT QUITE HANDSOMELY AND MR. MANTLE MADE SURE I GOT ALL OF IT.
I HEARD WHY YOU GUYS WANTED THE TRUCK. THIS MONEY SHOULD COVER ALL YOUR COSTS...
...AND STILL GET ME TO SPACE CAMP.
HOW DO I FEEL?
LIKE A WINNER.

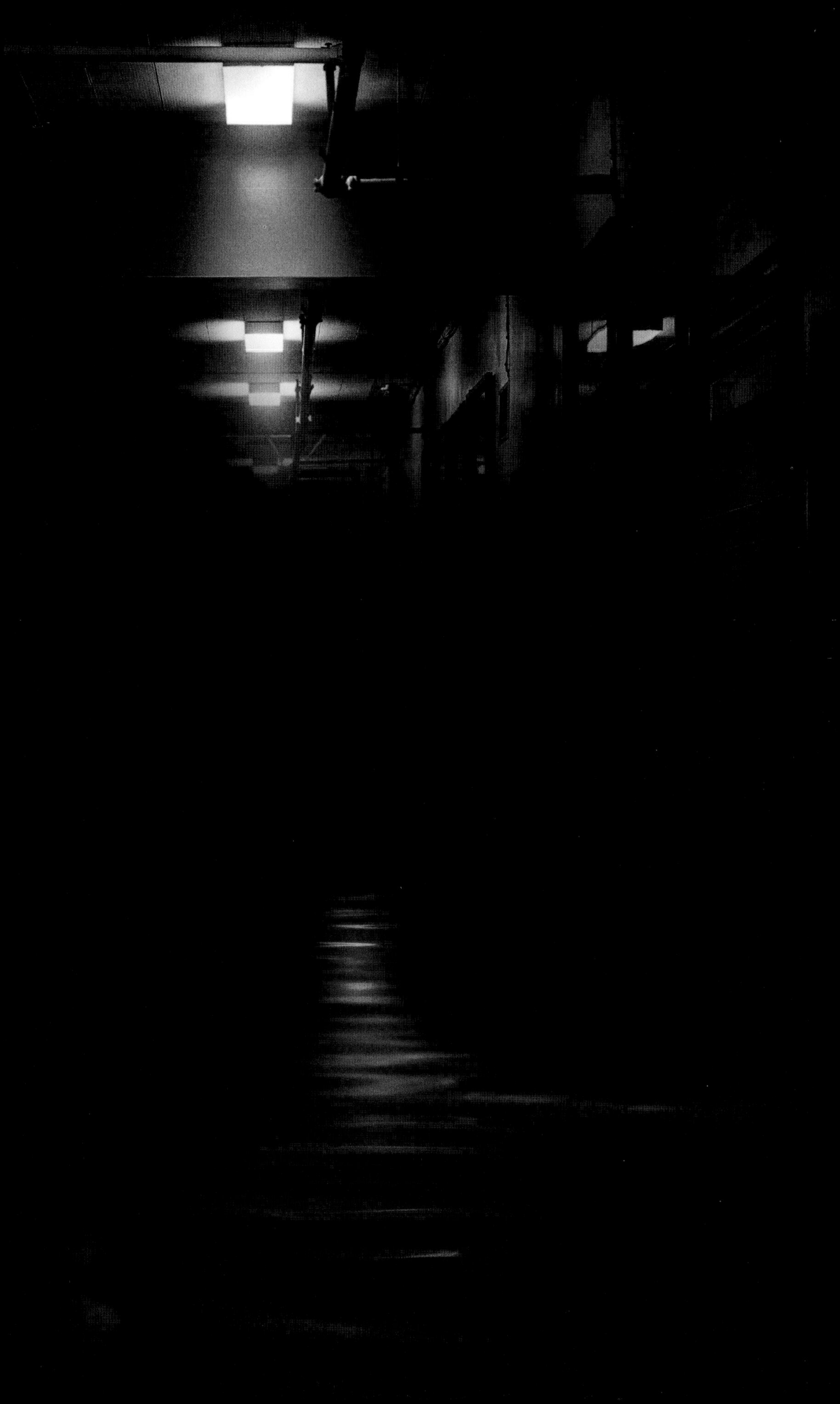

ISSUE TEN

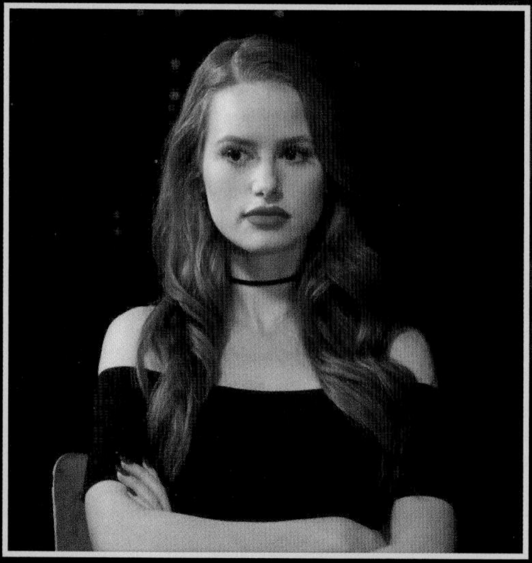

OUTBREAK

WRITER:
GREG MURRAY

ART:
THOMAS PITILLI

COLORS:
ANDRE SZYMANOWICZ

LETTERS:
JOHN WORKMAN

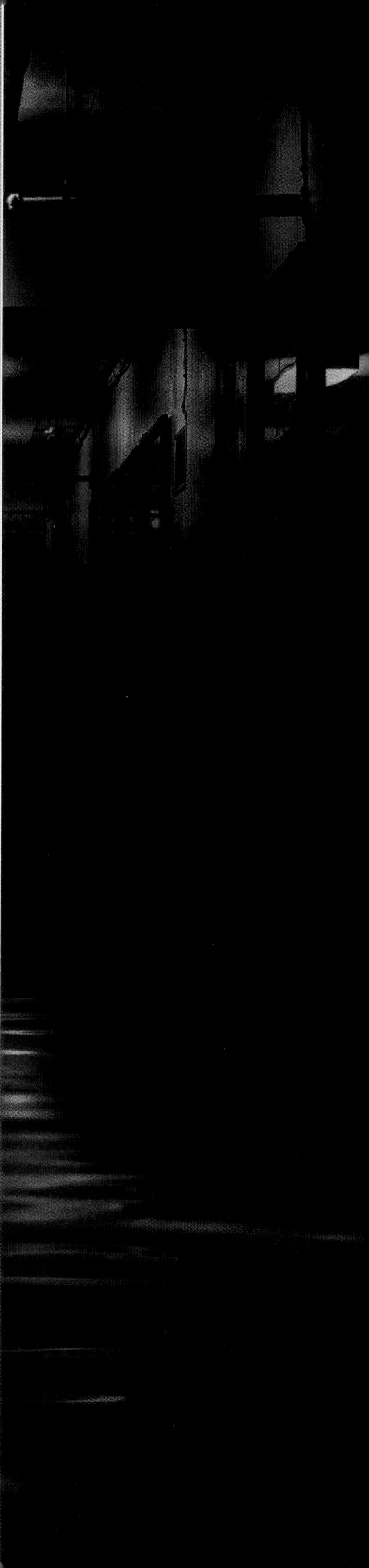

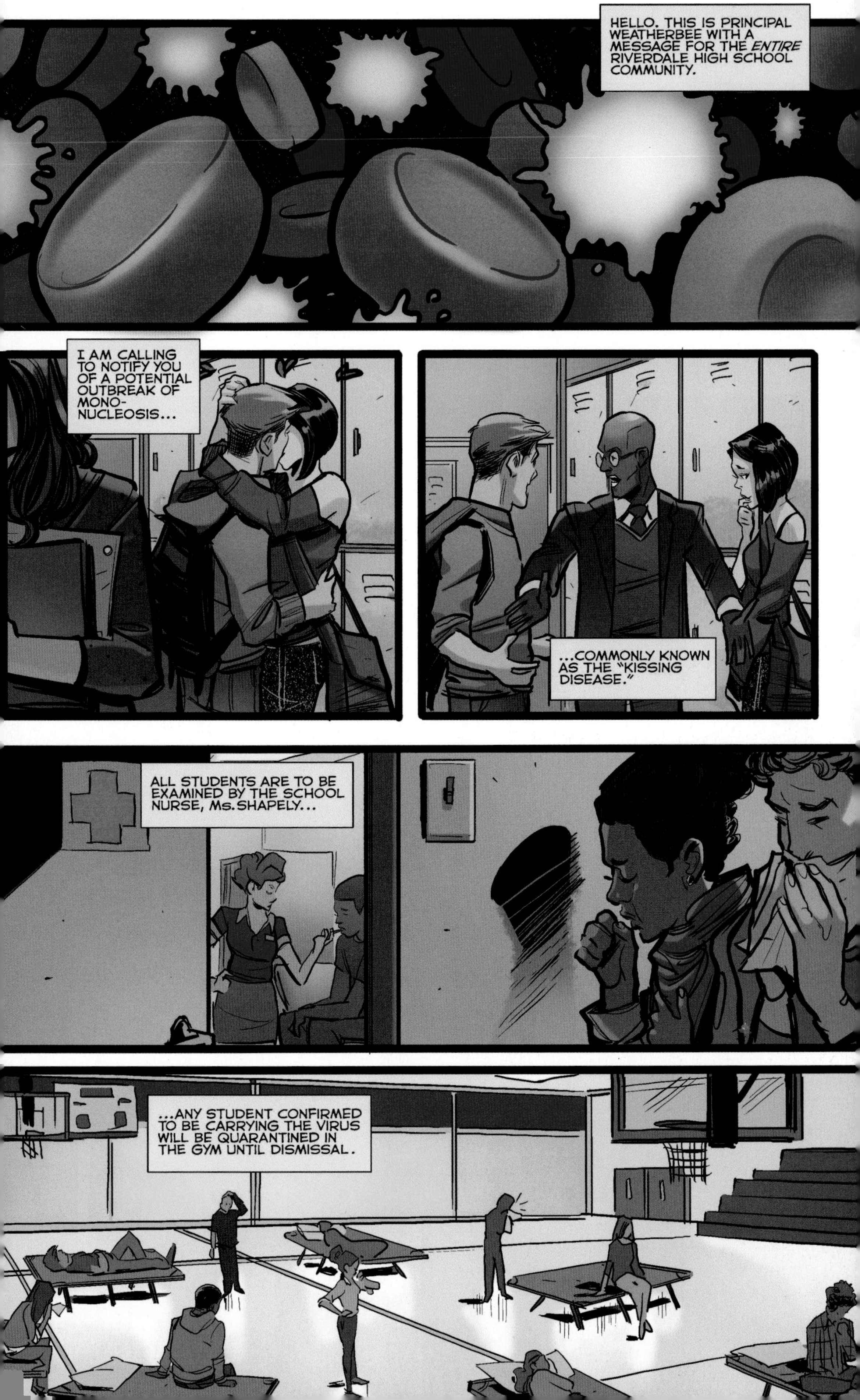
HELLO. THIS IS PRINCIPAL WEATHERBEE WITH A MESSAGE FOR THE *ENTIRE* RIVERDALE HIGH SCHOOL COMMUNITY.
I AM CALLING TO NOTIFY YOU OF A POTENTIAL OUTBREAK OF MONO-NUCLEOSIS...
...COMMONLY KNOWN AS THE "KISSING DISEASE."
ALL STUDENTS ARE TO BE EXAMINED BY THE SCHOOL NURSE, Ms. SHAPELY...
...ANY STUDENT CONFIRMED TO BE CARRYING THE VIRUS WILL BE QUARANTINED IN THE GYM UNTIL DISMISSAL.

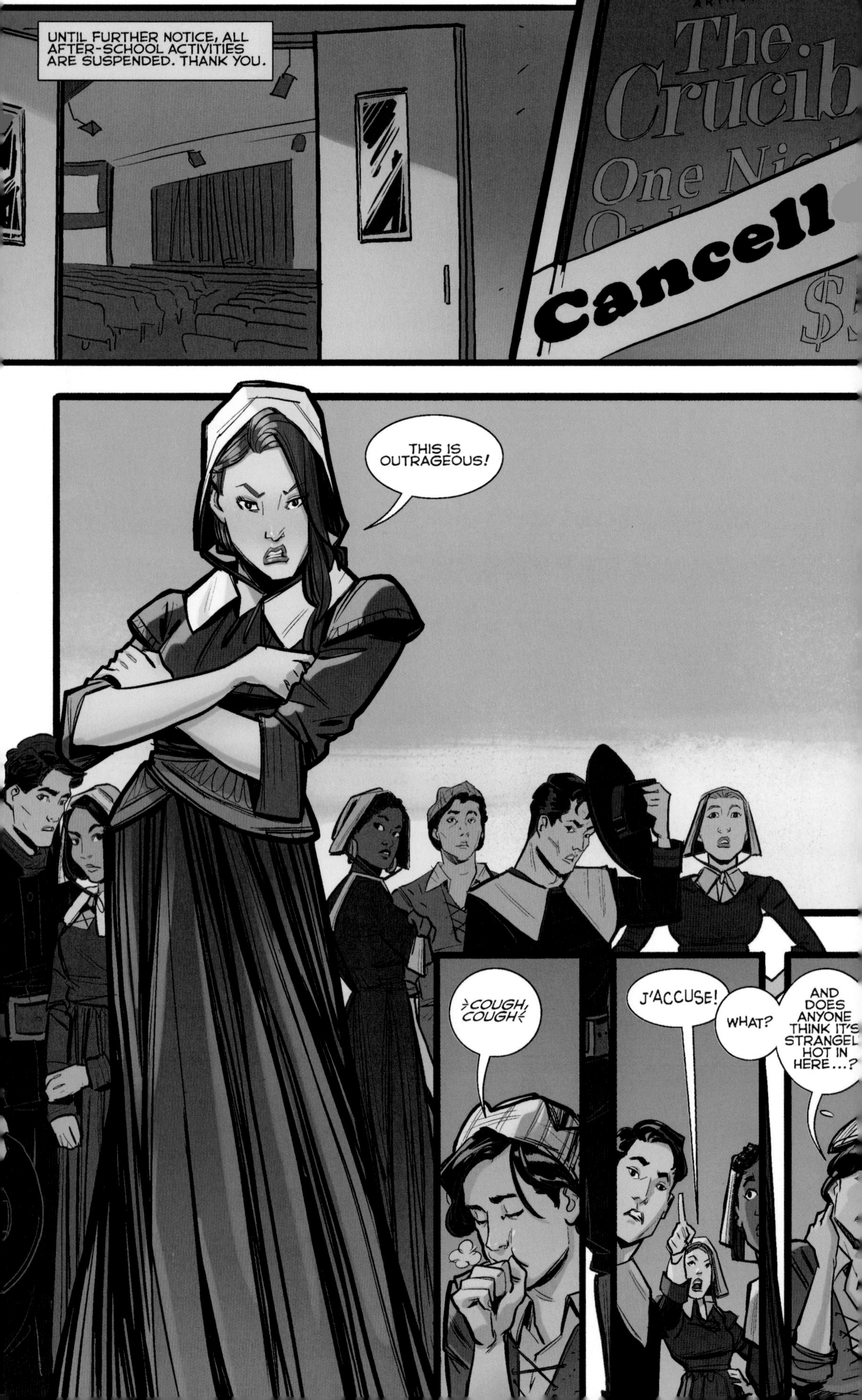

UNTIL FURTHER NOTICE, ALL AFTER-SCHOOL ACTIVITIES ARE SUSPENDED. THANK YOU.
ARTHUR MILLER'S
The Crucib
One Ni
Cancell
THIS IS OUTRAGEOUS!
COUGH, COUGH
J'ACCUSE!
WHAT?
AND DOES ANYONE THINK IT'S STRANGEL HOT IN HERE...?

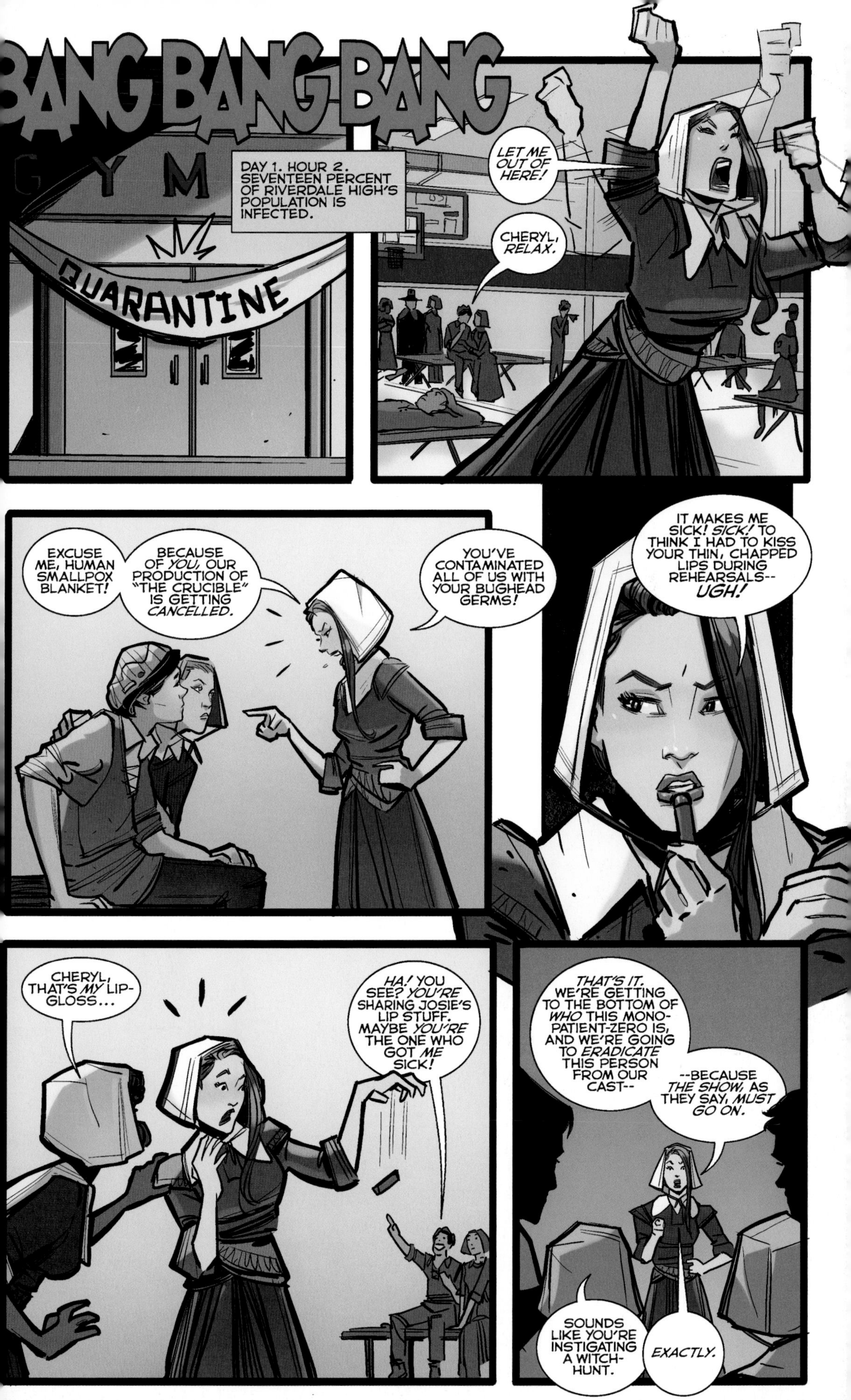
BANG BANG BANG
GYM
DAY 1. HOUR 2. SEVENTEEN PERCENT OF RIVERDALE HIGH'S POPULATION IS INFECTED.
QUARANTINE
LET ME OUT OF HERE!
CHERYL, RELAX.
EXCUSE ME, HUMAN SMALLPOX BLANKET!
BECAUSE OF YOU, OUR PRODUCTION OF "THE CRUCIBLE" IS GETTING CANCELLED.
YOU'VE CONTAMINATED ALL OF US WITH YOUR BUGHEAD GERMS!
IT MAKES ME SICK! SICK! TO THINK I HAD TO KISS YOUR THIN, CHAPPED LIPS DURING REHEARSALS-- UGH!
CHERYL, THAT'S MY LIP-GLOSS...
HA! YOU SEE? YOU'RE SHARING JOSIE'S LIP STUFF. MAYBE YOU'RE THE ONE WHO GOT ME SICK!
THAT'S IT. WE'RE GETTING TO THE BOTTOM OF WHO THIS MONO-PATIENT-ZERO IS, AND WE'RE GOING TO ERADICATE THIS PERSON FROM OUR CAST--
--BECAUSE THE SHOW, AS THEY SAY, MUST GO ON.
SOUNDS LIKE YOU'RE INSTIGATING A WITCH-HUNT.
EXACTLY.

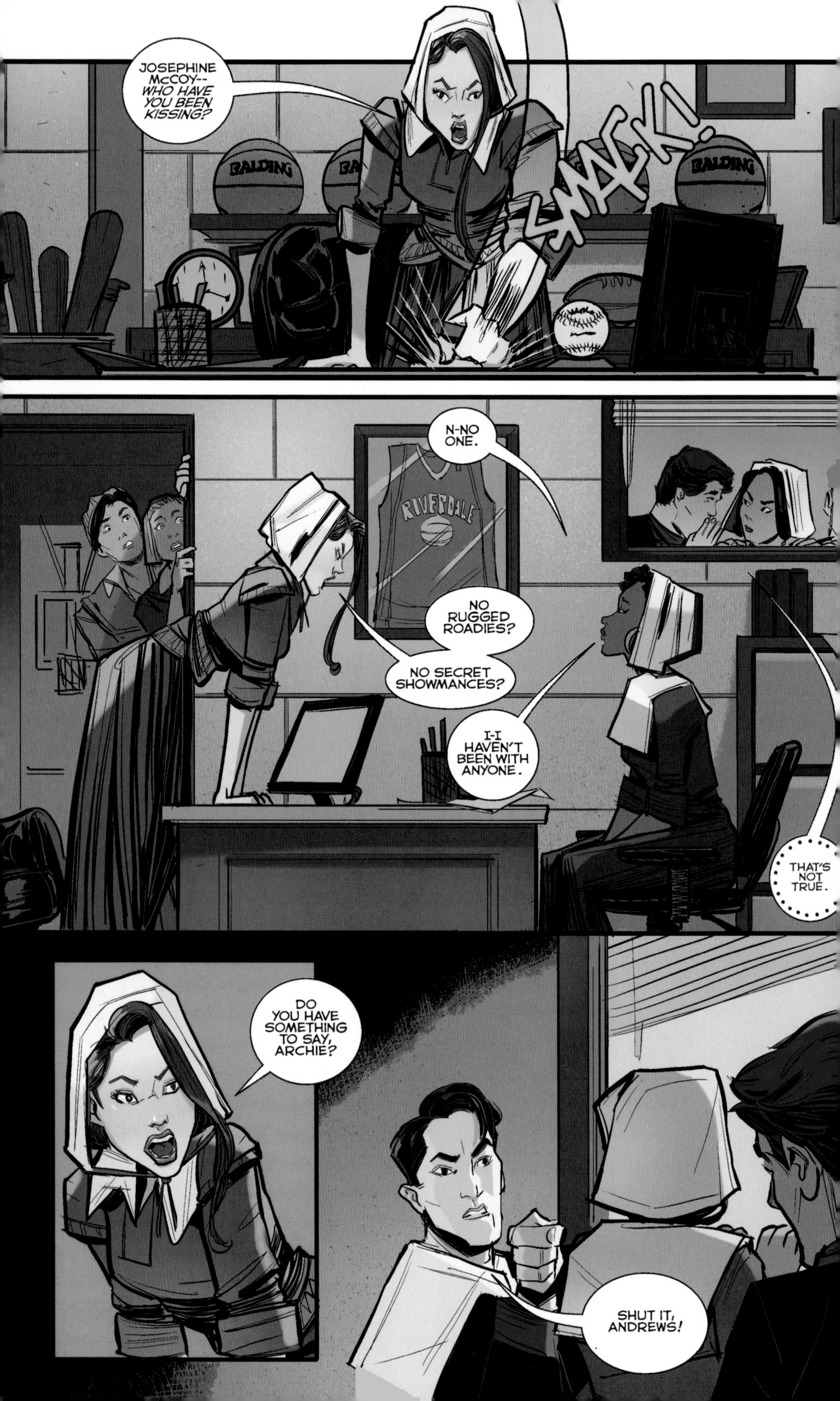
JOSEPHINE McCOY-- WHO HAVE YOU BEEN KISSING?
SMACK!
BALDING
N-NO ONE.
RIVERDALE
NO RUGGED ROADIES?
NO SECRET SHOWMANCES?
I-I HAVEN'T BEEN WITH ANYONE.
THAT'S NOT TRUE.
DO YOU HAVE SOMETHING TO SAY, ARCHIE?
SHUT IT, ANDREWS!

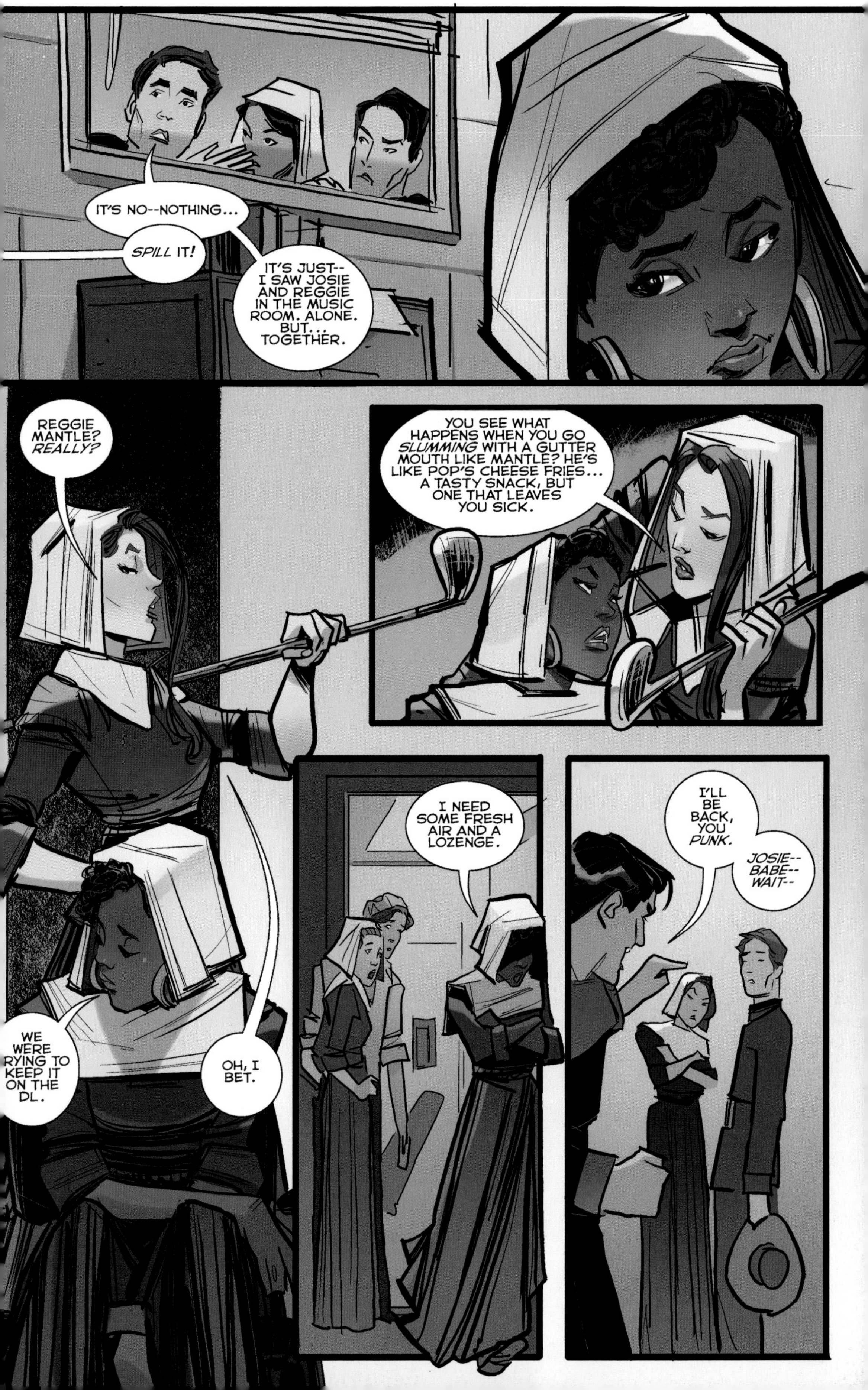
IT'S NO--NOTHING...
SPILL IT!
IT'S JUST-- I SAW JOSIE AND REGGIE IN THE MUSIC ROOM. ALONE. BUT... TOGETHER.
REGGIE MANTLE? REALLY?
YOU SEE WHAT HAPPENS WHEN YOU GO SLUMMING WITH A GUTTER MOUTH LIKE MANTLE? HE'S LIKE POP'S CHEESE FRIES... A TASTY SNACK, BUT ONE THAT LEAVES YOU SICK.
WE WERE RYING TO KEEP IT ON THE DL.
OH, I BET.
I NEED SOME FRESH AIR AND A LOZENGE.
I'LL BE BACK, YOU PUNK.
JOSIE-- BABE-- WAIT--

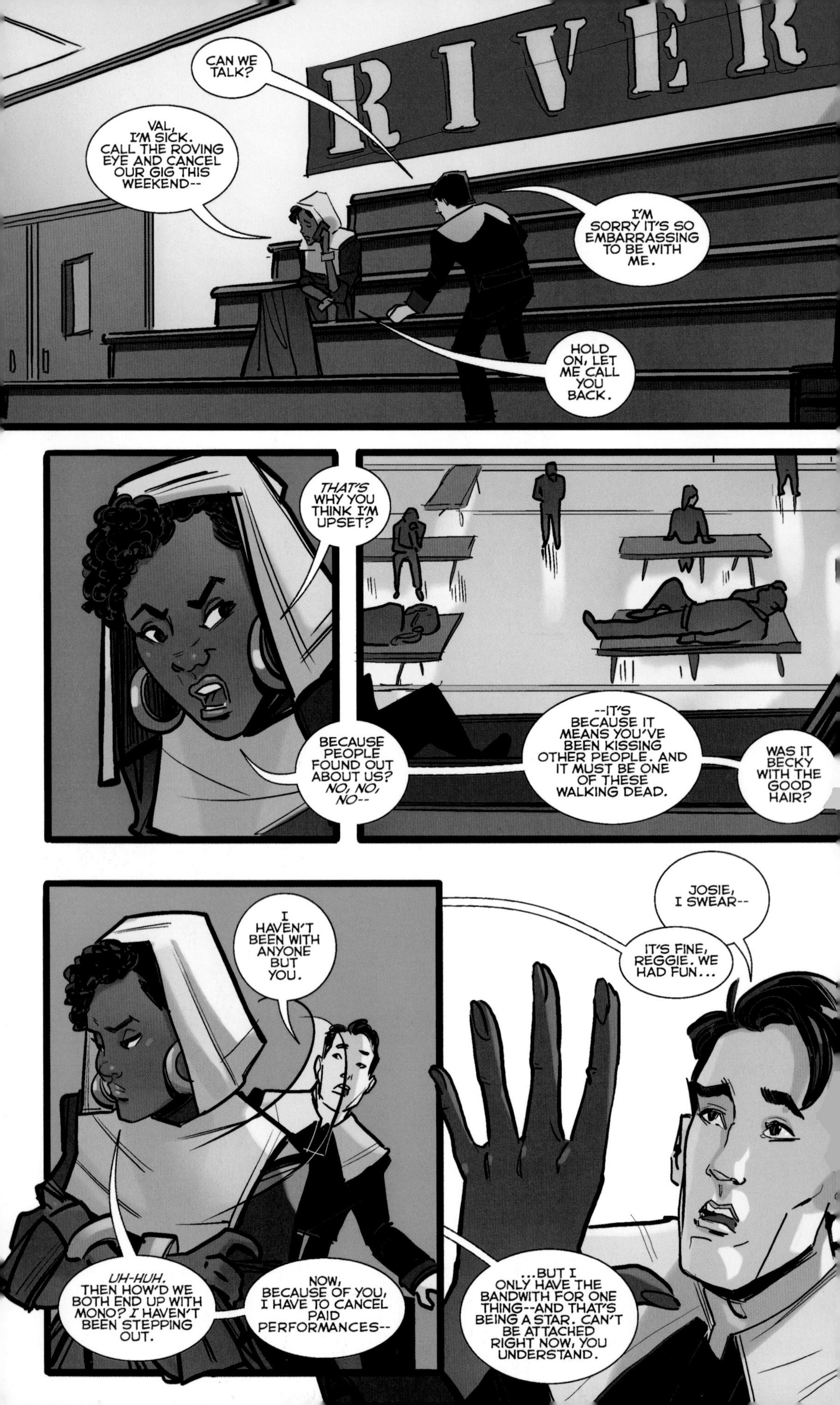

CAN WE TALK?
VAL, I'M SICK. CALL THE ROVING EYE AND CANCEL OUR GIG THIS WEEKEND--
I'M SORRY IT'S SO EMBARRASSING TO BE WITH ME.
HOLD ON, LET ME CALL YOU BACK.
THAT'S WHY YOU THINK I'M UPSET?
BECAUSE PEOPLE FOUND OUT ABOUT US? *NO, NO, NO*--
--IT'S BECAUSE IT MEANS YOU'VE BEEN KISSING OTHER PEOPLE. AND IT MUST BE ONE OF THESE WALKING DEAD.
WAS IT BECKY WITH THE GOOD HAIR?
I HAVEN'T BEEN WITH ANYONE BUT YOU.
UH-HUH. THEN HOW'D WE BOTH END UP WITH MONO? *I* HAVEN'T BEEN STEPPING OUT.
NOW, BECAUSE OF YOU, I HAVE TO CANCEL PAID PERFORMANCES--
JOSIE, I SWEAR--
IT'S FINE, REGGIE. WE HAD FUN...
...BUT I ONLY HAVE THE BANDWITH FOR ONE THING--AND THAT'S BEING A STAR. CAN'T BE ATTACHED RIGHT NOW, YOU UNDERSTAND.

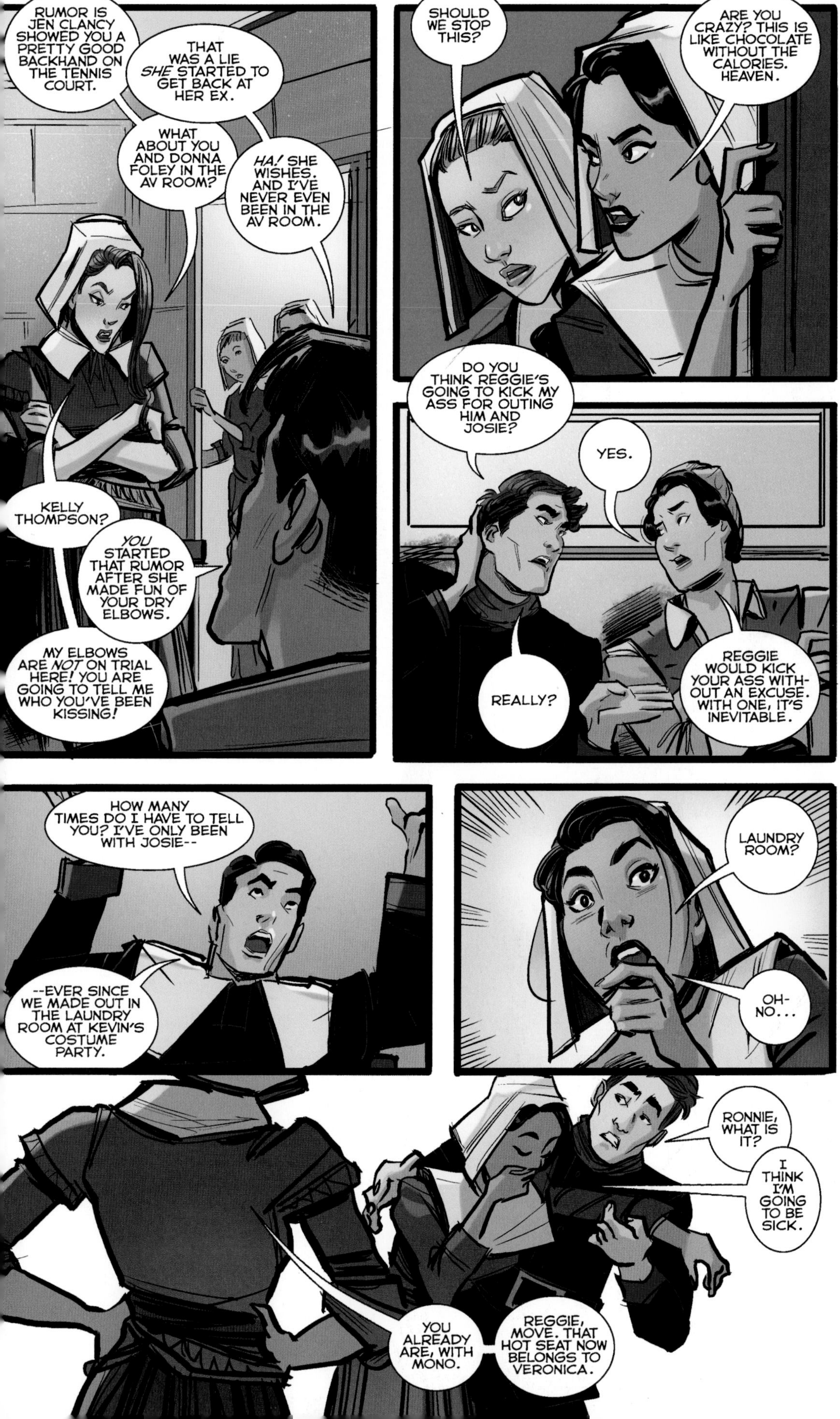

RUMOR IS JEN CLANCY SHOWED YOU A PRETTY GOOD BACKHAND ON THE TENNIS COURT.
THAT WAS A LIE *SHE* STARTED TO GET BACK AT HER EX.
WHAT ABOUT YOU AND DONNA FOLEY IN THE AV ROOM?
HA! SHE WISHES. AND I'VE NEVER EVEN BEEN IN THE AV ROOM.
KELLY THOMPSON?
YOU STARTED THAT RUMOR AFTER SHE MADE FUN OF YOUR DRY ELBOWS.
MY ELBOWS ARE *NOT* ON TRIAL HERE! YOU ARE GOING TO TELL ME WHO YOU'VE BEEN KISSING!
SHOULD WE STOP THIS?
ARE YOU CRAZY? THIS IS LIKE CHOCOLATE WITHOUT THE CALORIES. HEAVEN.
DO YOU THINK REGGIE'S GOING TO KICK MY ASS FOR OUTING HIM AND JOSIE?
YES.
REALLY?
REGGIE WOULD KICK YOUR ASS WITHOUT AN EXCUSE. WITH ONE, IT'S INEVITABLE.
HOW MANY TIMES DO I HAVE TO TELL YOU? I'VE ONLY BEEN WITH JOSIE--
--EVER SINCE WE MADE OUT IN THE LAUNDRY ROOM AT KEVIN'S COSTUME PARTY.
LAUNDRY ROOM?
OH-NO...
RONNIE, WHAT IS IT?
I THINK I'M GOING TO BE SICK.
YOU ALREADY ARE, WITH MONO.
REGGIE, MOVE. THAT HOT SEAT NOW BELONGS TO VERONICA.

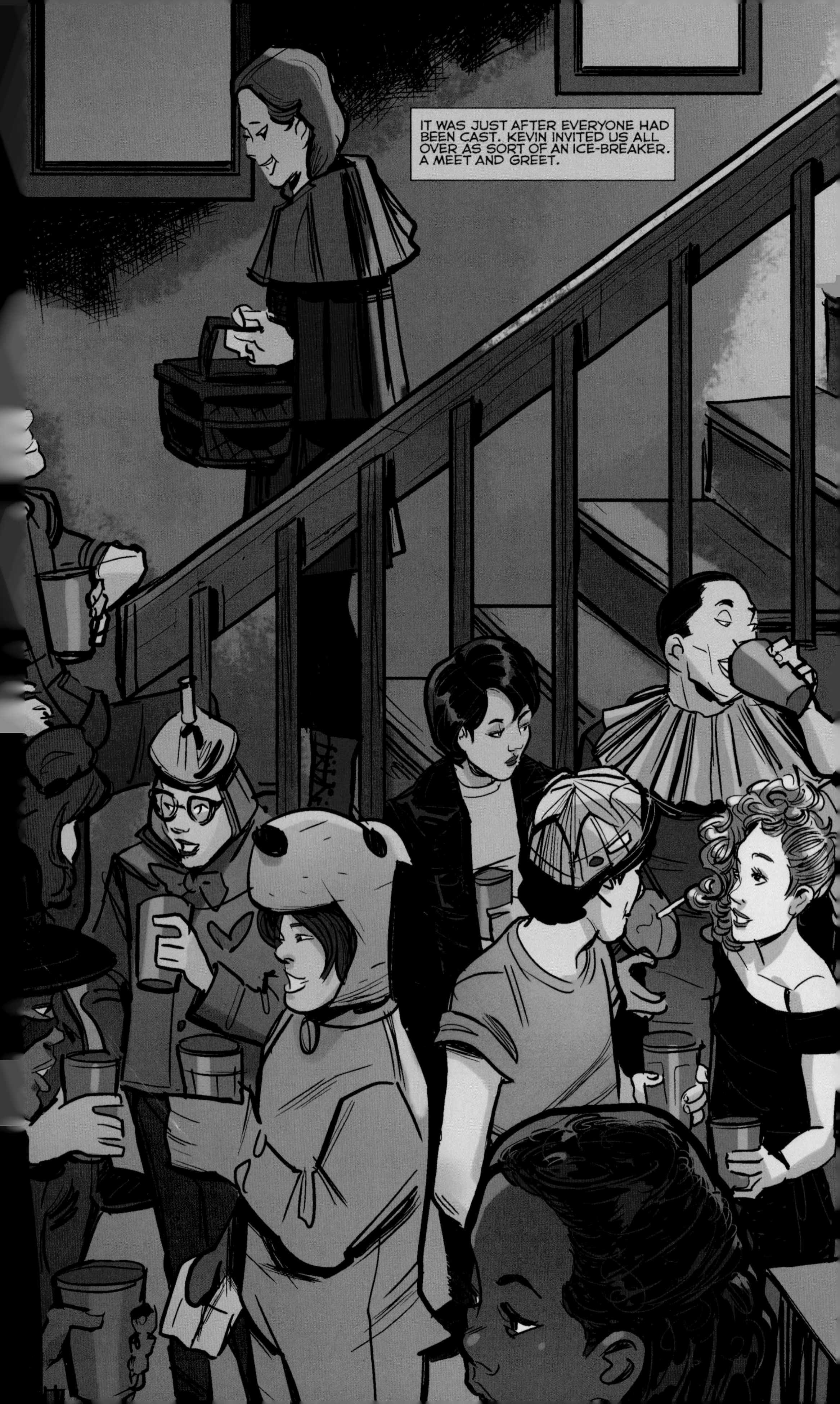
IT WAS JUST AFTER EVERYONE HAD BEEN CAST. KEVIN INVITED US ALL OVER AS SORT OF AN ICE-BREAKER. A MEET AND GREET.

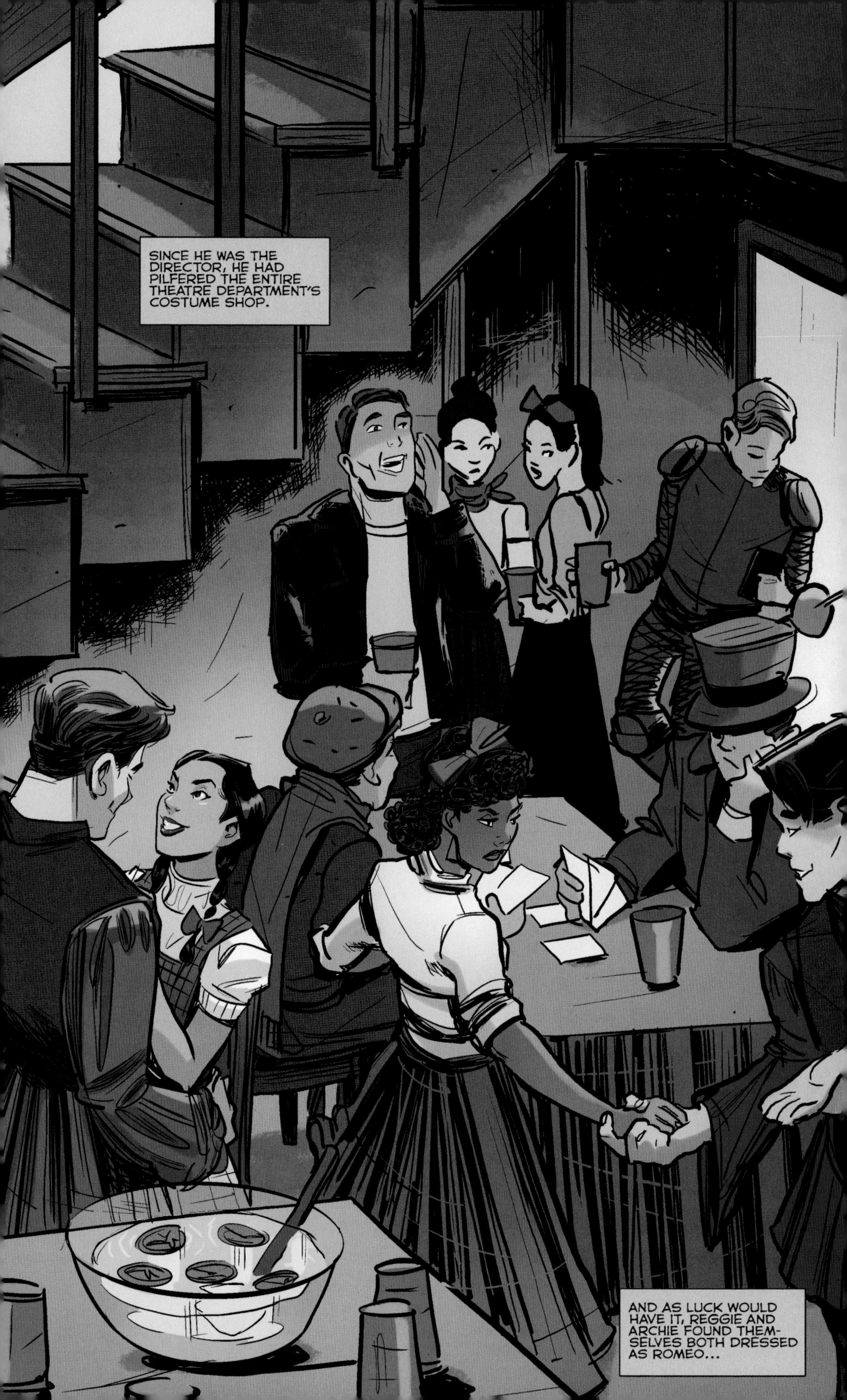
SINCE HE WAS THE DIRECTOR, HE HAD PILFERED THE ENTIRE THEATRE DEPARTMENT'S COSTUME SHOP.
AND AS LUCK WOULD HAVE IT, REGGIE AND ARCHIE FOUND THEMSELVES BOTH DRESSED AS ROMEO...

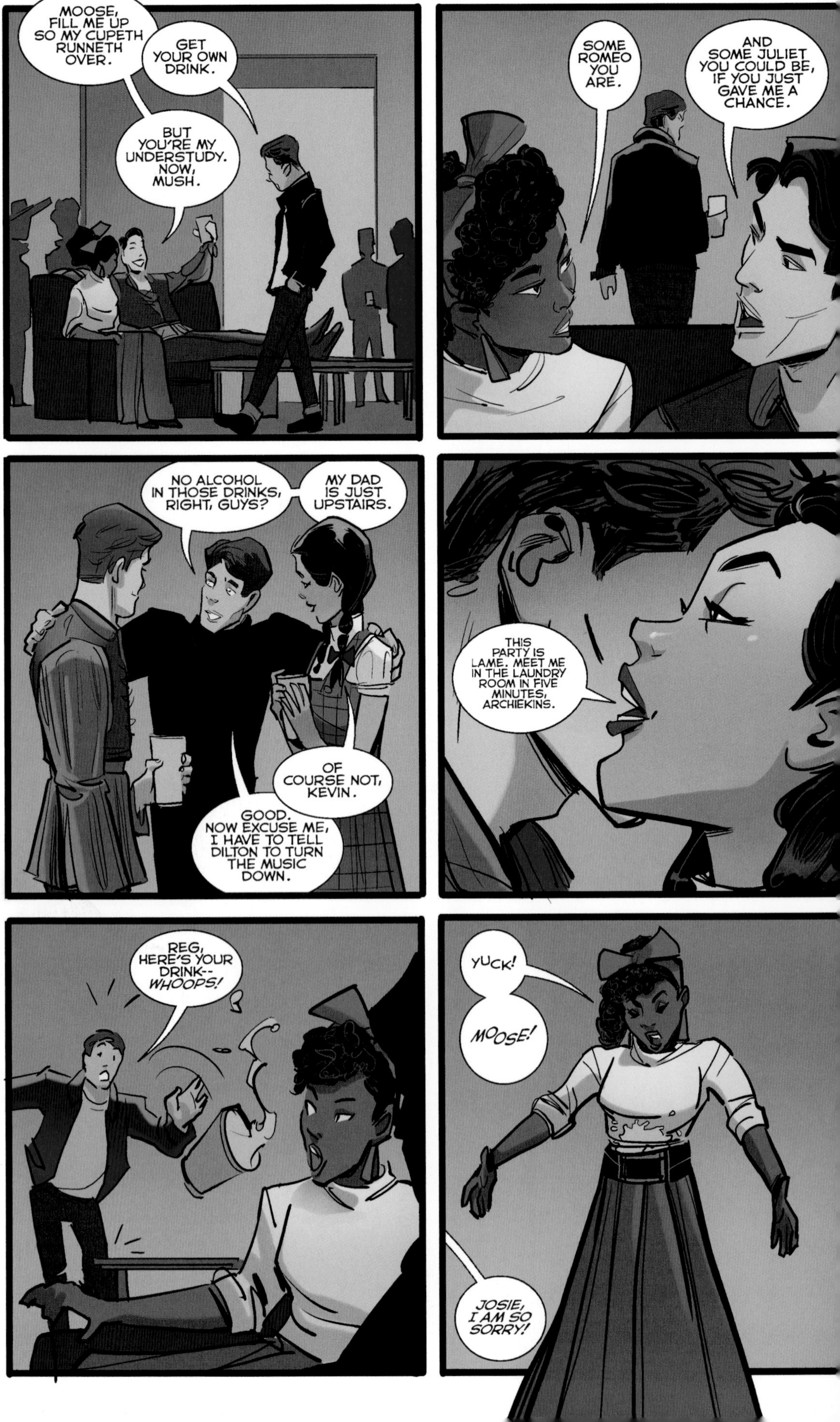

MOOSE, FILL ME UP SO MY CUPETH RUNNETH OVER.
GET YOUR OWN DRINK.
BUT YOU'RE MY UNDERSTUDY. NOW, MUSH.
SOME ROMEO YOU ARE.
AND SOME JULIET YOU COULD BE, IF YOU JUST GAVE ME A CHANCE.
NO ALCOHOL IN THOSE DRINKS, RIGHT, GUYS?
MY DAD IS JUST UPSTAIRS.
OF COURSE NOT, KEVIN.
GOOD. NOW EXCUSE ME, I HAVE TO TELL DILTON TO TURN THE MUSIC DOWN.
THIS PARTY IS LAME. MEET ME IN THE LAUNDRY ROOM IN FIVE MINUTES, ARCHIEKINS.
REG, HERE'S YOUR DRINK-- *WHOOPS!*
YUCK!
MOOSE!
JOSIE, I AM SO SORRY!

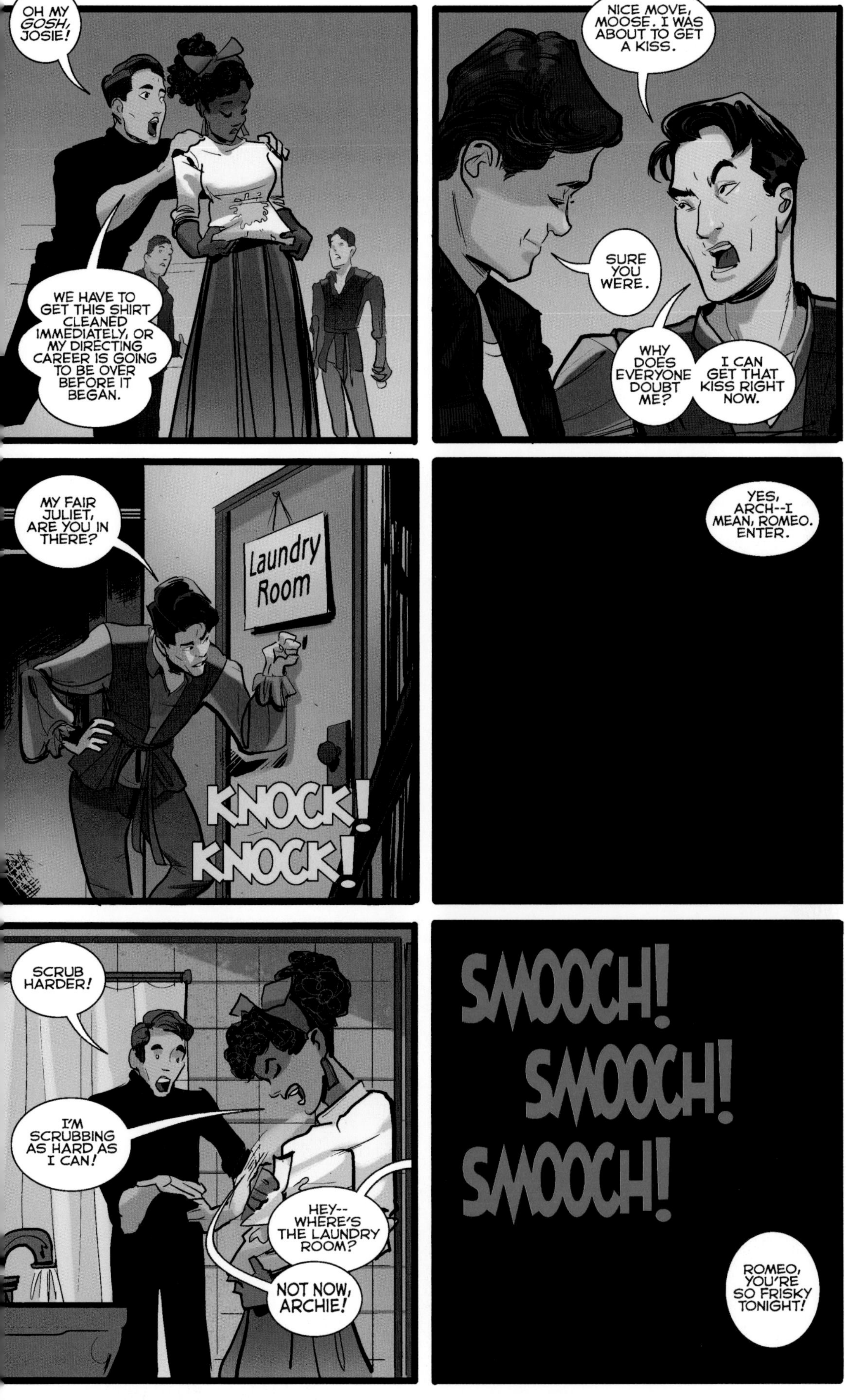
OH MY *GOSH*, JOSIE!
WE HAVE TO GET THIS SHIRT CLEANED IMMEDIATELY, OR MY DIRECTING CAREER IS GOING TO BE OVER BEFORE IT BEGAN.
NICE MOVE, MOOSE. I WAS ABOUT TO GET A KISS.
SURE YOU WERE.
WHY DOES EVERYONE DOUBT ME?
I CAN GET THAT KISS RIGHT NOW.
MY FAIR JULIET, ARE YOU IN THERE?
Laundry Room
KNOCK! KNOCK!
YES, ARCH--I MEAN, ROMEO. ENTER.
SCRUB HARDER!
I'M SCRUBBING AS HARD AS I CAN!
HEY--WHERE'S THE LAUNDRY ROOM?
NOT NOW, ARCHIE!
SMOOCH! SMOOCH! SMOOCH!
ROMEO, YOU'RE SO FRISKY TONIGHT!

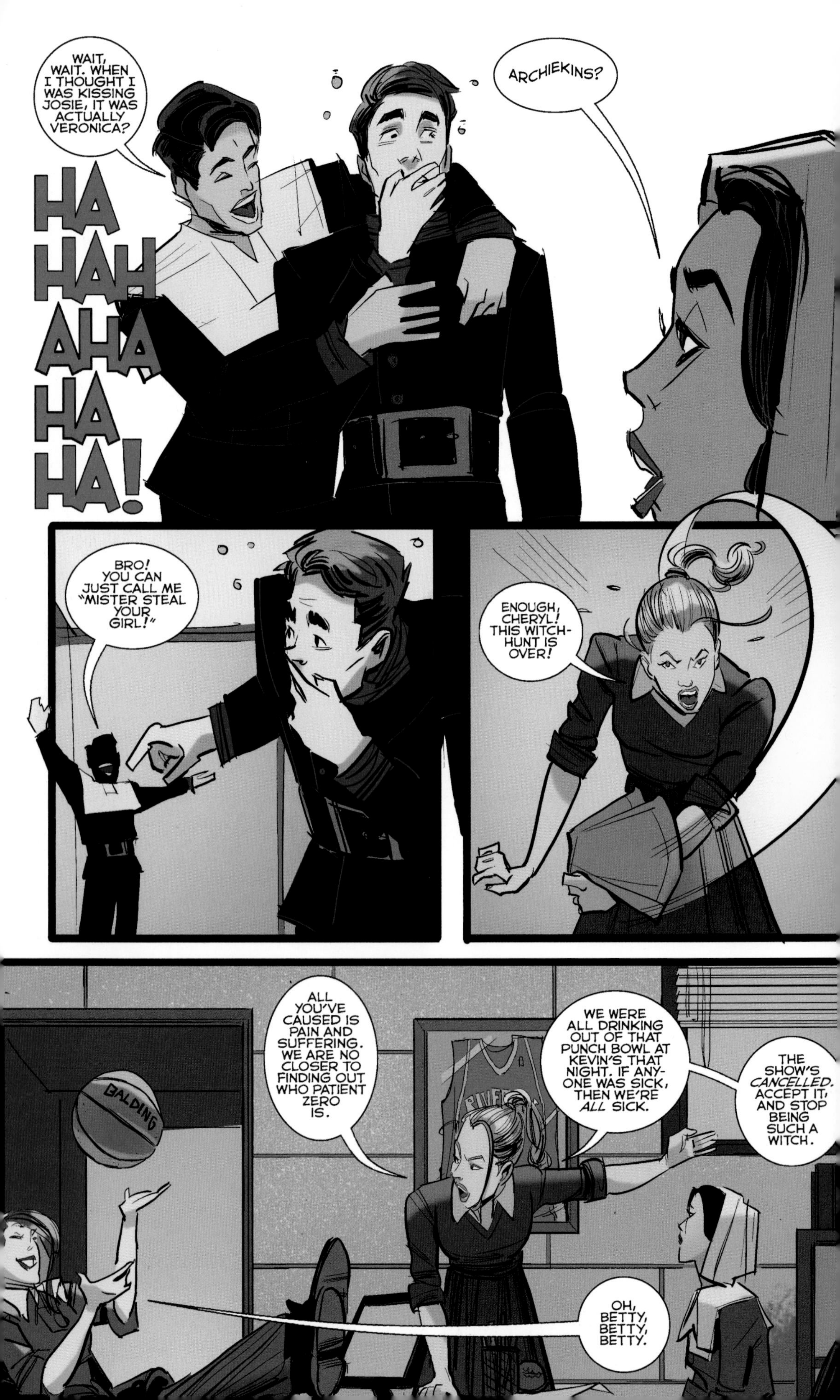

WAIT, WAIT. WHEN I THOUGHT I WAS KISSING JOSIE, IT WAS ACTUALLY VERONICA?
HA HAH AHA HA HA!
ARCHIEKINS?
BRO! YOU CAN JUST CALL ME "MISTER STEAL YOUR GIRL!"
ENOUGH, CHERYL! THIS WITCH-HUNT IS OVER!
ALL YOU'VE CAUSED IS PAIN AND SUFFERING. WE ARE NO CLOSER TO FINDING OUT WHO PATIENT ZERO IS.
WE WERE ALL DRINKING OUT OF THAT PUNCH BOWL AT KEVIN'S THAT NIGHT. IF ANY-ONE WAS SICK, THEN WE'RE *ALL* SICK.
THE SHOW'S *CANCELLED*. ACCEPT IT, AND STOP BEING SUCH A WITCH.
OH, BETTY, BETTY, BETTY.
BALDING

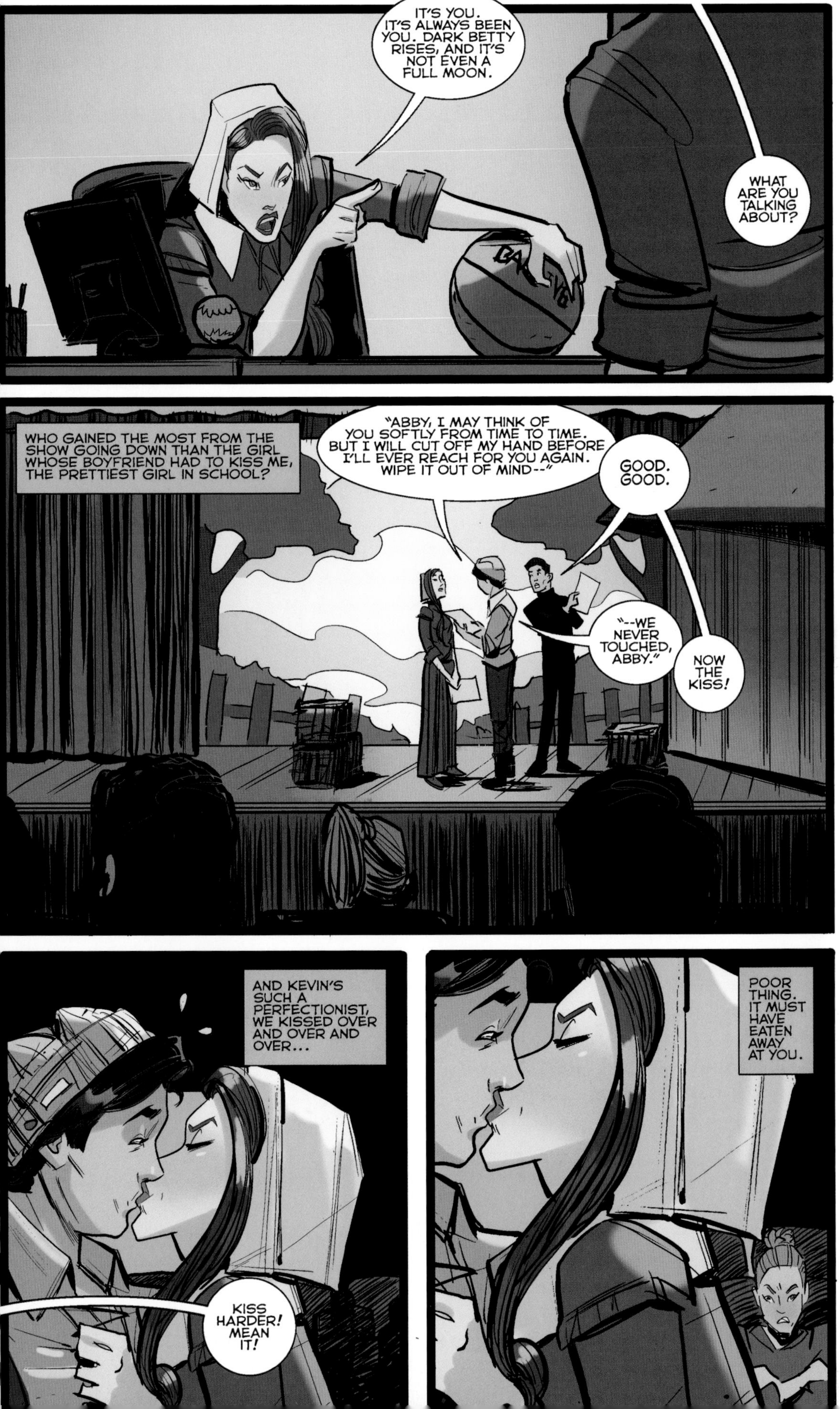
IT'S YOU. IT'S ALWAYS BEEN YOU. DARK BETTY RISES, AND IT'S NOT EVEN A FULL MOON.
WHAT ARE YOU TALKING ABOUT?
WHO GAINED THE MOST FROM THE SHOW GOING DOWN THAN THE GIRL WHOSE BOYFRIEND HAD TO KISS ME, THE PRETTIEST GIRL IN SCHOOL?
"ABBY, I MAY THINK OF YOU SOFTLY FROM TIME TO TIME. BUT I WILL CUT OFF MY HAND BEFORE I'LL EVER REACH FOR YOU AGAIN. WIPE IT OUT OF MIND--"
GOOD. GOOD.
"--WE NEVER TOUCHED, ABBY."
NOW THE KISS!
AND KEVIN'S SUCH A PERFECTIONIST, WE KISSED OVER AND OVER AND OVER...
KISS HARDER! MEAN IT!
POOR THING. IT MUST HAVE EATEN AWAY AT YOU.

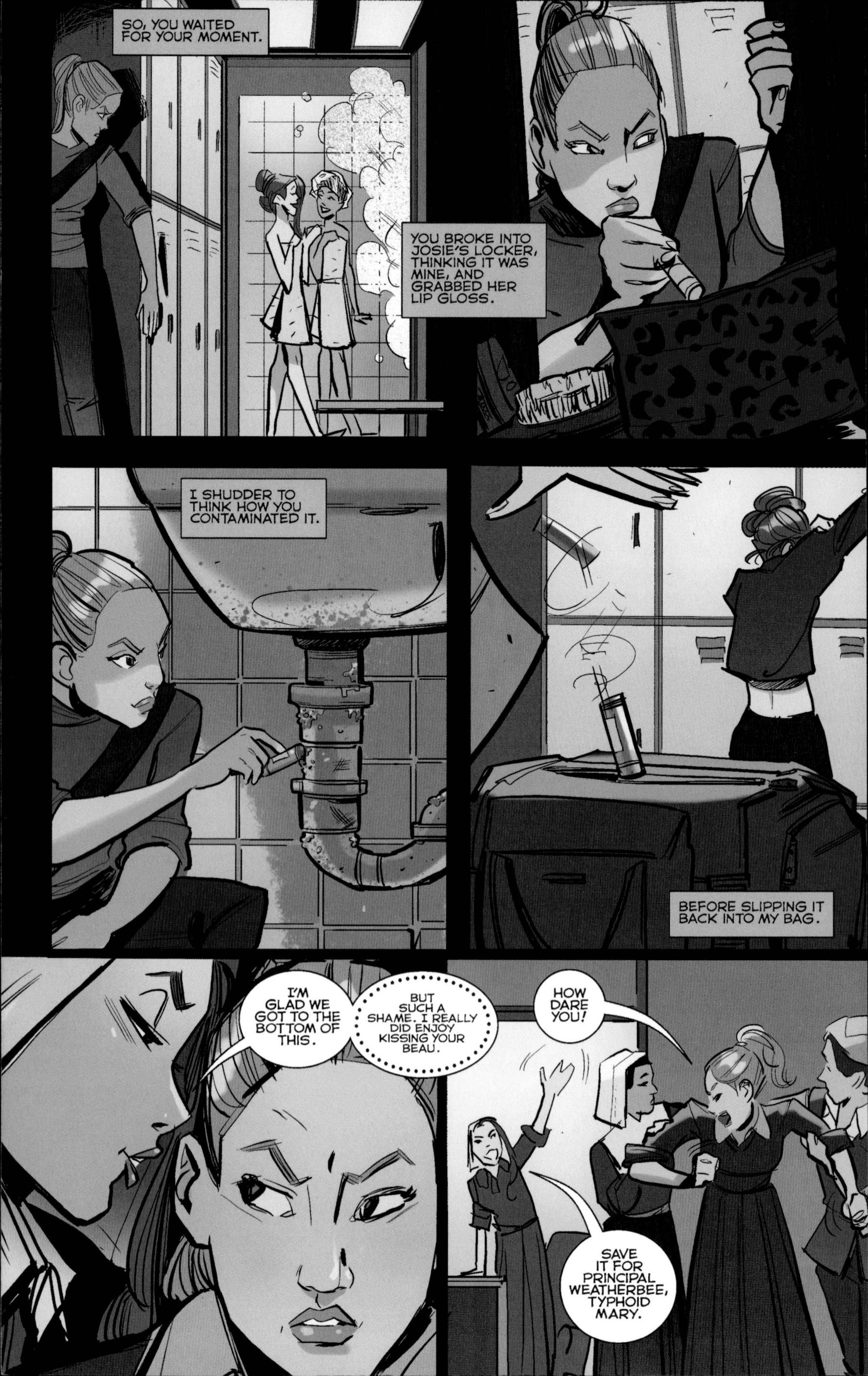
SO, YOU WAITED FOR YOUR MOMENT.
YOU BROKE INTO JOSIE'S LOCKER, THINKING IT WAS MINE, AND GRABBED HER LIP GLOSS.
I SHUDDER TO THINK HOW YOU CONTAMINATED IT.
BEFORE SLIPPING IT BACK INTO MY BAG.
I'M GLAD WE GOT TO THE BOTTOM OF THIS.
BUT SUCH A SHAME. I REALLY DID ENJOY KISSING YOUR BEAU.
HOW DARE YOU!
SAVE IT FOR PRINCIPAL WEATHERBEE, TYPHOID MARY.

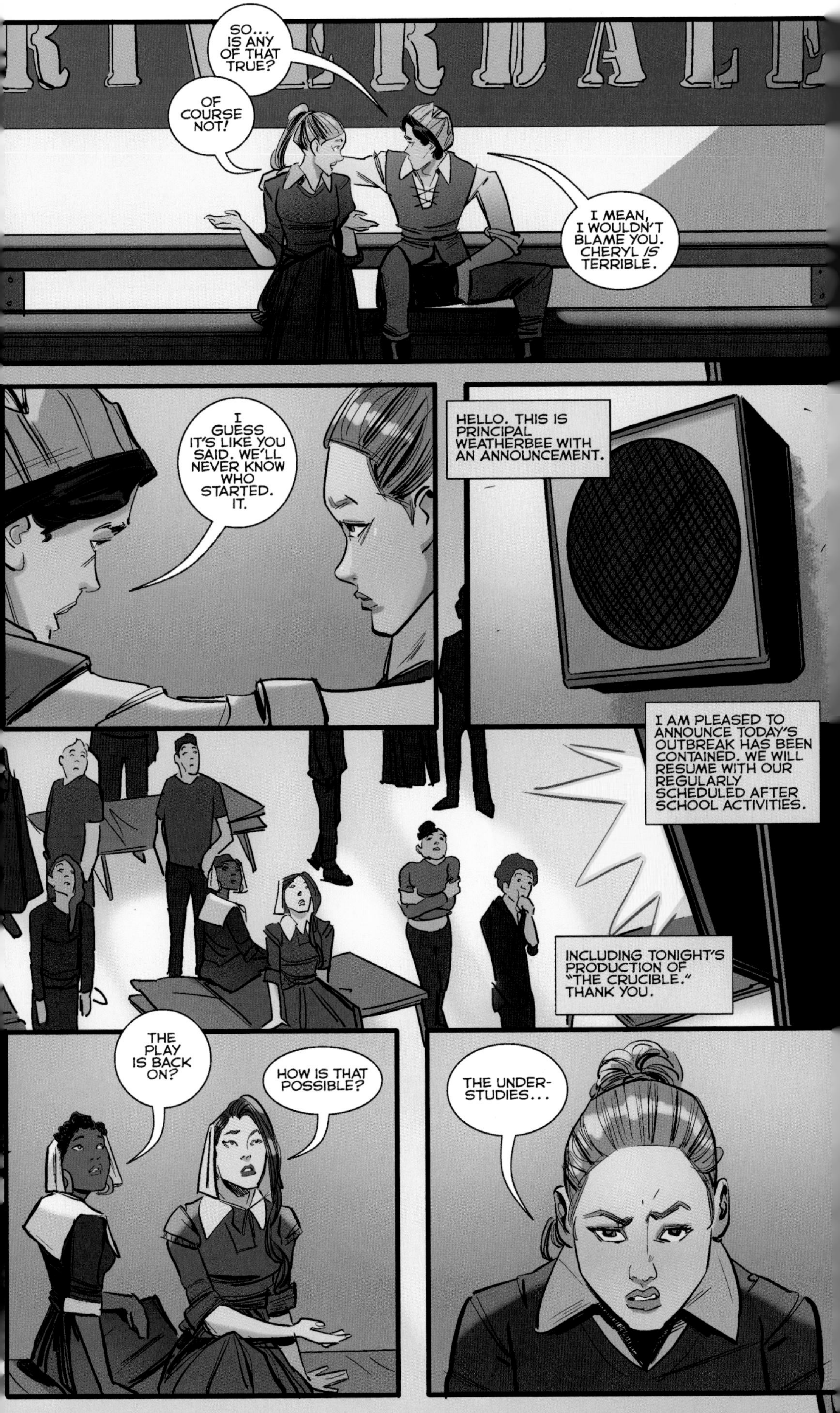
RIVERDALE
SO... IS ANY OF THAT TRUE?
OF COURSE NOT!
I MEAN, I WOULDN'T BLAME YOU. CHERYL *IS* TERRIBLE.
I GUESS IT'S LIKE YOU SAID. WE'LL NEVER KNOW WHO STARTED. IT.
HELLO. THIS IS PRINCIPAL WEATHERBEE WITH AN ANNOUNCEMENT.
I AM PLEASED TO ANNOUNCE TODAY'S OUTBREAK HAS BEEN CONTAINED. WE WILL RESUME WITH OUR REGULARLY SCHEDULED AFTER SCHOOL ACTIVITIES.
INCLUDING TONIGHT'S PRODUCTION OF "THE CRUCIBLE." THANK YOU.
THE PLAY IS BACK ON?
HOW IS THAT POSSIBLE?
THE UNDER-STUDIES...

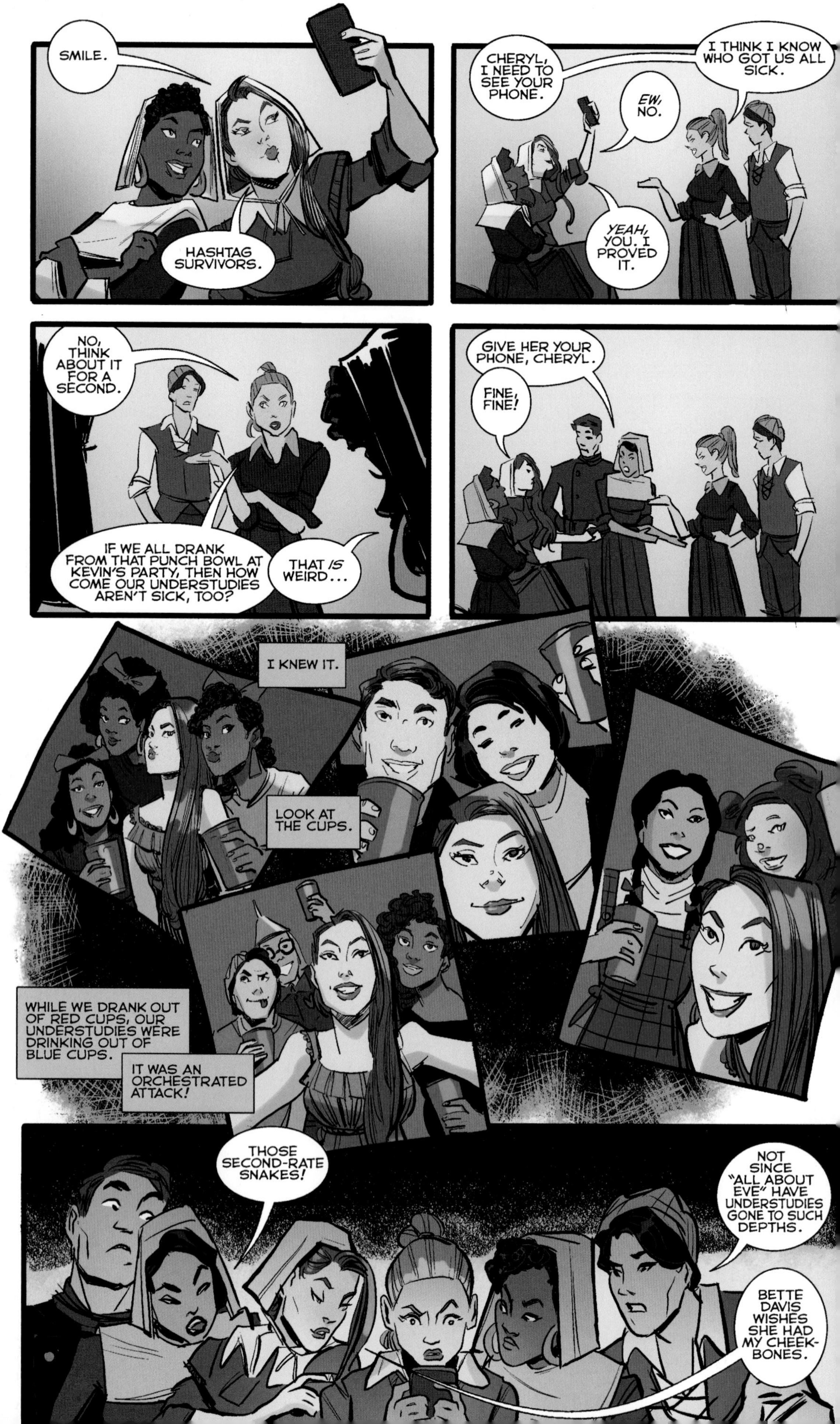
SMILE.
HASHTAG SURVIVORS.
CHERYL, I NEED TO SEE YOUR PHONE.
I THINK I KNOW WHO GOT US ALL SICK.
EW, NO.
YEAH, YOU. I PROVED IT.
NO, THINK ABOUT IT FOR A SECOND.
IF WE ALL DRANK FROM THAT PUNCH BOWL AT KEVIN'S PARTY, THEN HOW COME OUR UNDERSTUDIES AREN'T SICK, TOO?
THAT IS WEIRD...
GIVE HER YOUR PHONE, CHERYL.
FINE, FINE!
I KNEW IT.
LOOK AT THE CUPS.
WHILE WE DRANK OUT OF RED CUPS, OUR UNDERSTUDIES WERE DRINKING OUT OF BLUE CUPS.
IT WAS AN ORCHESTRATED ATTACK!
THOSE SECOND-RATE SNAKES!
NOT SINCE "ALL ABOUT EVE" HAVE UNDERSTUDIES GONE TO SUCH DEPTHS.
BETTE DAVIS WISHES SHE HAD MY CHEEK-BONES.

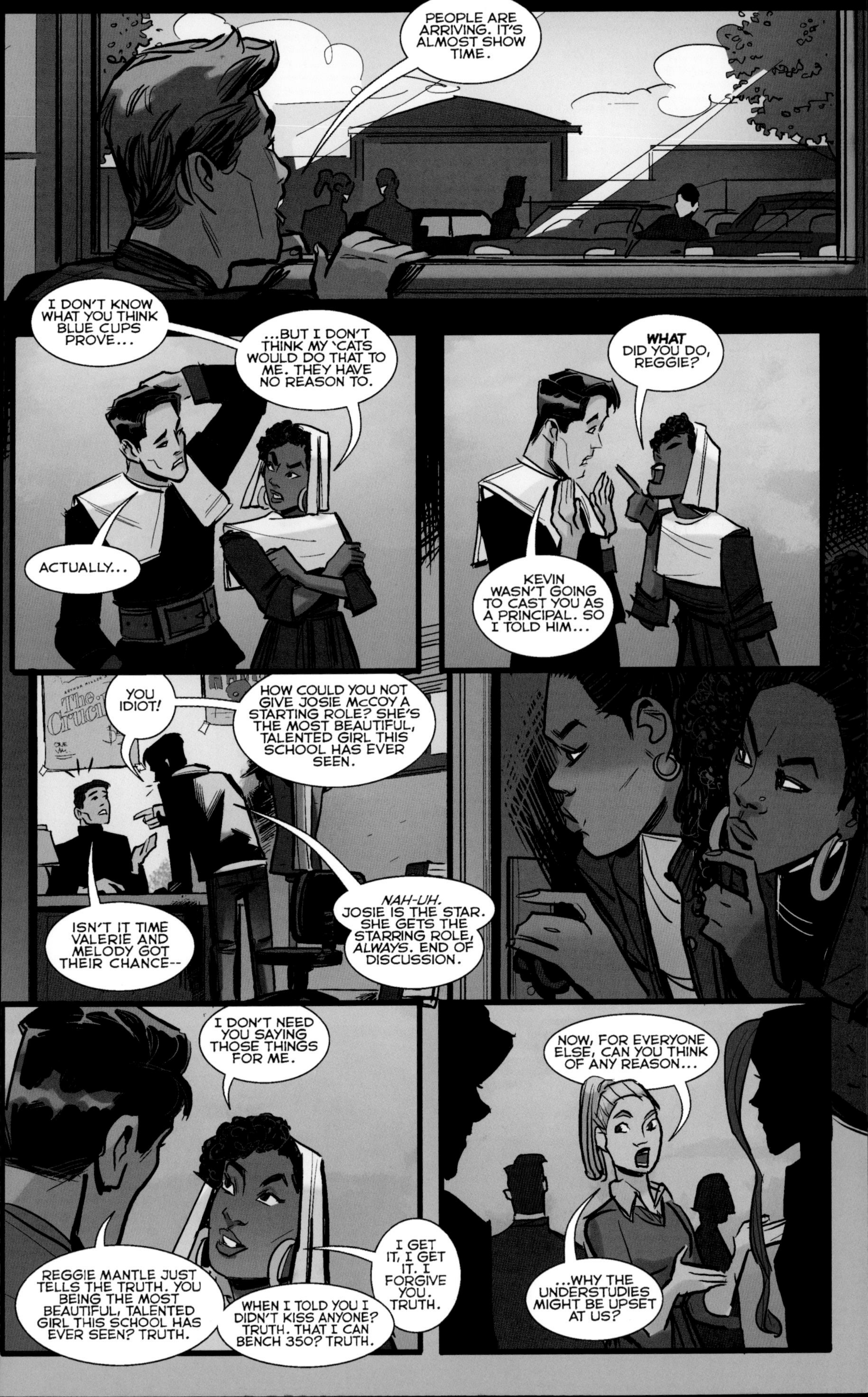
PEOPLE ARE ARRIVING. IT'S ALMOST SHOW TIME.
I DON'T KNOW WHAT YOU THINK BLUE CUPS PROVE...
...BUT I DON'T THINK MY 'CATS WOULD DO THAT TO ME. THEY HAVE NO REASON TO.
ACTUALLY...
WHAT DID YOU DO, REGGIE?
KEVIN WASN'T GOING TO CAST YOU AS A PRINCIPAL. SO I TOLD HIM...
YOU IDIOT!
HOW COULD YOU NOT GIVE JOSIE McCOY A STARTING ROLE? SHE'S THE MOST BEAUTIFUL, TALENTED GIRL THIS SCHOOL HAS EVER SEEN.
ISN'T IT TIME VALERIE AND MELODY GOT THEIR CHANCE--
NAH-UH. JOSIE IS THE STAR. SHE GETS THE STARRING ROLE, ALWAYS. END OF DISCUSSION.
I DON'T NEED YOU SAYING THOSE THINGS FOR ME.
REGGIE MANTLE JUST TELLS THE TRUTH. YOU BEING THE MOST BEAUTIFUL, TALENTED GIRL THIS SCHOOL HAS EVER SEEN? TRUTH.
WHEN I TOLD YOU I DIDN'T KISS ANYONE? TRUTH. THAT I CAN BENCH 350? TRUTH.
I GET IT, I GET IT. I FORGIVE YOU. TRUTH.
NOW, FOR EVERYONE ELSE, CAN YOU THINK OF ANY REASON...
...WHY THE UNDERSTUDIES MIGHT BE UPSET AT US?

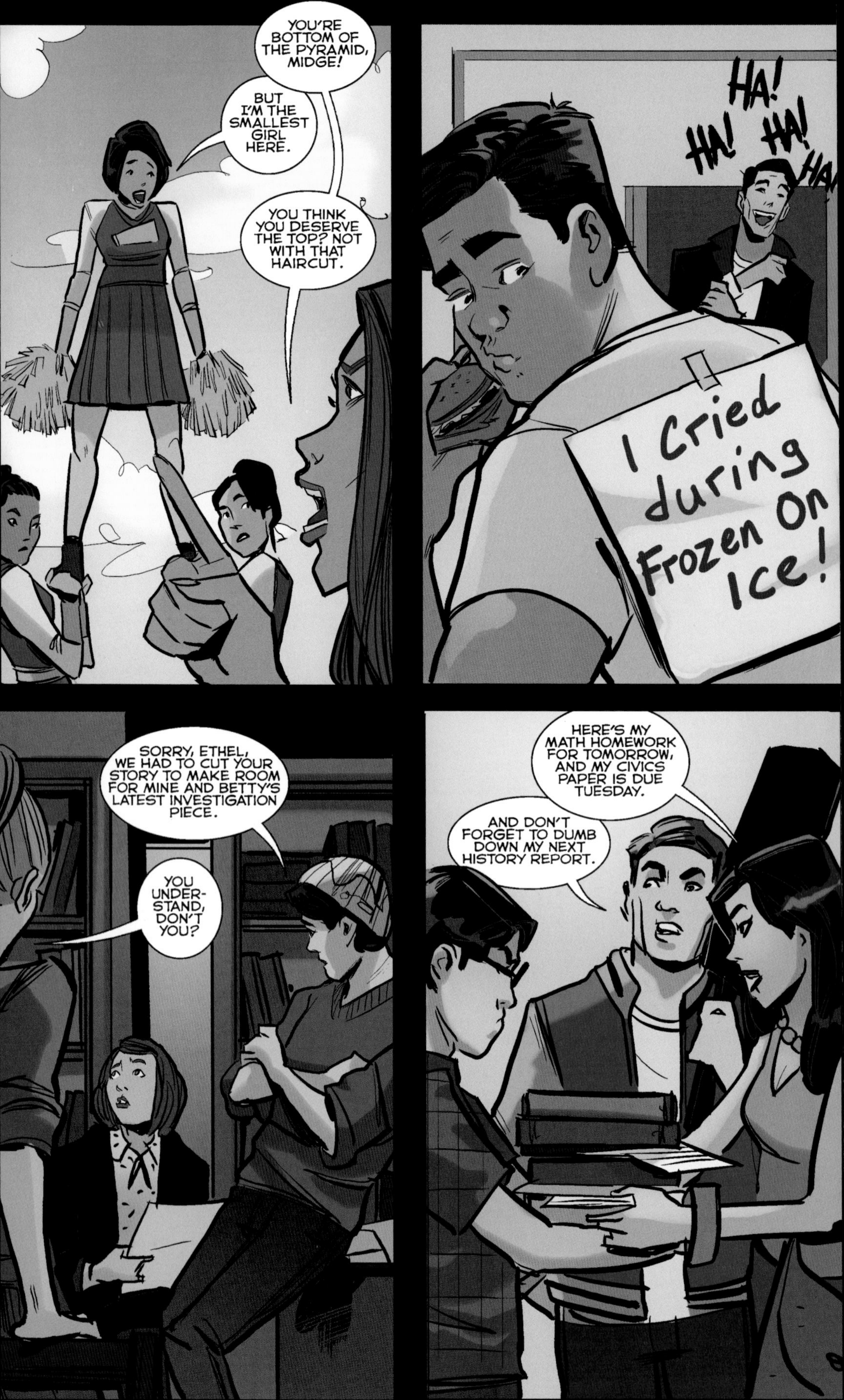
YOU'RE BOTTOM OF THE PYRAMID, MIDGE!
BUT I'M THE SMALLEST GIRL HERE.
YOU THINK YOU DESERVE THE TOP? NOT WITH THAT HAIRCUT.
HA! HA! HA! HA!
I Cried during Frozen On Ice!
SORRY, ETHEL, WE HAD TO CUT YOUR STORY TO MAKE ROOM FOR MINE AND BETTY'S LATEST INVESTIGATION PIECE.
YOU UNDER-STAND, DON'T YOU?
HERE'S MY MATH HOMEWORK FOR TOMORROW, AND MY CIVICS PAPER IS DUE TUESDAY.
AND DON'T FORGET TO DUMB DOWN MY NEXT HISTORY REPORT.

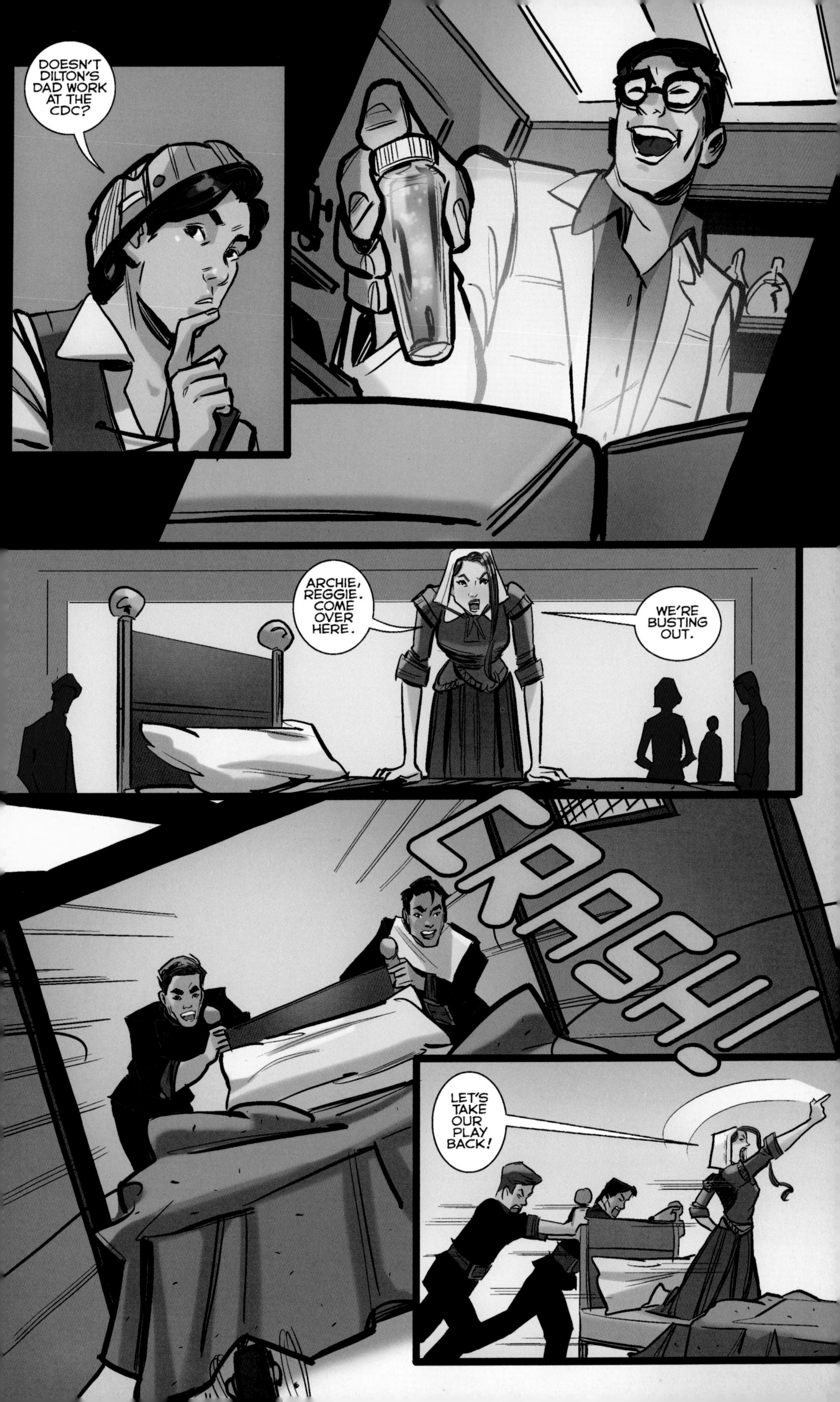
DOESN'T DILTON'S DAD WORK AT THE CDC?
ARCHIE, REGGIE. COME OVER HERE.
WE'RE BUSTING OUT.
CRASH!!
LET'S TAKE OUR PLAY BACK!

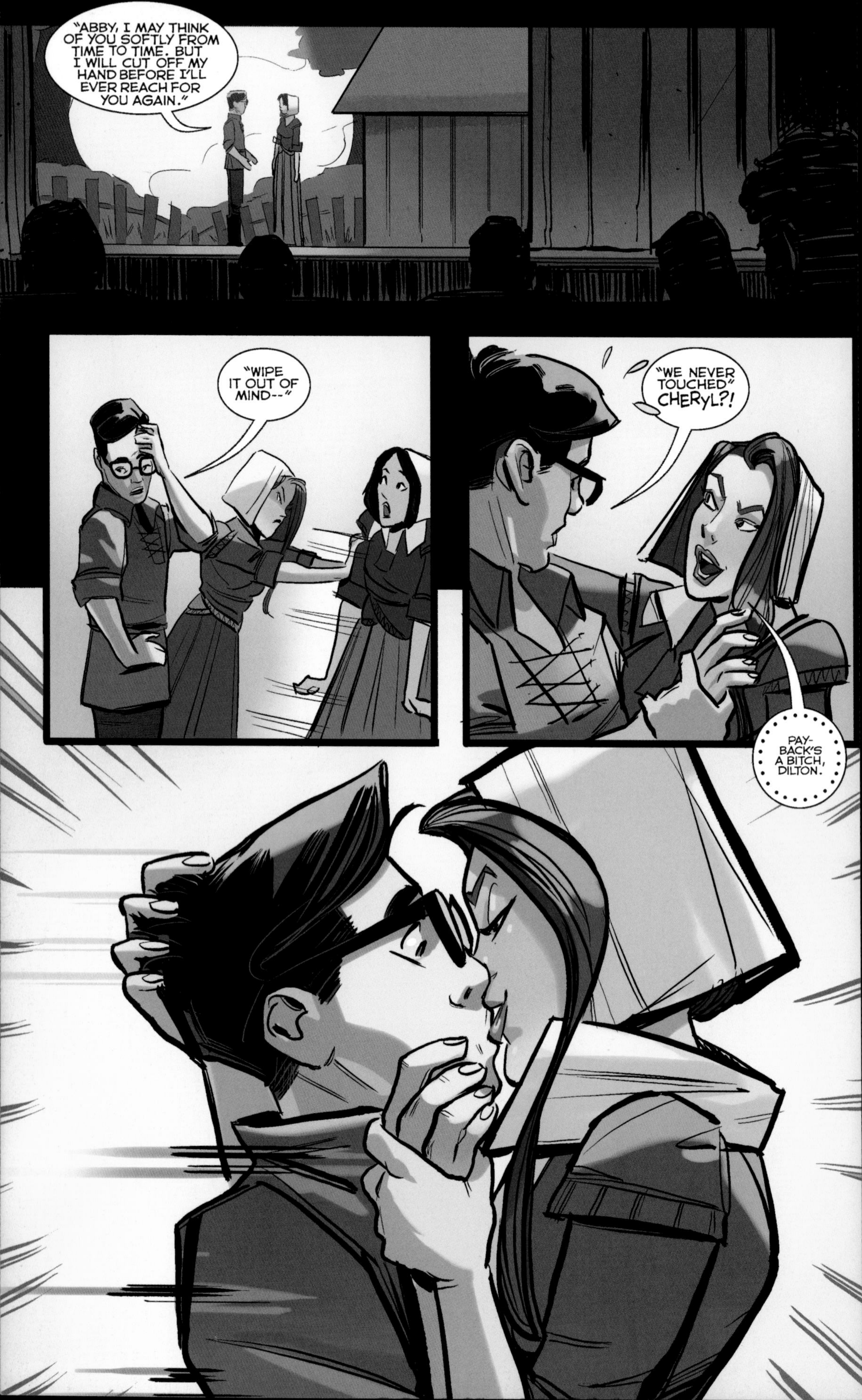
"ABBY, I MAY THINK OF YOU SOFTLY FROM TIME TO TIME. BUT I WILL CUT OFF MY HAND BEFORE I'LL EVER REACH FOR YOU AGAIN."
"WIPE IT OUT OF MIND--"
"WE NEVER TOUCHED" CHERyL?!
PAY-BACK'S A BITCH, DILTON.

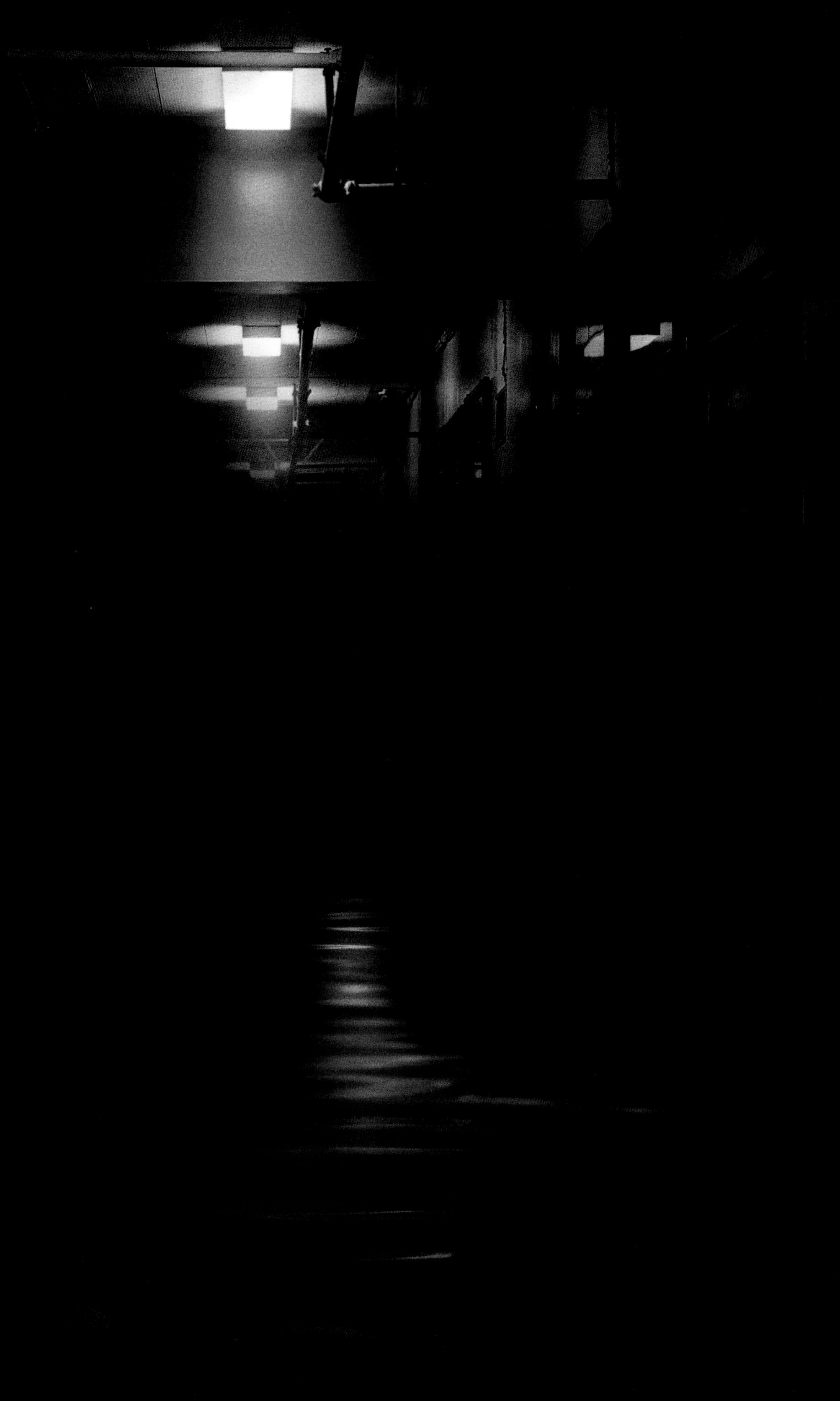

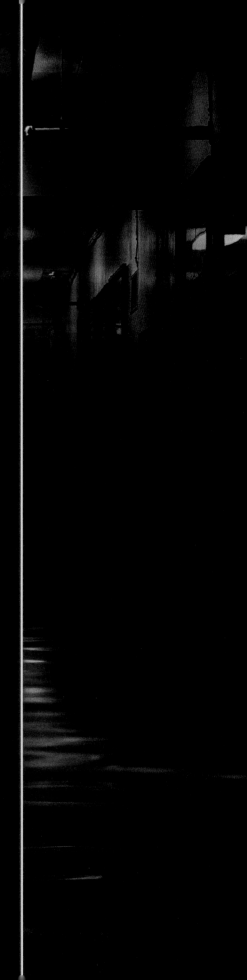

ISSUE ELEVEN

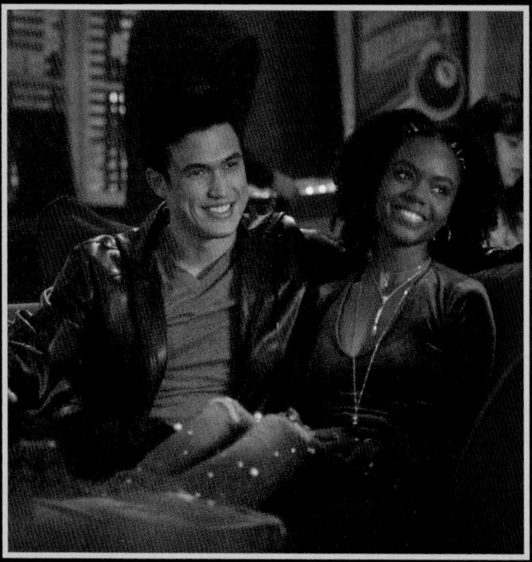

THE LAST WILL AND TESTAMENT OF REGGIE MANTLE

WRITER:
GREG MURRAY

ART:
THOMAS PITILLI

COLORS:
ANDRE SZYMANOWICZ

LETTERS:
JANICE CHIANG

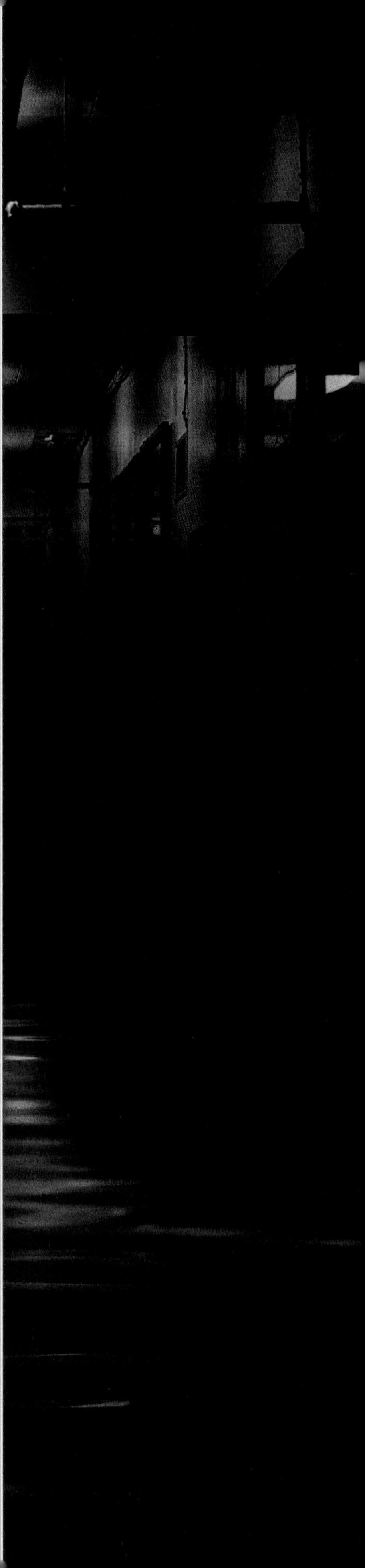

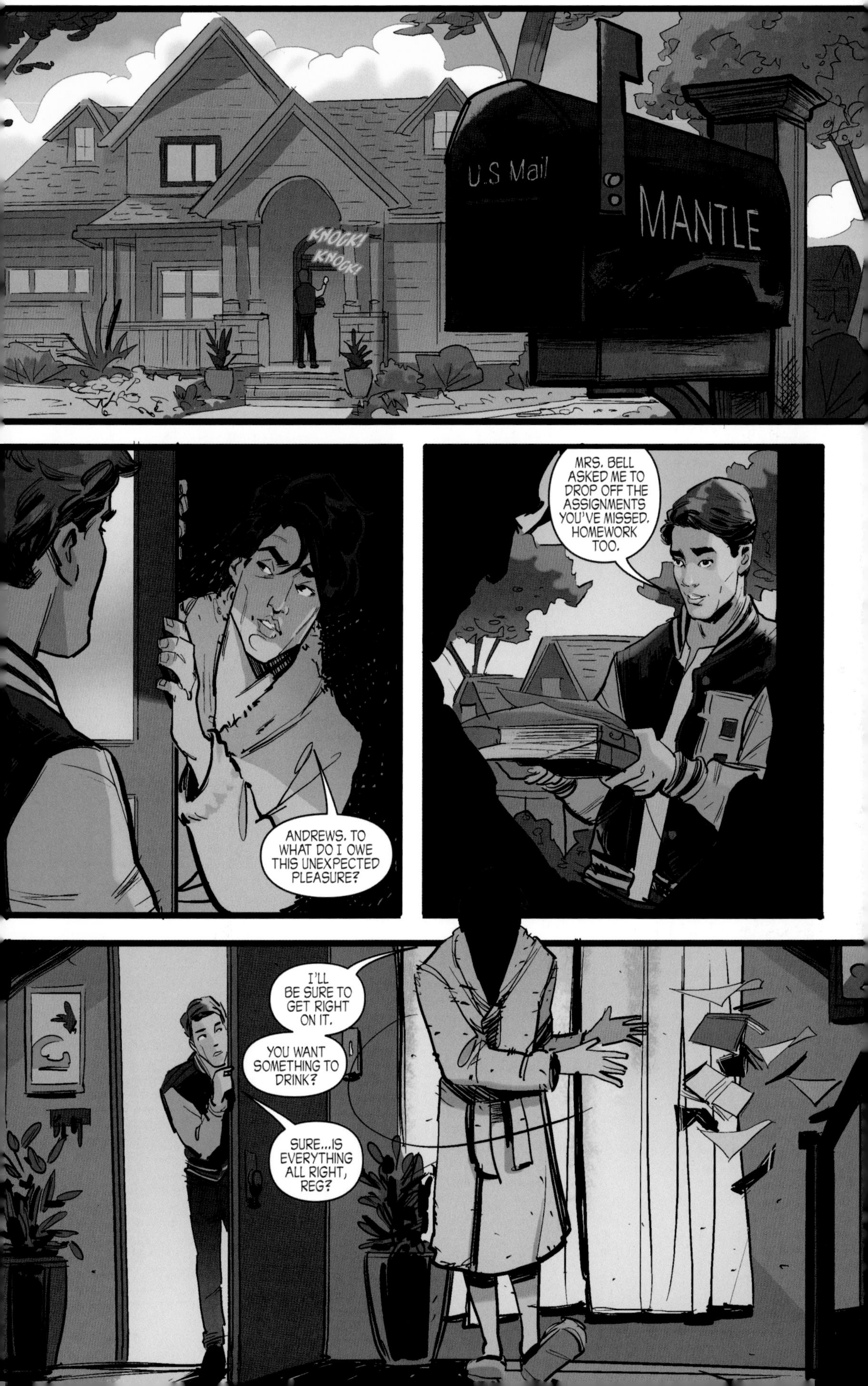
U.S Mail
MANTLE
KNOCK! KNOCK!
ANDREWS. TO WHAT DO I OWE THIS UNEXPECTED PLEASURE?
MRS. BELL ASKED ME TO DROP OFF THE ASSIGNMENTS YOU'VE MISSED. HOMEWORK TOO.
I'LL BE SURE TO GET RIGHT ON IT.
YOU WANT SOMETHING TO DRINK?
SURE...IS EVERYTHING ALL RIGHT, REG?

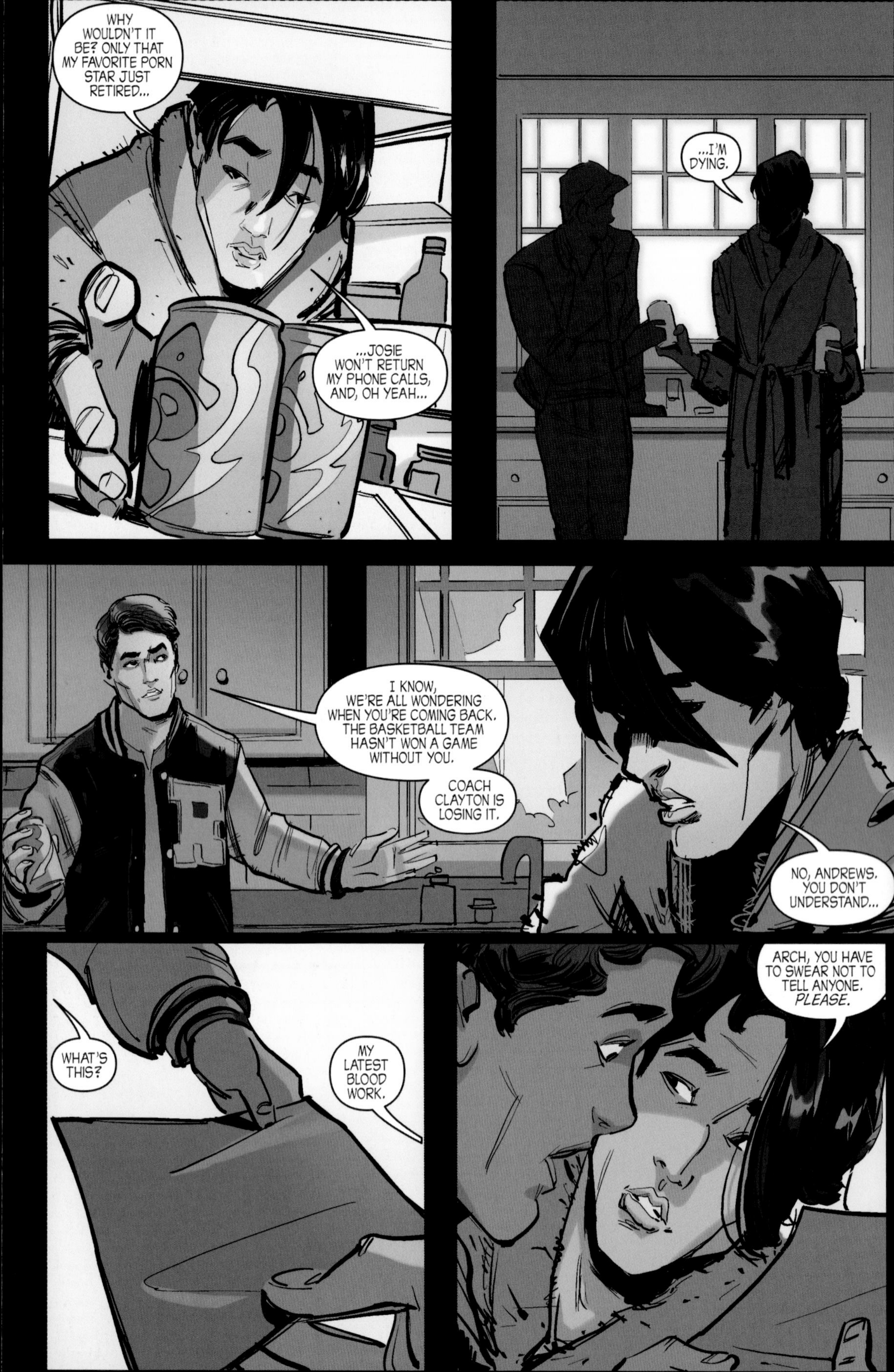
WHY WOULDN'T IT BE? ONLY THAT MY FAVORITE PORN STAR JUST RETIRED...
...JOSIE WON'T RETURN MY PHONE CALLS, AND, OH YEAH...
...I'M DYING.
I KNOW, WE'RE ALL WONDERING WHEN YOU'RE COMING BACK. THE BASKETBALL TEAM HASN'T WON A GAME WITHOUT YOU.
COACH CLAYTON IS LOSING IT.
NO, ANDREWS. YOU DON'T UNDERSTAND...
WHAT'S THIS?
MY LATEST BLOOD WORK.
ARCH, YOU HAVE TO SWEAR NOT TO TELL ANYONE. *PLEASE*.

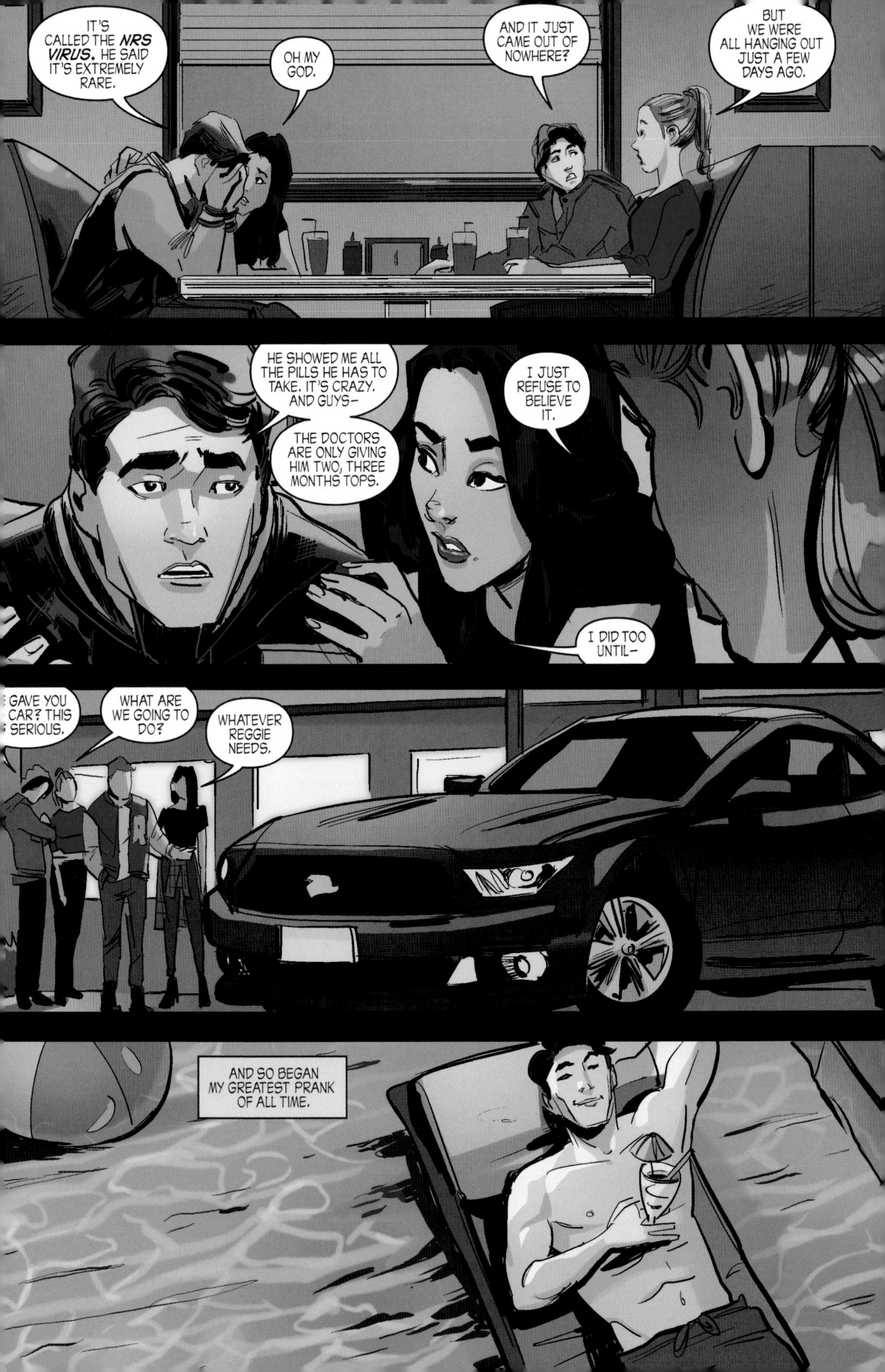
IT'S CALLED THE NRS VIRUS. HE SAID IT'S EXTREMELY RARE.
OH MY GOD.
AND IT JUST CAME OUT OF NOWHERE?
BUT WE WERE ALL HANGING OUT JUST A FEW DAYS AGO.
HE SHOWED ME ALL THE PILLS HE HAS TO TAKE. IT'S CRAZY. AND GUYS–
THE DOCTORS ARE ONLY GIVING HIM TWO, THREE MONTHS TOPS.
I JUST REFUSE TO BELIEVE IT.
I DID TOO UNTIL–
GAVE YOU CAR? THIS SERIOUS.
WHAT ARE WE GOING TO DO?
WHATEVER REGGIE NEEDS.
AND SO BEGAN MY GREATEST PRANK OF ALL TIME.

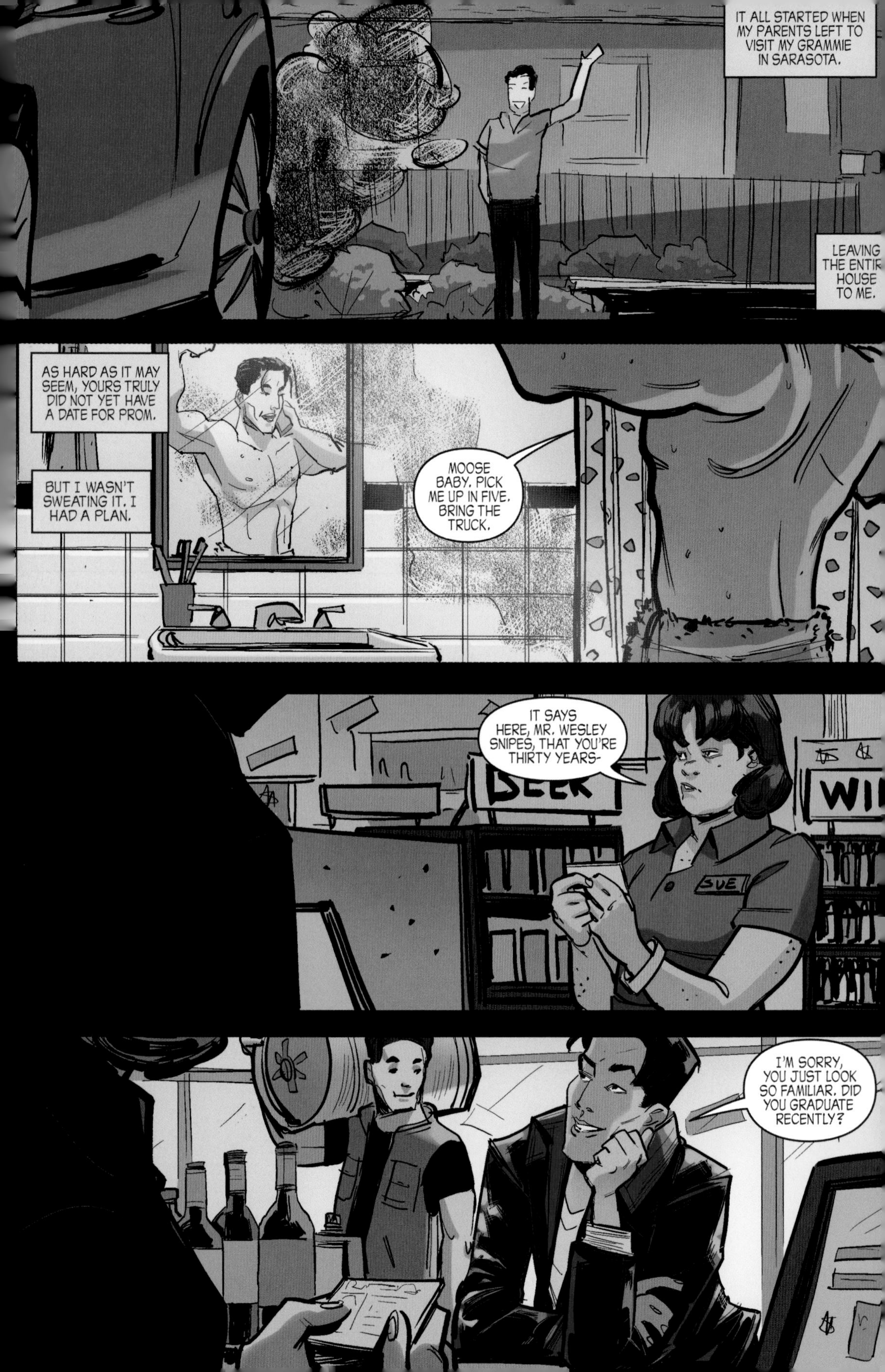
IT ALL STARTED WHEN MY PARENTS LEFT TO VISIT MY GRAMMIE IN SARASOTA.
LEAVING THE ENTIR HOUSE TO ME.
AS HARD AS IT MAY SEEM, YOURS TRULY DID NOT YET HAVE A DATE FOR PROM.
BUT I WASN'T SWEATING IT. I HAD A PLAN.
MOOSE BABY. PICK ME UP IN FIVE. BRING THE TRUCK.
IT SAYS HERE, MR. WESLEY SNIPES, THAT YOU'RE THIRTY YEARS-
SUE
I'M SORRY, YOU JUST LOOK SO FAMILIAR. DID YOU GRADUATE RECENTLY?

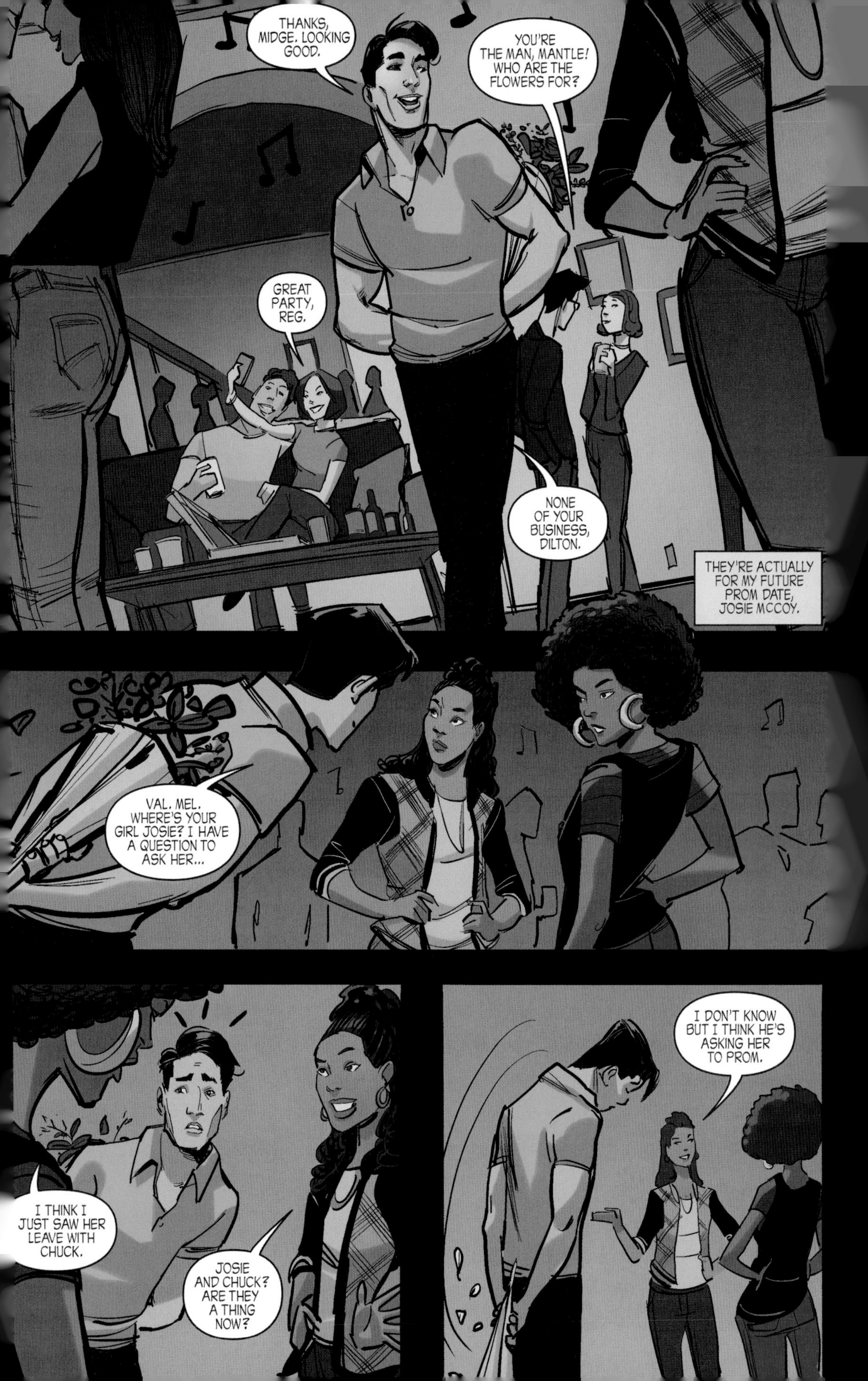
THANKS, MIDGE. LOOKING GOOD.
YOU'RE THE MAN, MANTLE! WHO ARE THE FLOWERS FOR?
GREAT PARTY, REG.
NONE OF YOUR BUSINESS, DILTON.
THEY'RE ACTUALLY FOR MY FUTURE PROM DATE, JOSIE MCCOY.
VAL. MEL. WHERE'S YOUR GIRL JOSIE? I HAVE A QUESTION TO ASK HER...
I THINK I JUST SAW HER LEAVE WITH CHUCK.
JOSIE AND CHUCK? ARE THEY A THING NOW?
I DON'T KNOW BUT I THINK HE'S ASKING HER TO PROM.

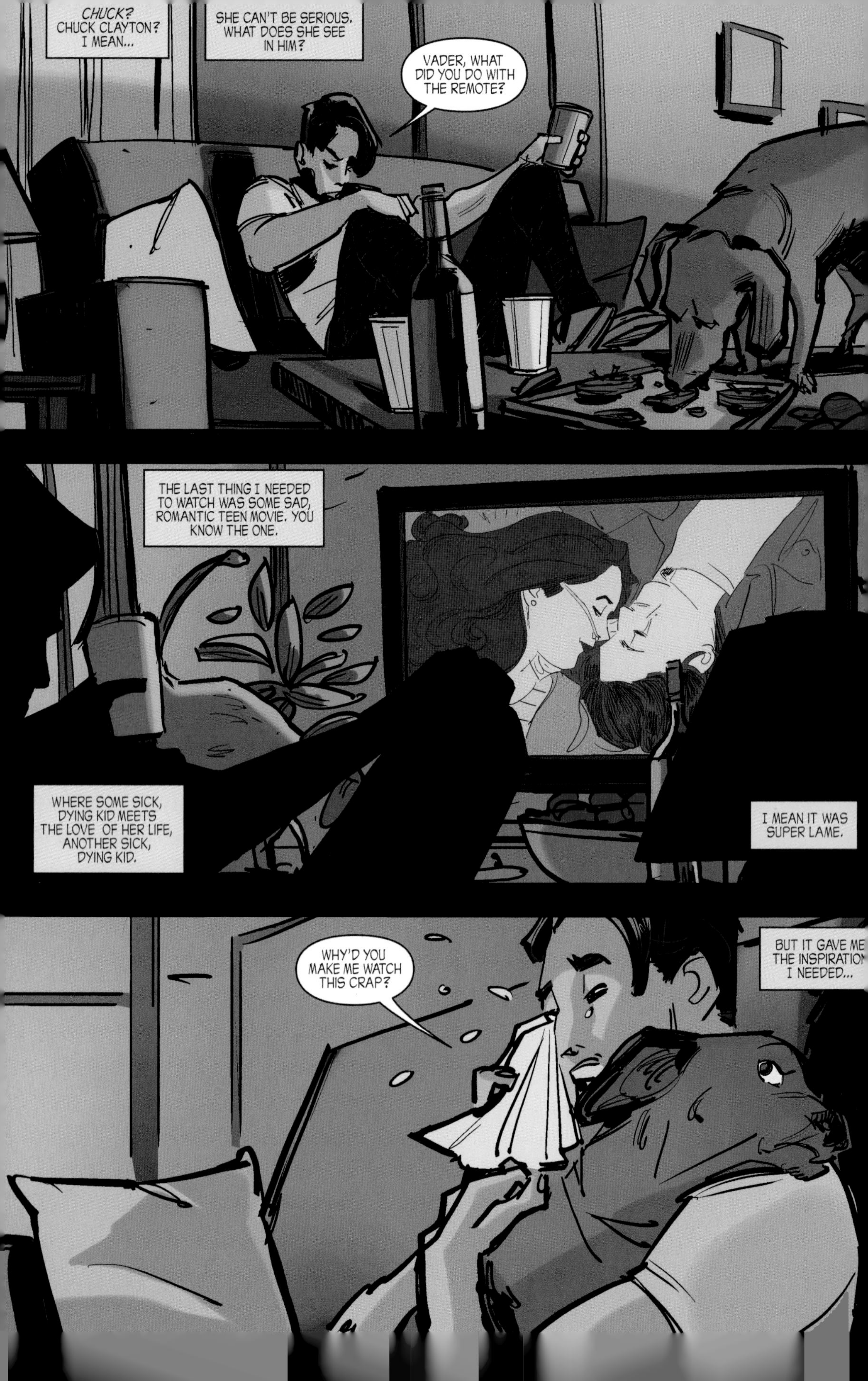
CHUCK? CHUCK CLAYTON? I MEAN...
SHE CAN'T BE SERIOUS. WHAT DOES SHE SEE IN HIM?
VADER, WHAT DID YOU DO WITH THE REMOTE?
THE LAST THING I NEEDED TO WATCH WAS SOME SAD, ROMANTIC TEEN MOVIE. YOU KNOW THE ONE.
WHERE SOME SICK, DYING KID MEETS THE LOVE OF HER LIFE, ANOTHER SICK, DYING KID.
I MEAN IT WAS SUPER LAME.
WHY'D YOU MAKE ME WATCH THIS CRAP?
BUT IT GAVE ME THE INSPIRATION I NEEDED...

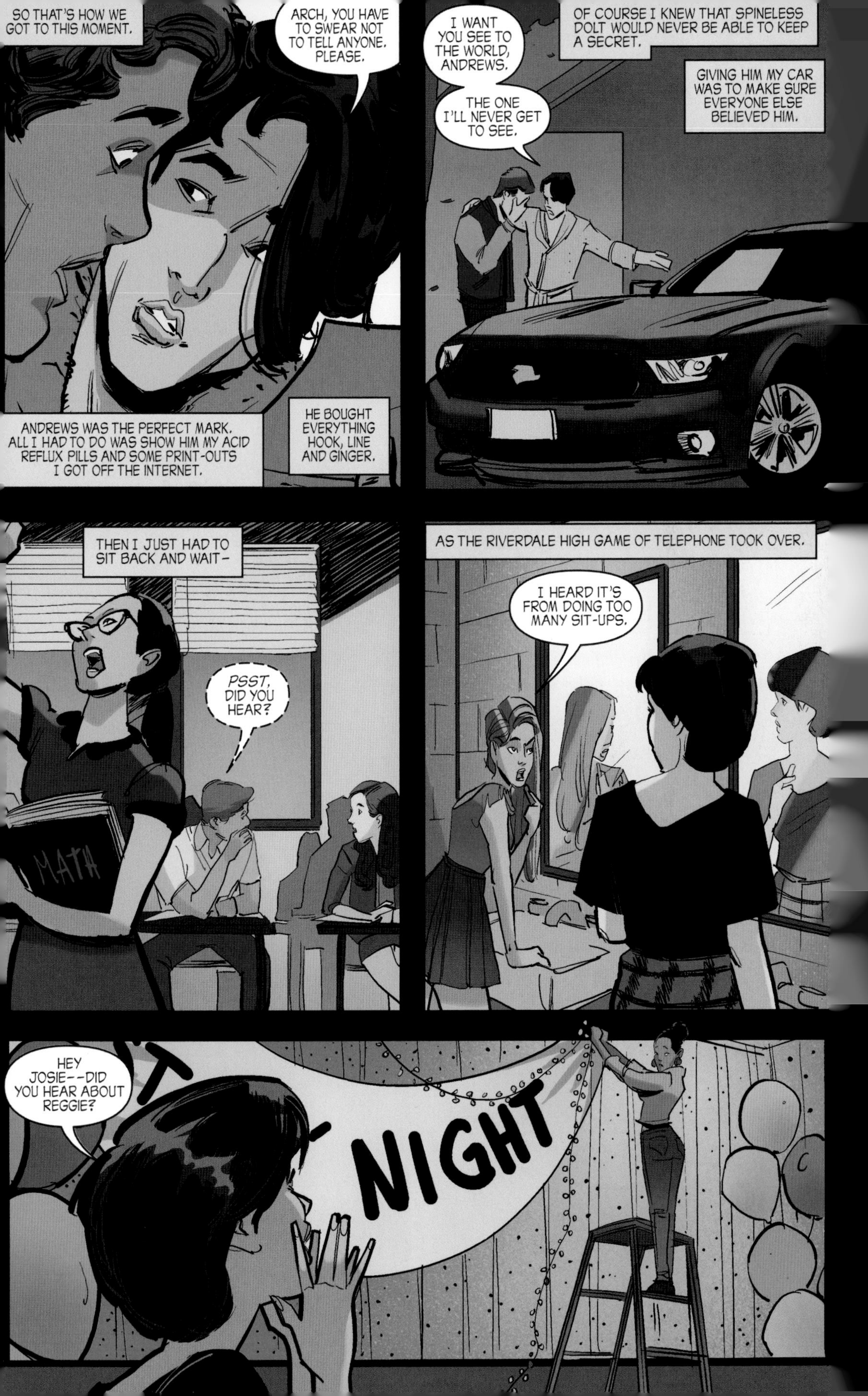
SO THAT'S HOW WE GOT TO THIS MOMENT.
ARCH, YOU HAVE TO SWEAR NOT TO TELL ANYONE. PLEASE.
ANDREWS WAS THE PERFECT MARK. ALL I HAD TO DO WAS SHOW HIM MY ACID REFLUX PILLS AND SOME PRINT-OUTS I GOT OFF THE INTERNET.
HE BOUGHT EVERYTHING HOOK, LINE AND GINGER.
I WANT YOU SEE TO THE WORLD, ANDREWS.
THE ONE I'LL NEVER GET TO SEE.
OF COURSE I KNEW THAT SPINELESS DOLT WOULD NEVER BE ABLE TO KEEP A SECRET.
GIVING HIM MY CAR WAS TO MAKE SURE EVERYONE ELSE BELIEVED HIM.
THEN I JUST HAD TO SIT BACK AND WAIT-
MATH
PSST, DID YOU HEAR?
AS THE RIVERDALE HIGH GAME OF TELEPHONE TOOK OVER.
I HEARD IT'S FROM DOING TOO MANY SIT-UPS.
HEY JOSIE--DID YOU HEAR ABOUT REGGIE?
NIGHT

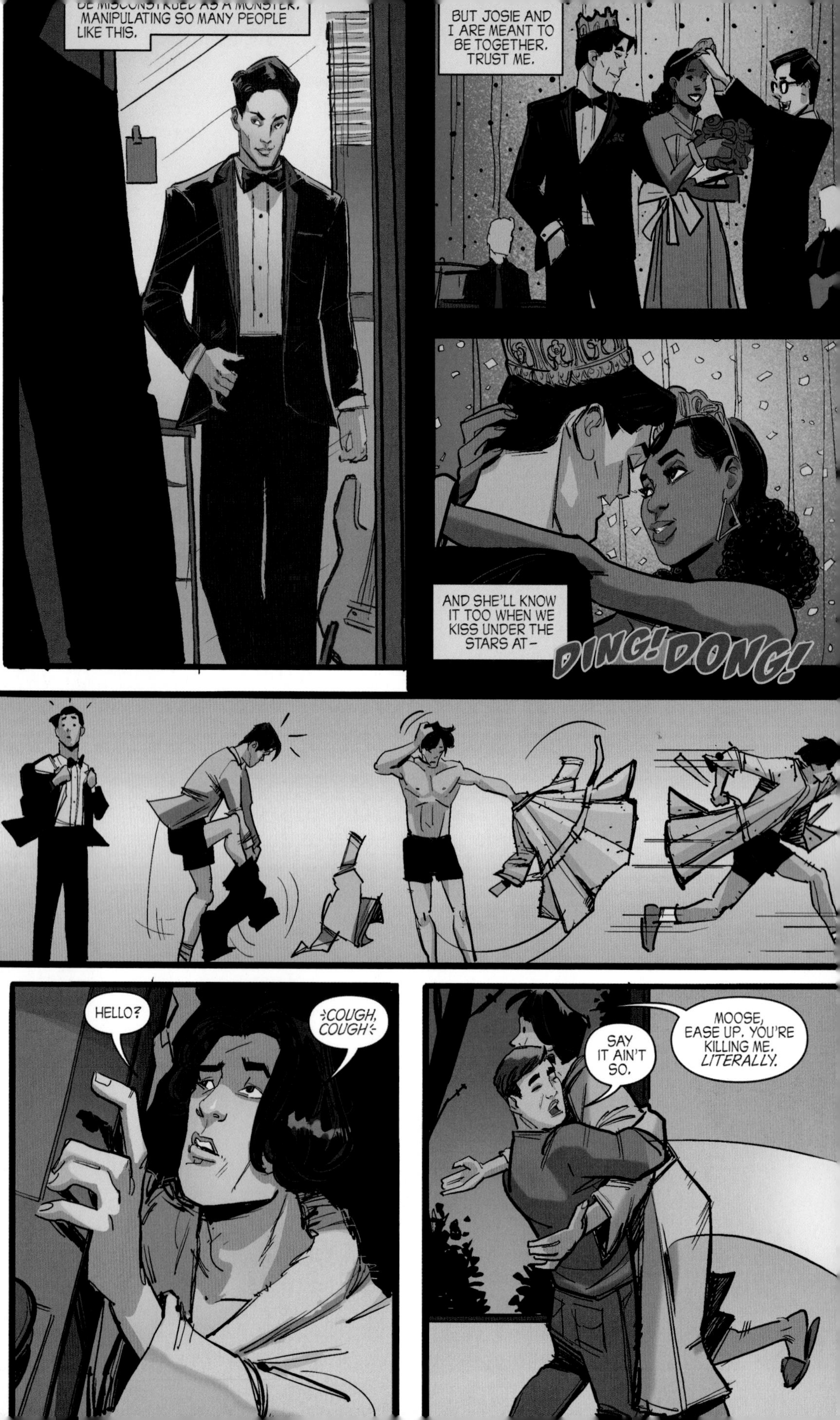
MANIPULATING SO MANY PEOPLE LIKE THIS.
BUT JOSIE AND I ARE MEANT TO BE TOGETHER. TRUST ME.
AND SHE'LL KNOW IT TOO WHEN WE KISS UNDER THE STARS AT–
DING! DONG!
HELLO?
-COUGH, COUGH-
SAY IT AIN'T SO.
MOOSE, EASE UP. YOU'RE KILLING ME. *LITERALLY.*

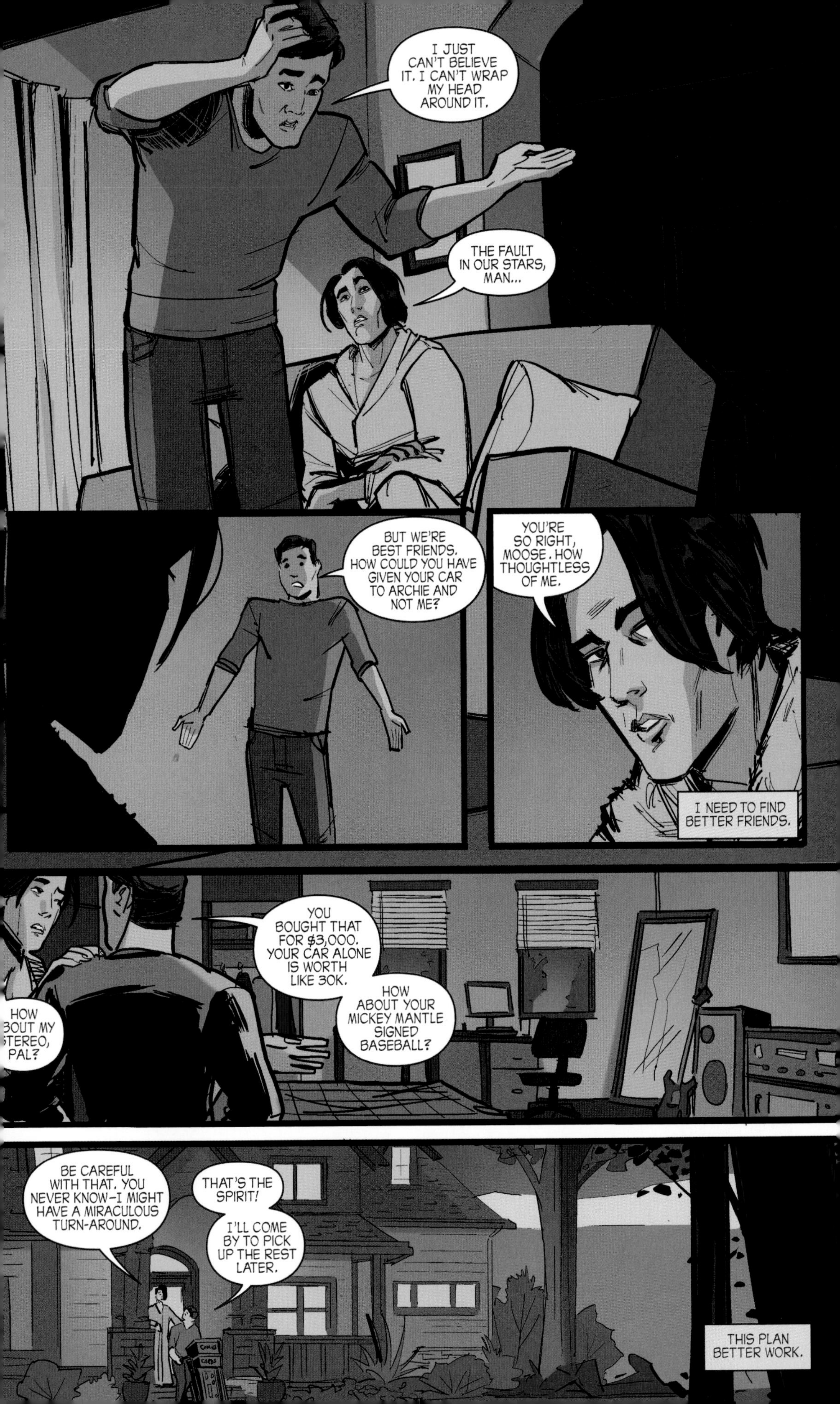
I JUST CAN'T BELIEVE IT. I CAN'T WRAP MY HEAD AROUND IT.
THE FAULT IN OUR STARS, MAN...
BUT WE'RE BEST FRIENDS. HOW COULD YOU HAVE GIVEN YOUR CAR TO ARCHIE AND NOT ME?
YOU'RE SO RIGHT, MOOSE. HOW THOUGHTLESS OF ME.
I NEED TO FIND BETTER FRIENDS.
HOW BOUT MY STEREO, PAL?
YOU BOUGHT THAT FOR $3,000. YOUR CAR ALONE IS WORTH LIKE 30K.
HOW ABOUT YOUR MICKEY MANTLE SIGNED BASEBALL?
BE CAREFUL WITH THAT. YOU NEVER KNOW—I MIGHT HAVE A MIRACULOUS TURN-AROUND.
THAT'S THE SPIRIT!
I'LL COME BY TO PICK UP THE REST LATER.
THIS PLAN BETTER WORK.

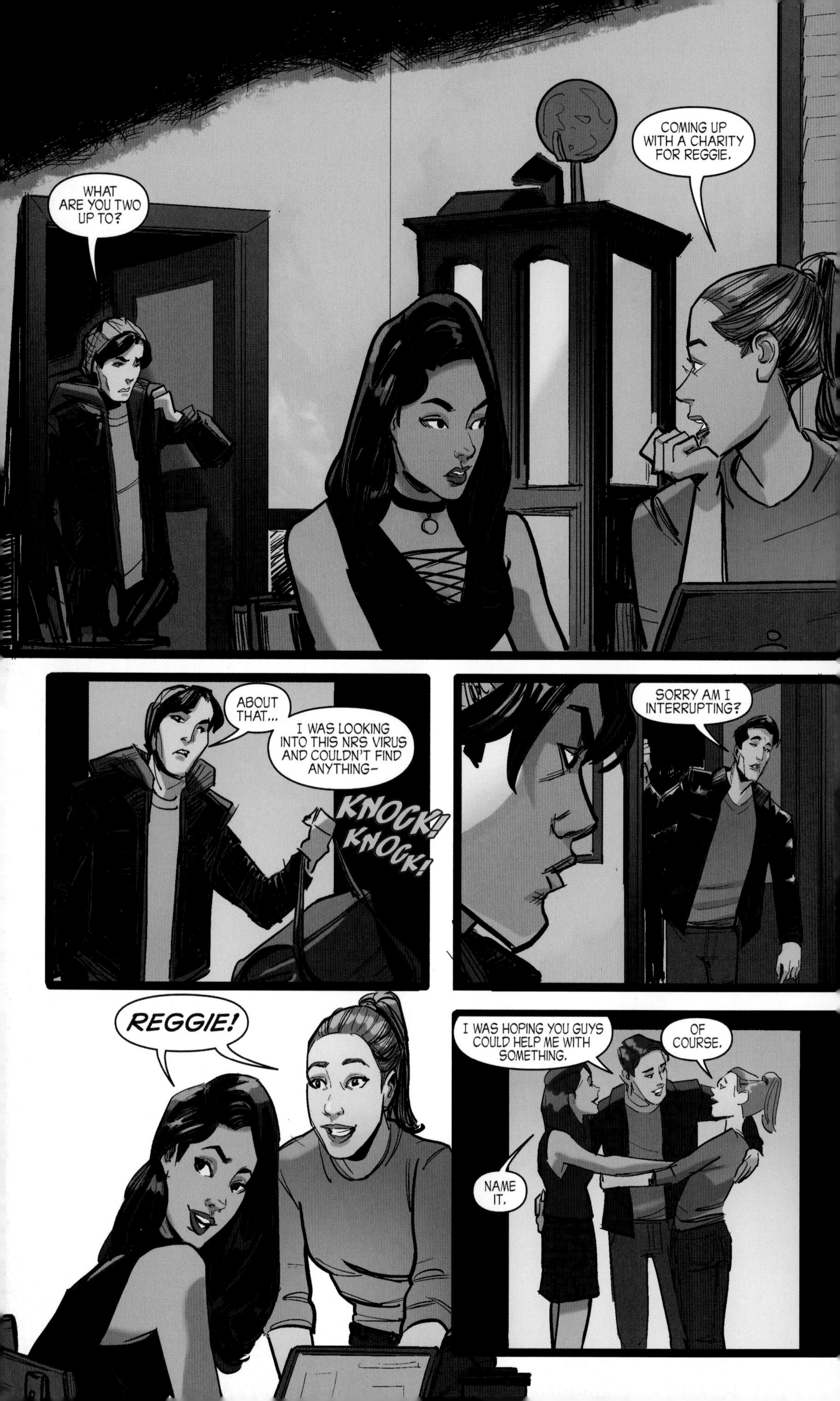
WHAT ARE YOU TWO UP TO?
COMING UP WITH A CHARITY FOR REGGIE.
ABOUT THAT...
I WAS LOOKING INTO THIS NRS VIRUS AND COULDN'T FIND ANYTHING–
KNOCK! KNOCK!
SORRY AM I INTERRUPTING?
REGGIE!
I WAS HOPING YOU GUYS COULD HELP ME WITH SOMETHING.
OF COURSE.
NAME IT.

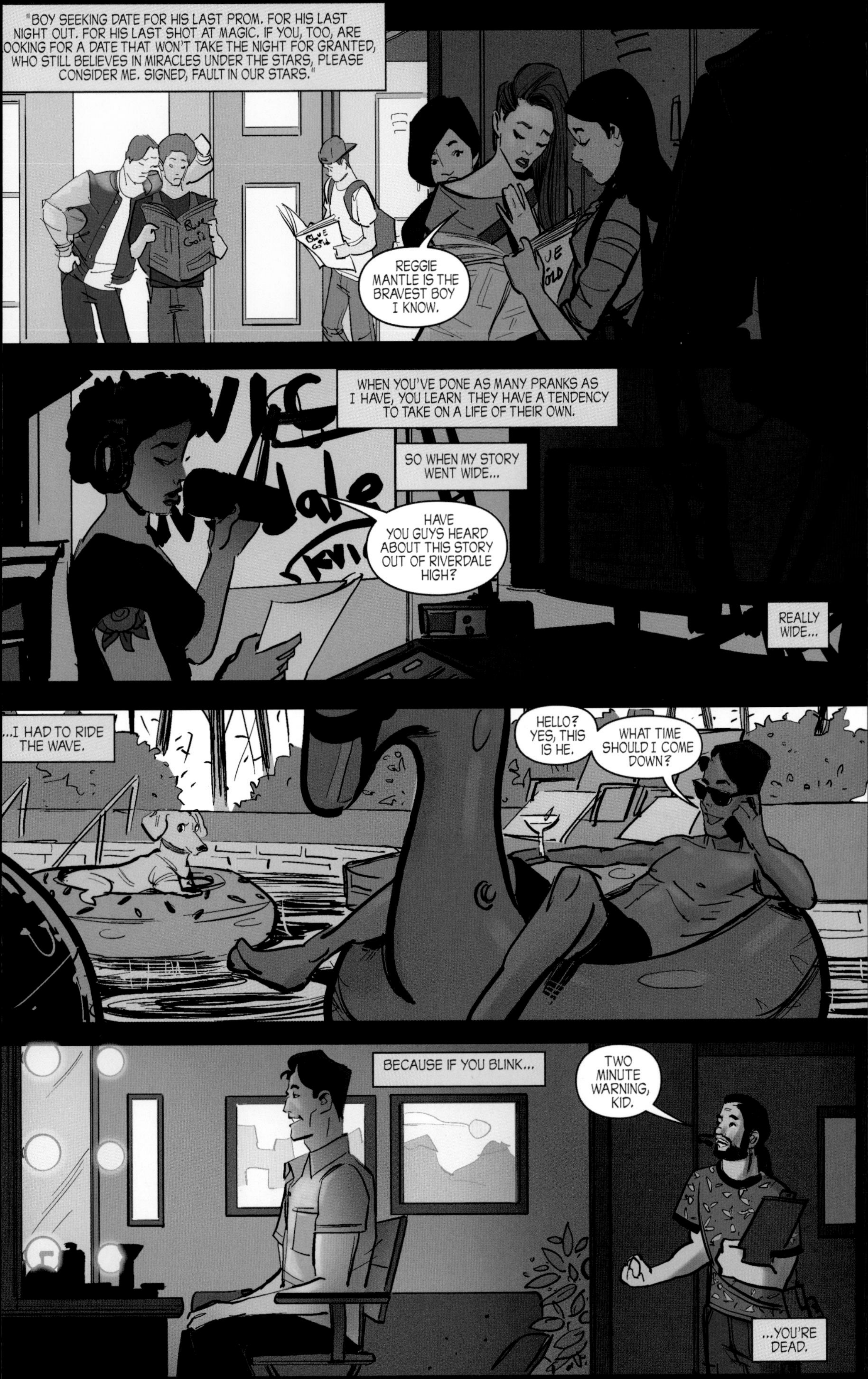

"BOY SEEKING DATE FOR HIS LAST PROM. FOR HIS LAST NIGHT OUT. FOR HIS LAST SHOT AT MAGIC. IF YOU, TOO, ARE LOOKING FOR A DATE THAT WON'T TAKE THE NIGHT FOR GRANTED, WHO STILL BELIEVES IN MIRACLES UNDER THE STARS, PLEASE CONSIDER ME. SIGNED, FAULT IN OUR STARS."
REGGIE MANTLE IS THE BRAVEST BOY I KNOW.
WHEN YOU'VE DONE AS MANY PRANKS AS I HAVE, YOU LEARN THEY HAVE A TENDENCY TO TAKE ON A LIFE OF THEIR OWN.
SO WHEN MY STORY WENT WIDE...
HAVE YOU GUYS HEARD ABOUT THIS STORY OUT OF RIVERDALE HIGH?
REALLY WIDE...
...I HAD TO RIDE THE WAVE.
HELLO? YES, THIS IS HE.
WHAT TIME SHOULD I COME DOWN?
BECAUSE IF YOU BLINK...
TWO MINUTE WARNING, KID.
...YOU'RE DEAD.

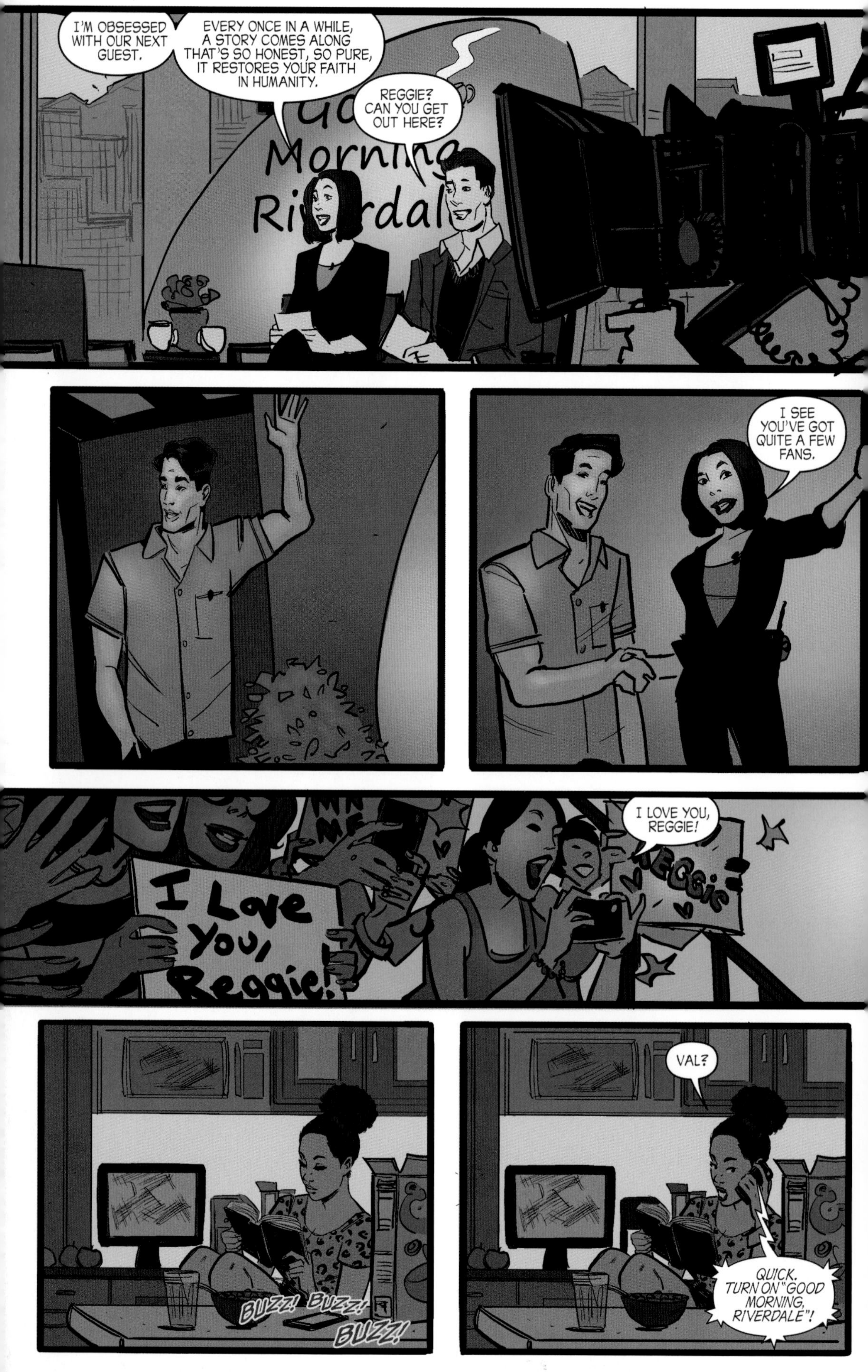
I'M OBSESSED WITH OUR NEXT GUEST.
EVERY ONCE IN A WHILE, A STORY COMES ALONG THAT'S SO HONEST, SO PURE, IT RESTORES YOUR FAITH IN HUMANITY.
REGGIE? CAN YOU GET OUT HERE?
Good Morning Riverdale
I SEE YOU'VE GOT QUITE A FEW FANS.
I LOVE YOU, REGGIE!
I Love you, Reggie!
REGGIE
BUZZ! BUZZ! BUZZ!
VAL?
QUICK. TURN ON "GOOD MORNING, RIVERDALE"!

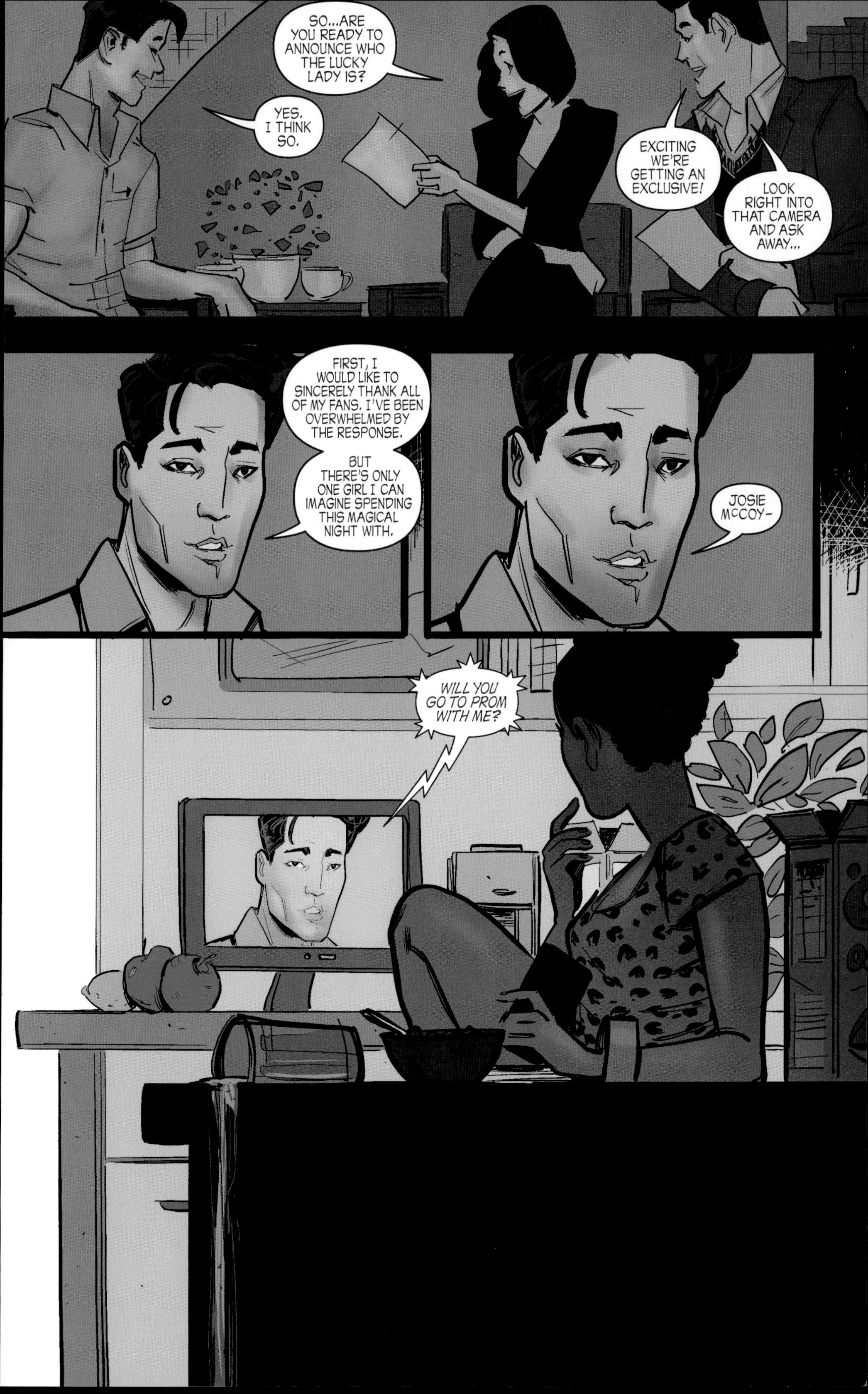
SO...ARE YOU READY TO ANNOUNCE WHO THE LUCKY LADY IS?
YES. I THINK SO.
EXCITING WE'RE GETTING AN EXCLUSIVE!
LOOK RIGHT INTO THAT CAMERA AND ASK AWAY...
FIRST, I WOULD LIKE TO SINCERELY THANK ALL OF MY FANS. I'VE BEEN OVERWHELMED BY THE RESPONSE.
BUT THERE'S ONLY ONE GIRL I CAN IMAGINE SPENDING THIS MAGICAL NIGHT WITH.
JOSIE McCOY-
WILL YOU GO TO PROM WITH ME?

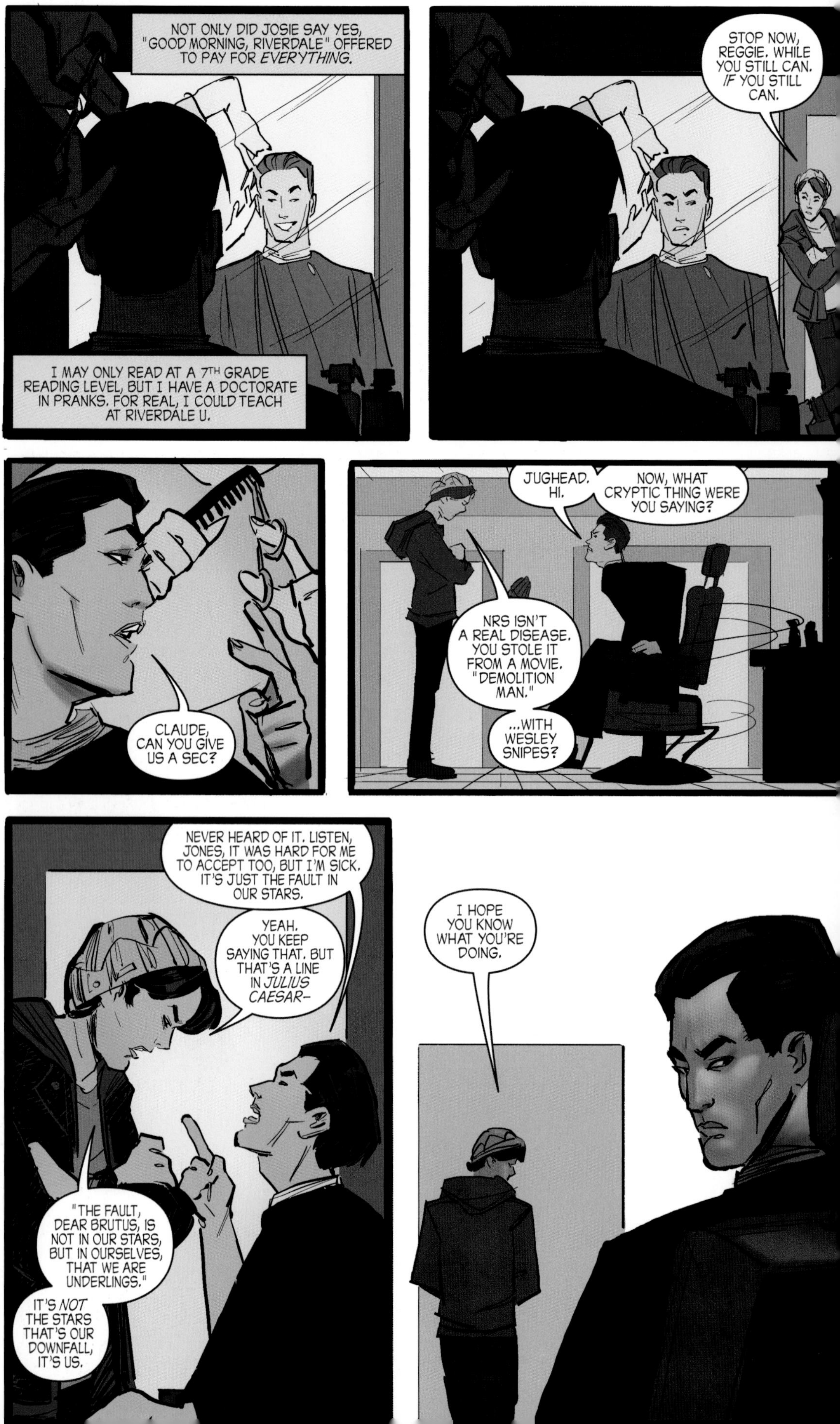
NOT ONLY DID JOSIE SAY YES, "GOOD MORNING, RIVERDALE" OFFERED TO PAY FOR *EVERYTHING.*
I MAY ONLY READ AT A 7TH GRADE READING LEVEL, BUT I HAVE A DOCTORATE IN PRANKS. FOR REAL, I COULD TEACH AT RIVERDALE U.
STOP NOW, REGGIE. WHILE YOU STILL CAN. *IF* YOU STILL CAN.
CLAUDE, CAN YOU GIVE US A SEC?
JUGHEAD. HI.
NOW, WHAT CRYPTIC THING WERE YOU SAYING?
NRS ISN'T A REAL DISEASE. YOU STOLE IT FROM A MOVIE. "DEMOLITION MAN."
...WITH WESLEY SNIPES?
NEVER HEARD OF IT. LISTEN, JONES, IT WAS HARD FOR ME TO ACCEPT TOO, BUT I'M SICK. IT'S JUST THE FAULT IN OUR STARS.
YEAH. YOU KEEP SAYING THAT. BUT THAT'S A LINE IN *JULIUS CAESAR*-
"THE FAULT, DEAR BRUTUS, IS NOT IN OUR STARS, BUT IN OURSELVES, THAT WE ARE UNDERLINGS."
IT'S *NOT* THE STARS THAT'S OUR DOWNFALL, IT'S US.
I HOPE YOU KNOW WHAT YOU'RE DOING.

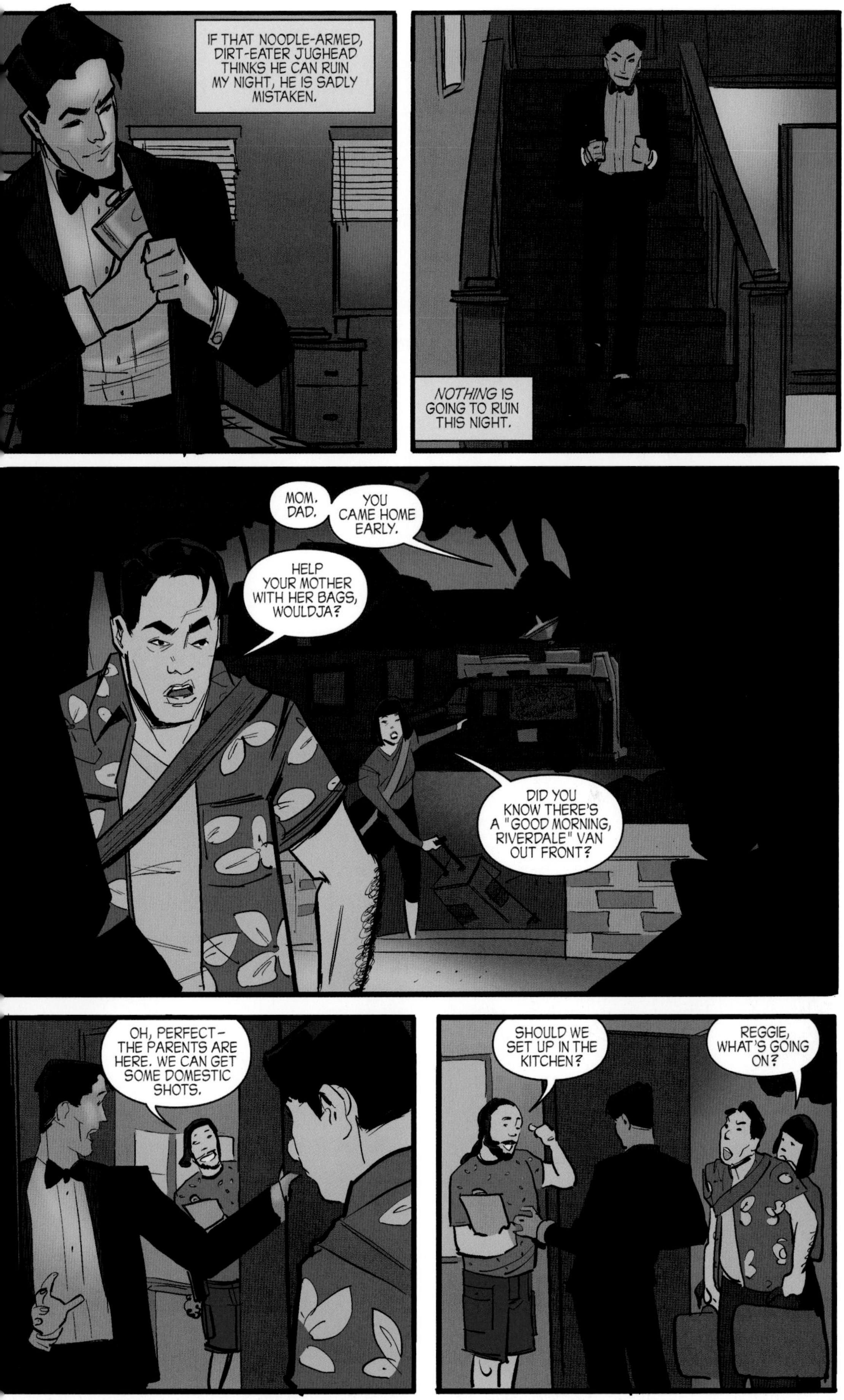

IF THAT NOODLE-ARMED, DIRT-EATER JUGHEAD THINKS HE CAN RUIN MY NIGHT, HE IS SADLY MISTAKEN.
NOTHING IS GOING TO RUIN THIS NIGHT.
MOM. DAD.
YOU CAME HOME EARLY.
HELP YOUR MOTHER WITH HER BAGS, WOULDJA?
DID YOU KNOW THERE'S A "GOOD MORNING, RIVERDALE" VAN OUT FRONT?
OH, PERFECT-THE PARENTS ARE HERE. WE CAN GET SOME DOMESTIC SHOTS.
SHOULD WE SET UP IN THE KITCHEN?
REGGIE, WHAT'S GOING ON?

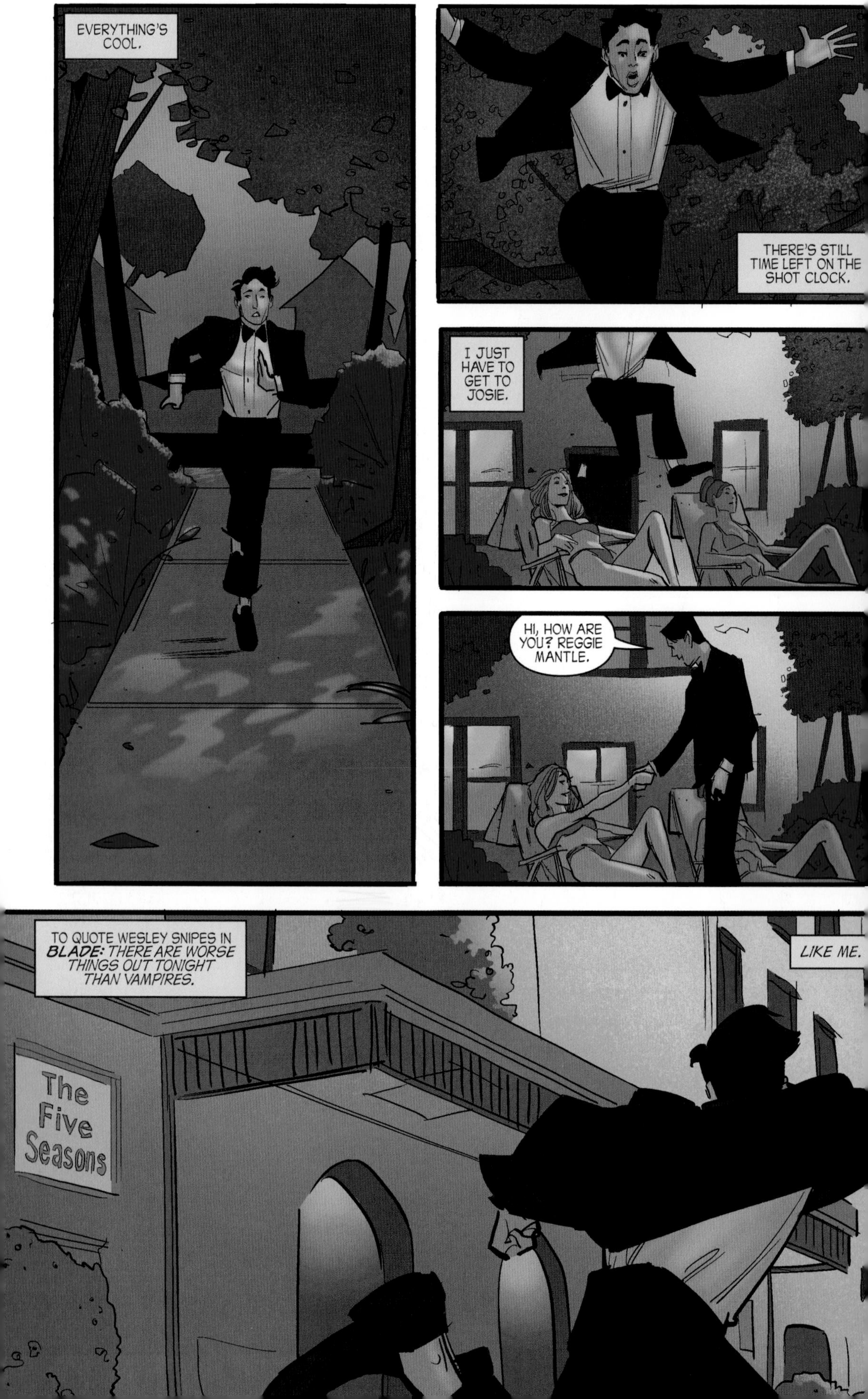

EVERYTHING'S COOL.
THERE'S STILL TIME LEFT ON THE SHOT CLOCK.
I JUST HAVE TO GET TO JOSIE.
HI, HOW ARE YOU? REGGIE MANTLE.
TO QUOTE WESLEY SNIPES IN BLADE: THERE ARE WORSE THINGS OUT TONIGHT THAN VAMPIRES.
LIKE ME.
The Five Seasons

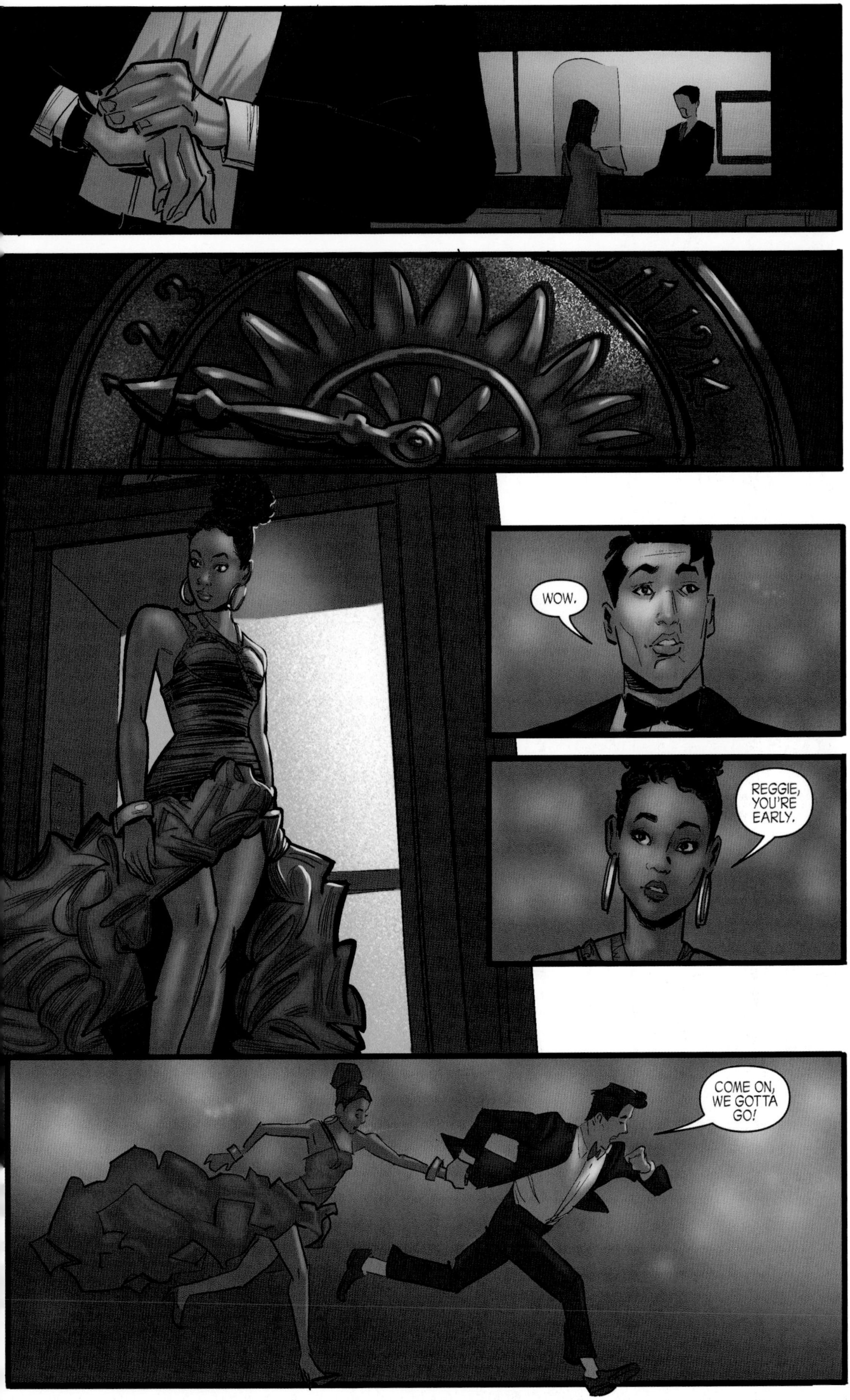
WOW.
REGGIE, YOU'RE EARLY.
COME ON, WE GOTTA GO!

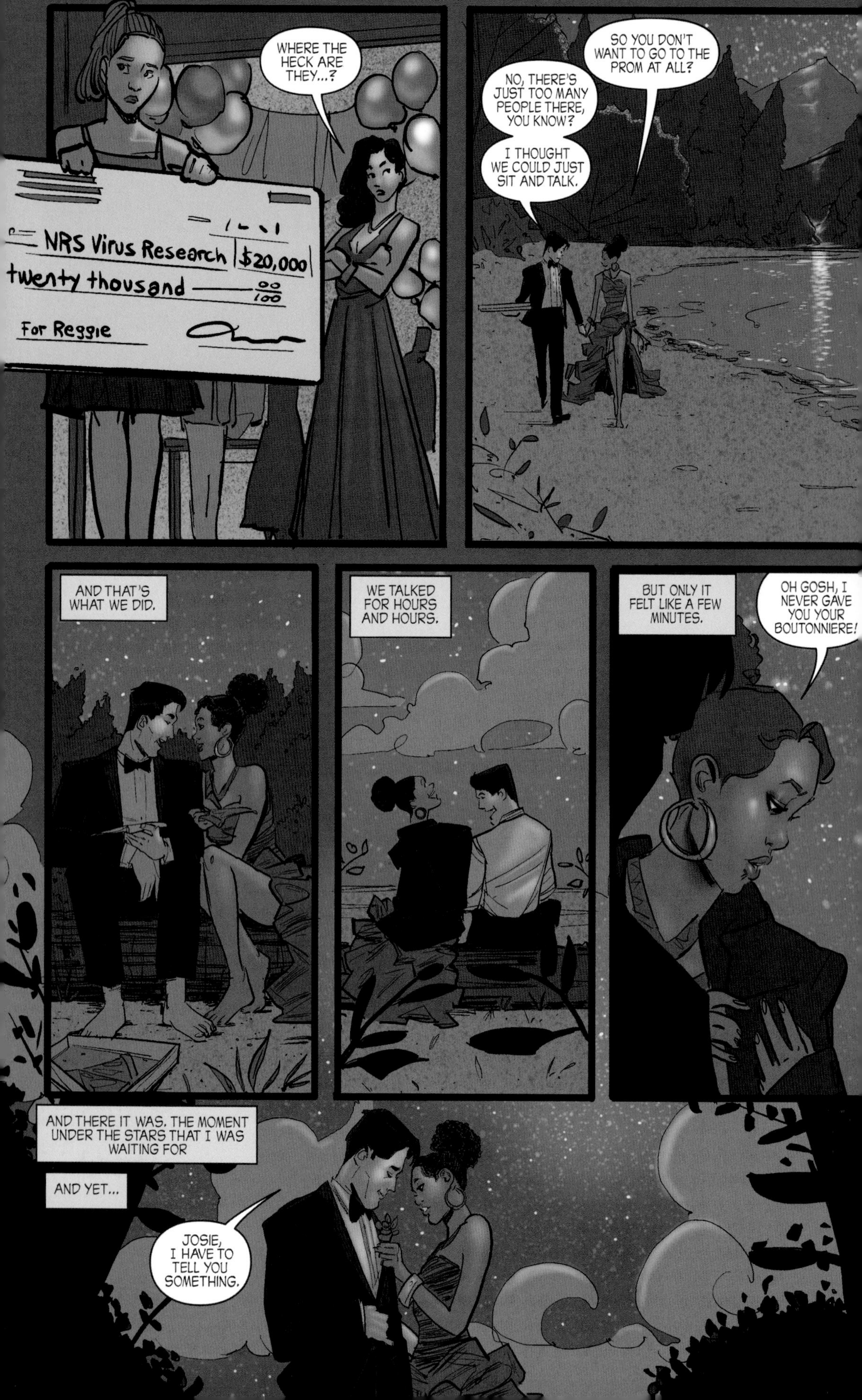
WHERE THE HECK ARE THEY...?
NRS Virus Research
$20,000
twenty thousand
00/100
For Reggie
SO YOU DON'T WANT TO GO TO THE PROM AT ALL?
NO, THERE'S JUST TOO MANY PEOPLE THERE, YOU KNOW?
I THOUGHT WE COULD JUST SIT AND TALK.
AND THAT'S WHAT WE DID.
WE TALKED FOR HOURS AND HOURS.
BUT ONLY IT FELT LIKE A FEW MINUTES.
OH GOSH, I NEVER GAVE YOU YOUR BOUTONNIERE!
AND THERE IT WAS. THE MOMENT UNDER THE STARS THAT I WAS WAITING FOR
AND YET...
JOSIE, I HAVE TO TELL YOU SOMETHING.

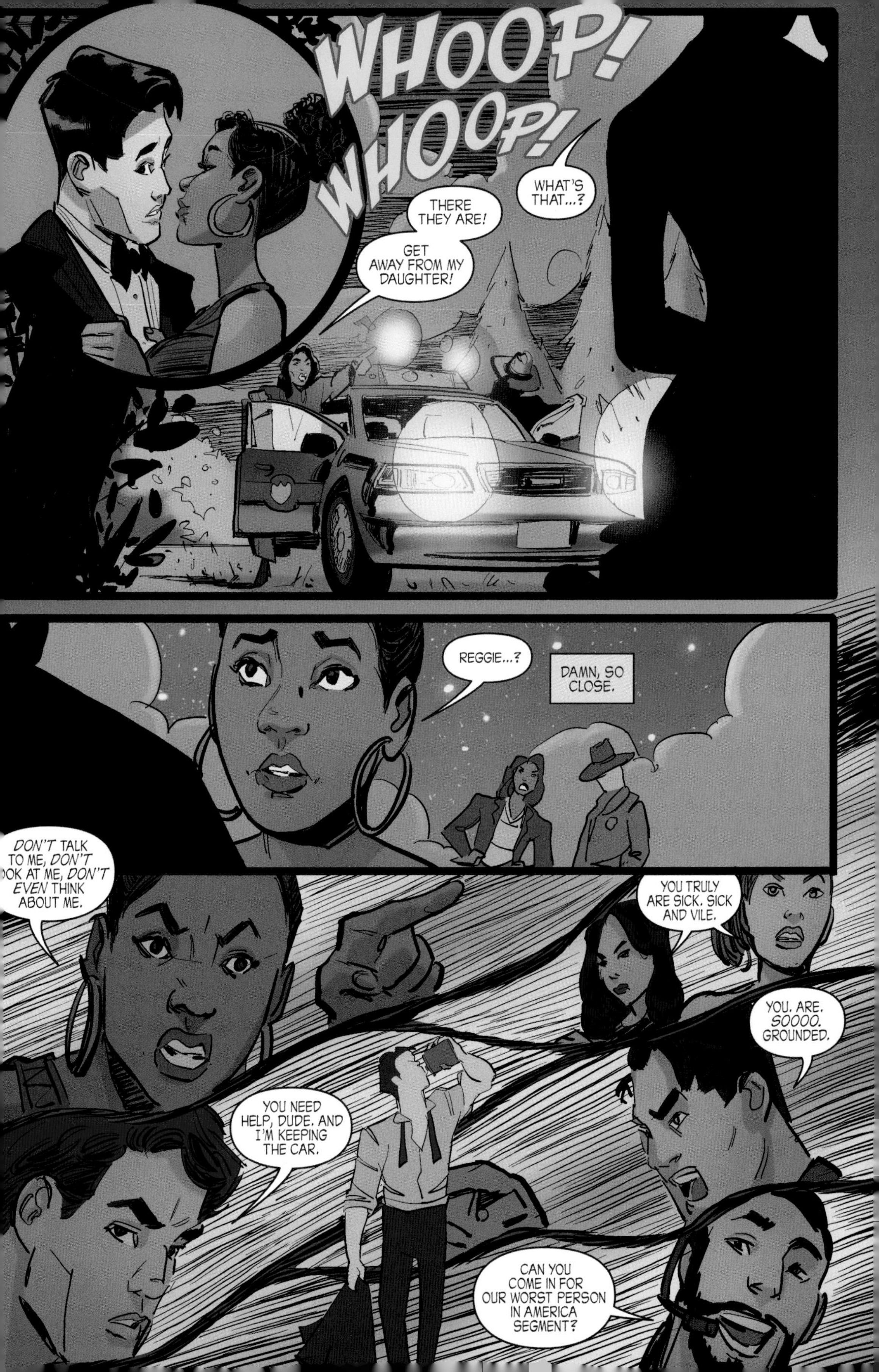
WHOOP! WHOOP!
WHAT'S THAT...?
THERE THEY ARE!
GET AWAY FROM MY DAUGHTER!
REGGIE...?
DAMN, SO CLOSE.
DON'T TALK TO ME, DON'T OOK AT ME, DON'T EVEN THINK ABOUT ME.
YOU TRULY ARE SICK. SICK AND VILE.
YOU. ARE. SOOOO. GROUNDED.
YOU NEED HELP, DUDE. AND I'M KEEPING THE CAR.
CAN YOU COME IN FOR OUR WORST PERSON IN AMERICA SEGMENT?

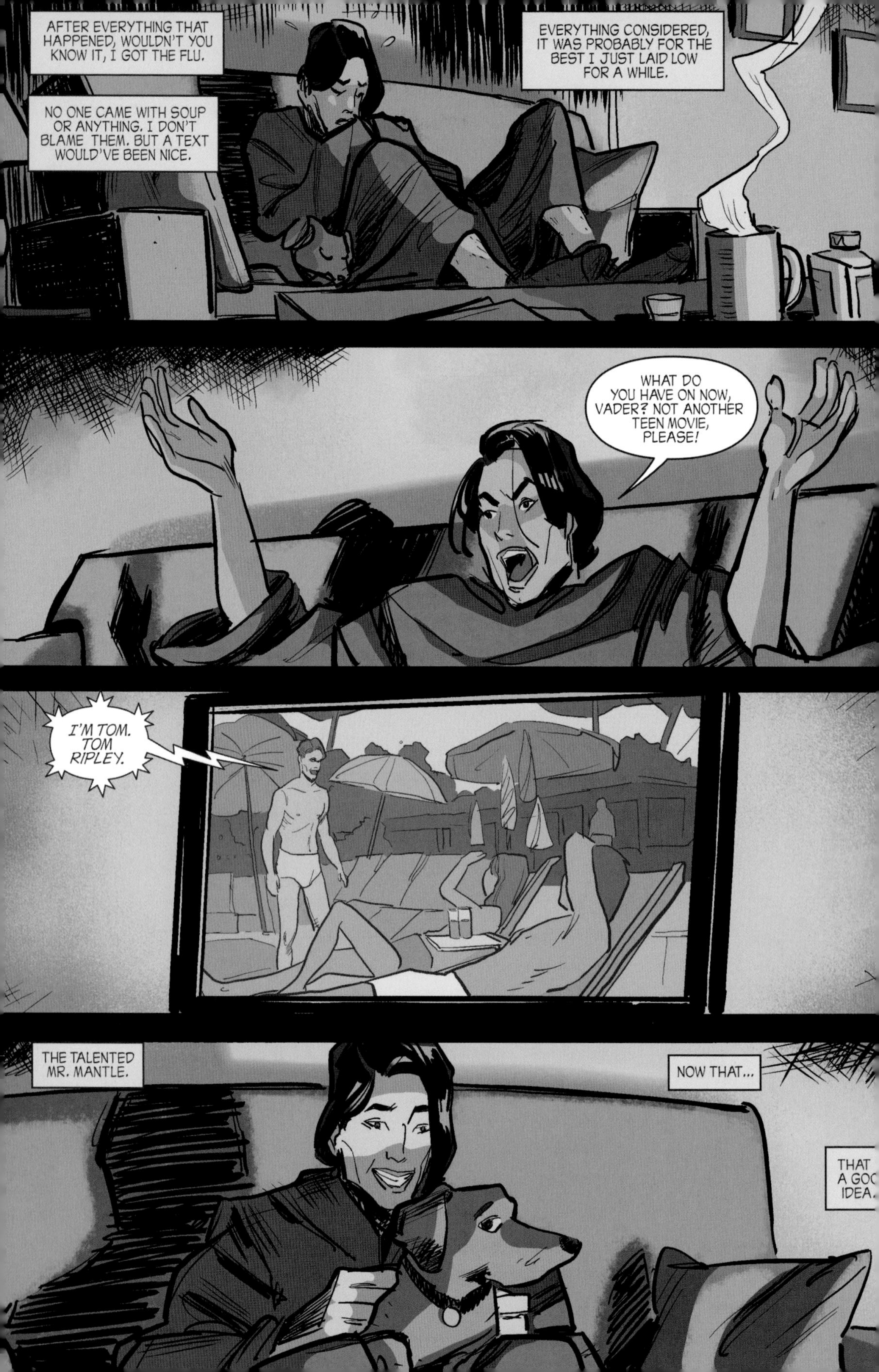
AFTER EVERYTHING THAT HAPPENED, WOULDN'T YOU KNOW IT, I GOT THE FLU.
NO ONE CAME WITH SOUP OR ANYTHING. I DON'T BLAME THEM. BUT A TEXT WOULD'VE BEEN NICE.
EVERYTHING CONSIDERED, IT WAS PROBABLY FOR THE BEST I JUST LAID LOW FOR A WHILE.
WHAT DO YOU HAVE ON NOW, VADER? NOT ANOTHER TEEN MOVIE, PLEASE!
I'M TOM. TOM RIPLEY.
THE TALENTED MR. MANTLE.
NOW THAT...
THAT

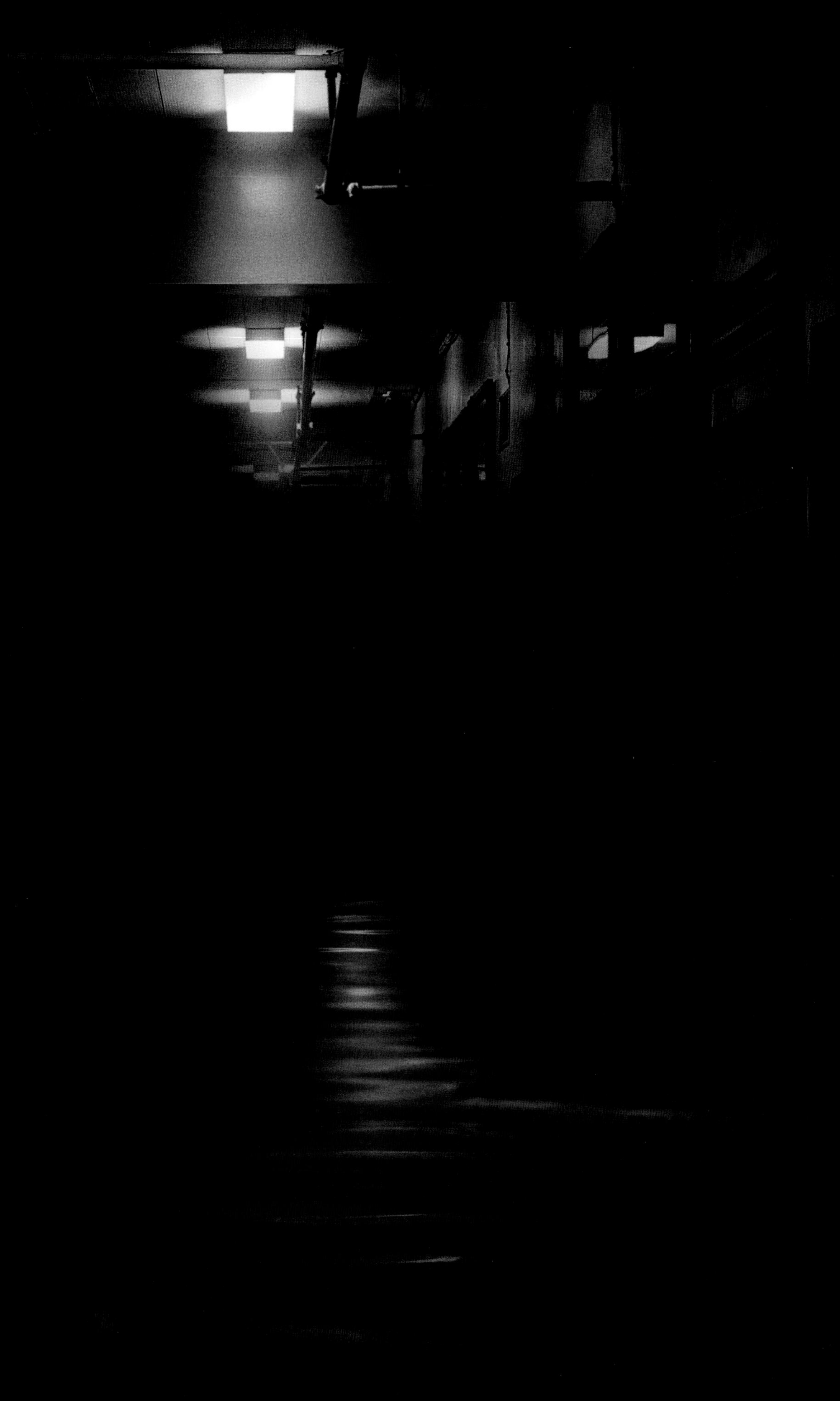

PVP

WRITER:
AARON ALLEN

ART:
THOMAS PITILLI

COLORS:
ANDRE SZYMANOWICZ

LETTERS:
JOHN WORKMAN

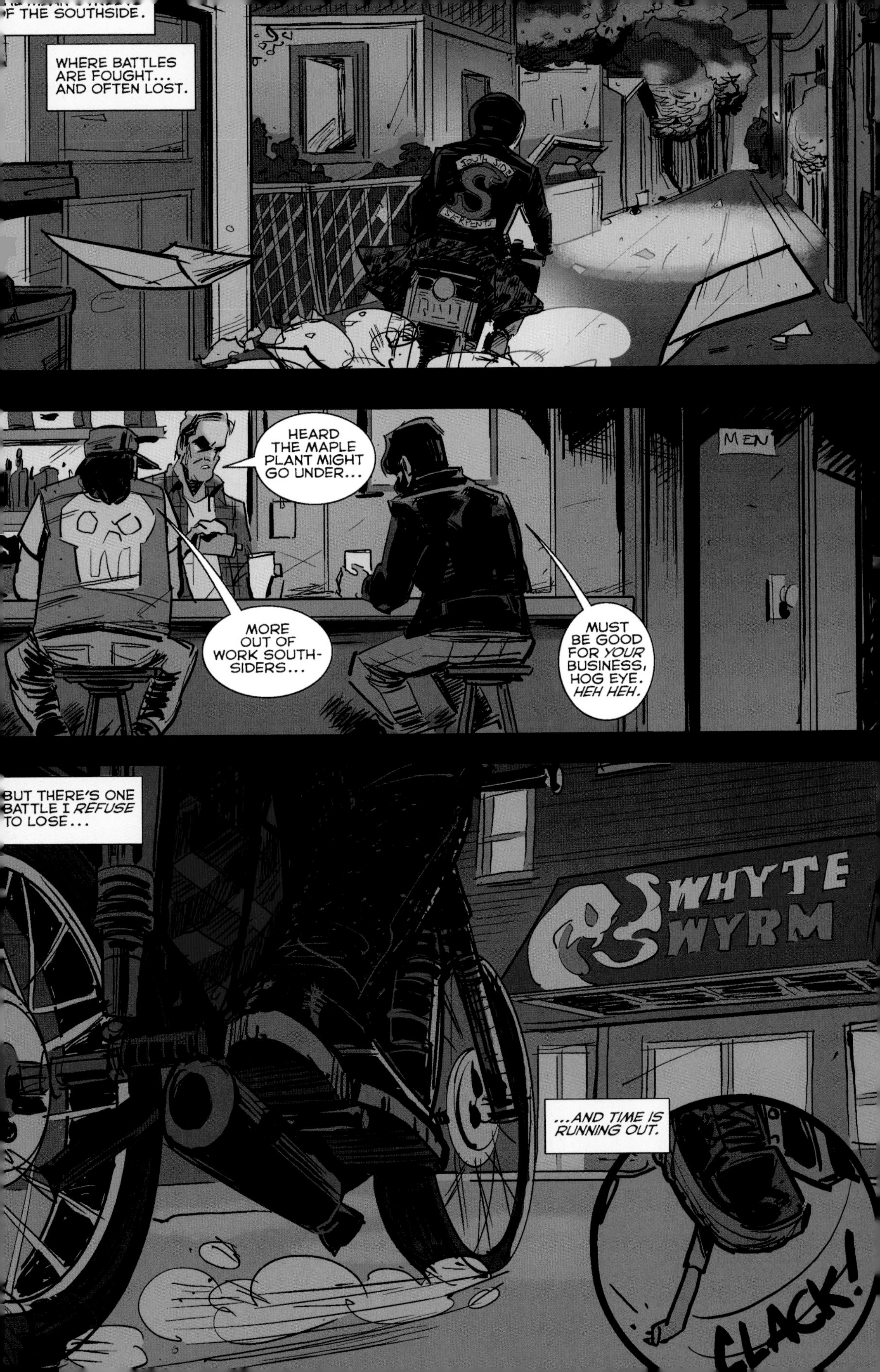
F THE SOUTHSIDE.
WHERE BATTLES ARE FOUGHT... AND OFTEN LOST.
SOUTH SIDE
SERPENTS
MEN
HEARD THE MAPLE PLANT MIGHT GO UNDER...
MORE OUT OF WORK SOUTH-SIDERS...
MUST BE GOOD FOR *YOUR* BUSINESS, HOG EYE. *HEH HEH.*
BUT THERE'S ONE BATTLE I *REFUSE* TO LOSE...
WHYTE WYRM
...AND TIME IS RUNNING OUT.
CLACK!

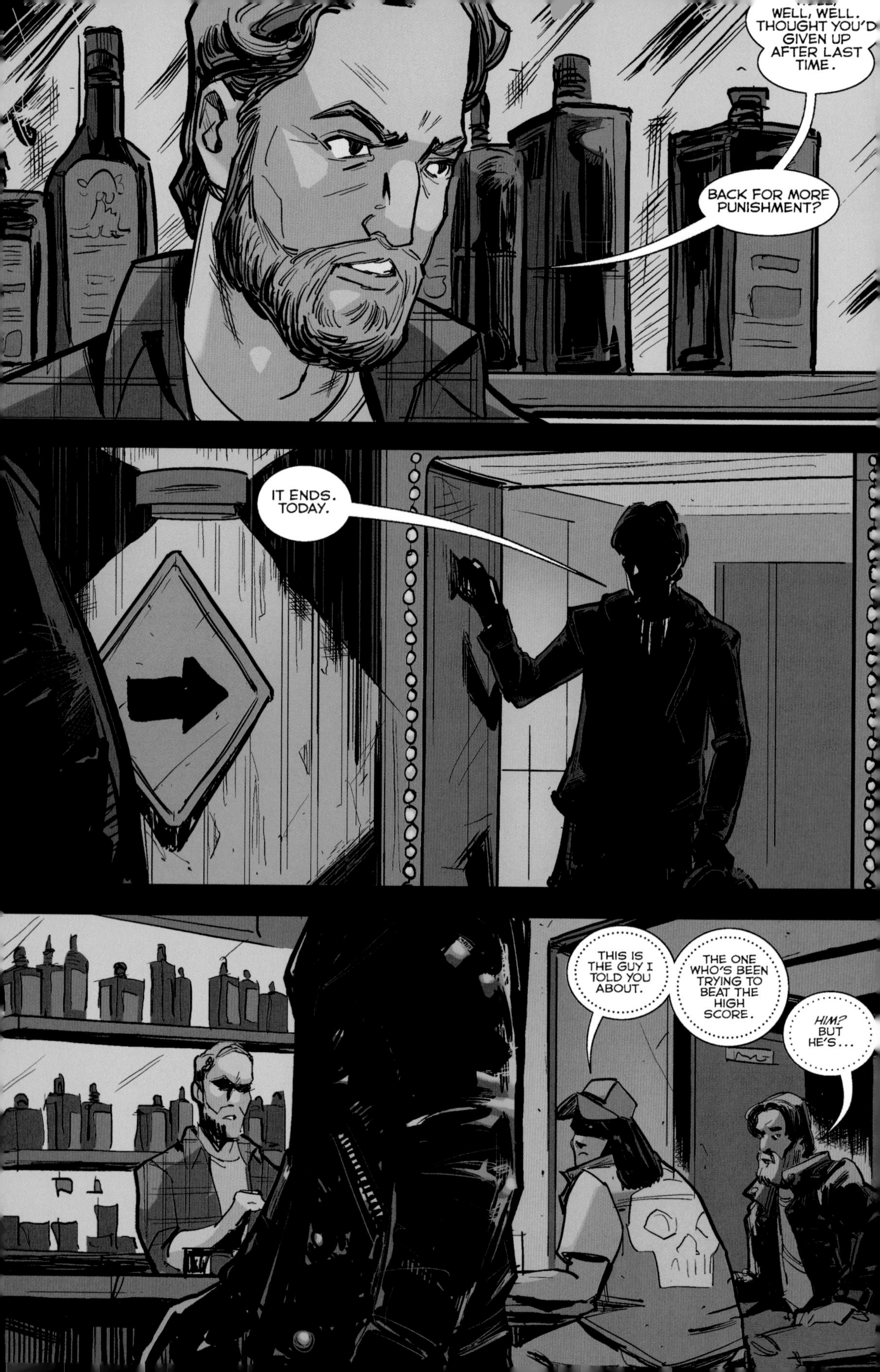
WELL, WELL. THOUGHT YOU'D GIVEN UP AFTER LAST TIME.
BACK FOR MORE PUNISHMENT?
IT ENDS. TODAY.
THIS IS THE GUY I TOLD YOU ABOUT.
THE ONE WHO'S BEEN TRYING TO BEAT THE HIGH SCORE.
HIM? BUT HE'S...

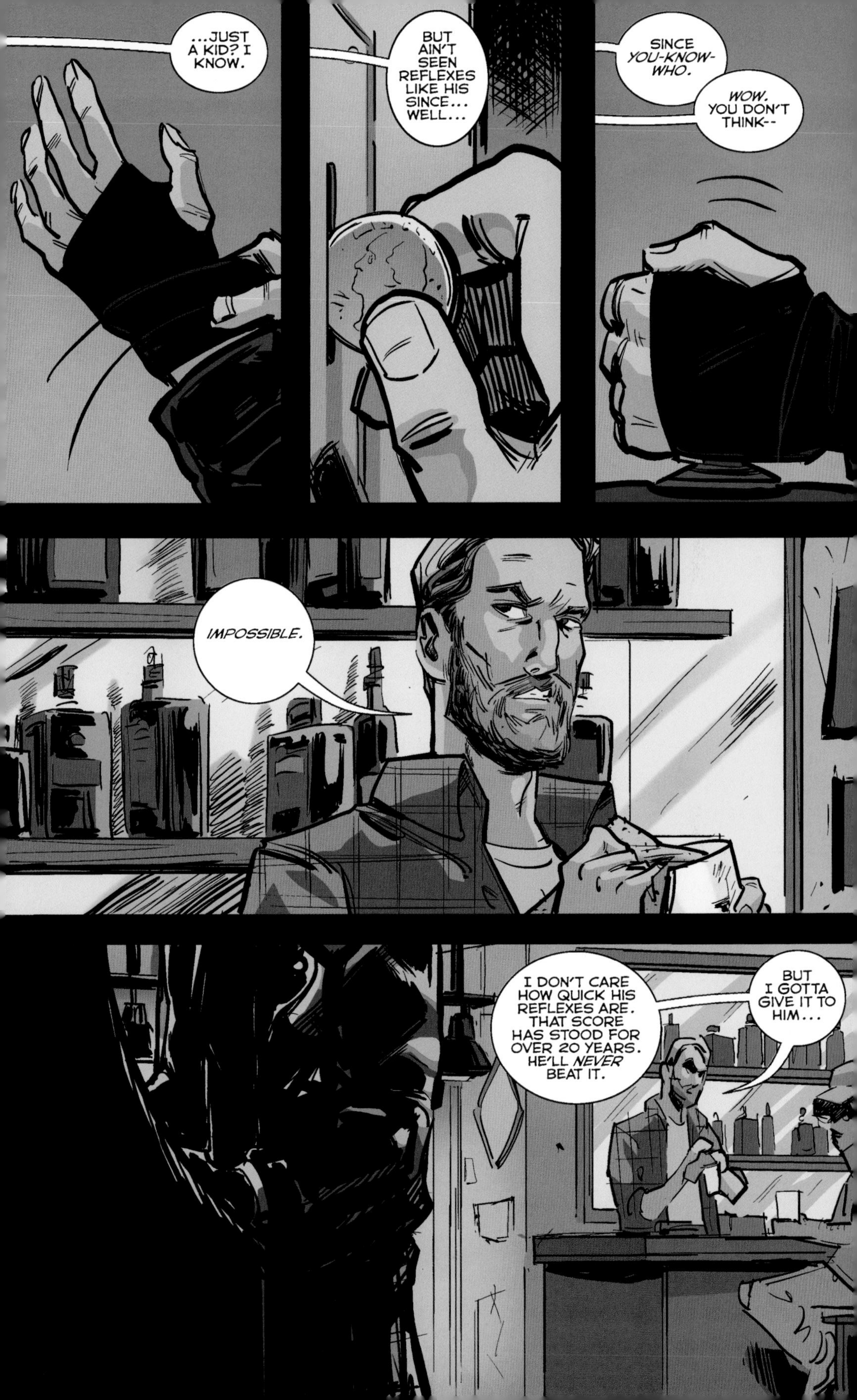
...JUST A KID? I KNOW.
BUT AIN'T SEEN REFLEXES LIKE HIS SINCE... WELL...
SINCE *YOU-KNOW-WHO.*
WOW. YOU DON'T THINK--
IMPOSSIBLE.
I DON'T CARE HOW QUICK HIS REFLEXES ARE. THAT SCORE HAS STOOD FOR OVER 20 YEARS. HE'LL *NEVER* BEAT IT.
BUT I GOTTA GIVE IT TO HIM...

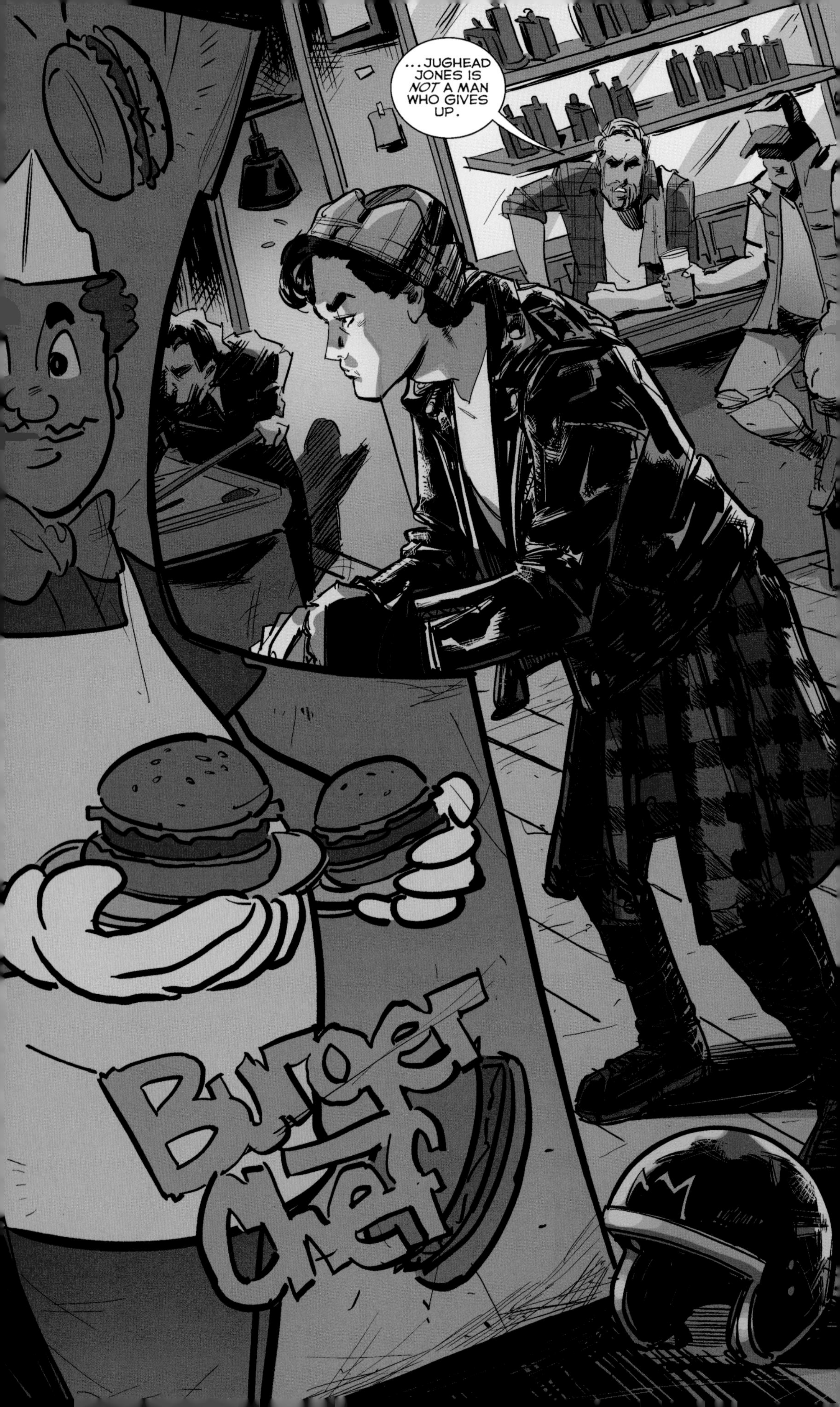
...JUGHEAD JONES IS *NOT* A MAN WHO GIVES UP.

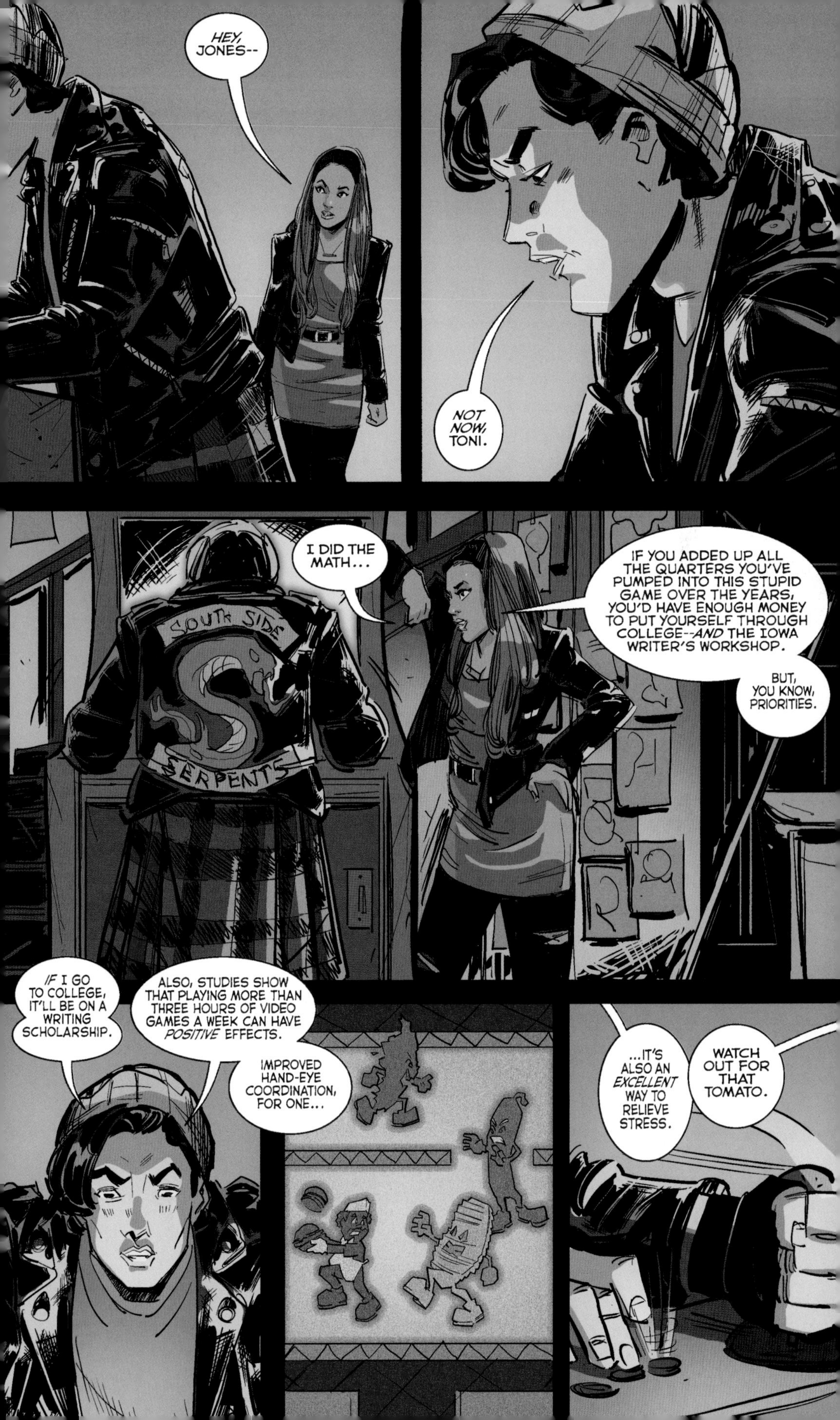
HEY, JONES--
NOT NOW, TONI.
I DID THE MATH...
IF YOU ADDED UP ALL THE QUARTERS YOU'VE PUMPED INTO THIS STUPID GAME OVER THE YEARS, YOU'D HAVE ENOUGH MONEY TO PUT YOURSELF THROUGH COLLEGE--AND THE IOWA WRITER'S WORKSHOP.
BUT, YOU KNOW, PRIORITIES.
SOUTH SIDE SERPENTS
IF I GO TO COLLEGE, IT'LL BE ON A WRITING SCHOLARSHIP.
ALSO, STUDIES SHOW THAT PLAYING MORE THAN THREE HOURS OF VIDEO GAMES A WEEK CAN HAVE POSITIVE EFFECTS.
IMPROVED HAND-EYE COORDINATION, FOR ONE...
...IT'S ALSO AN EXCELLENT WAY TO RELIEVE STRESS.
WATCH OUT FOR THAT TOMATO.

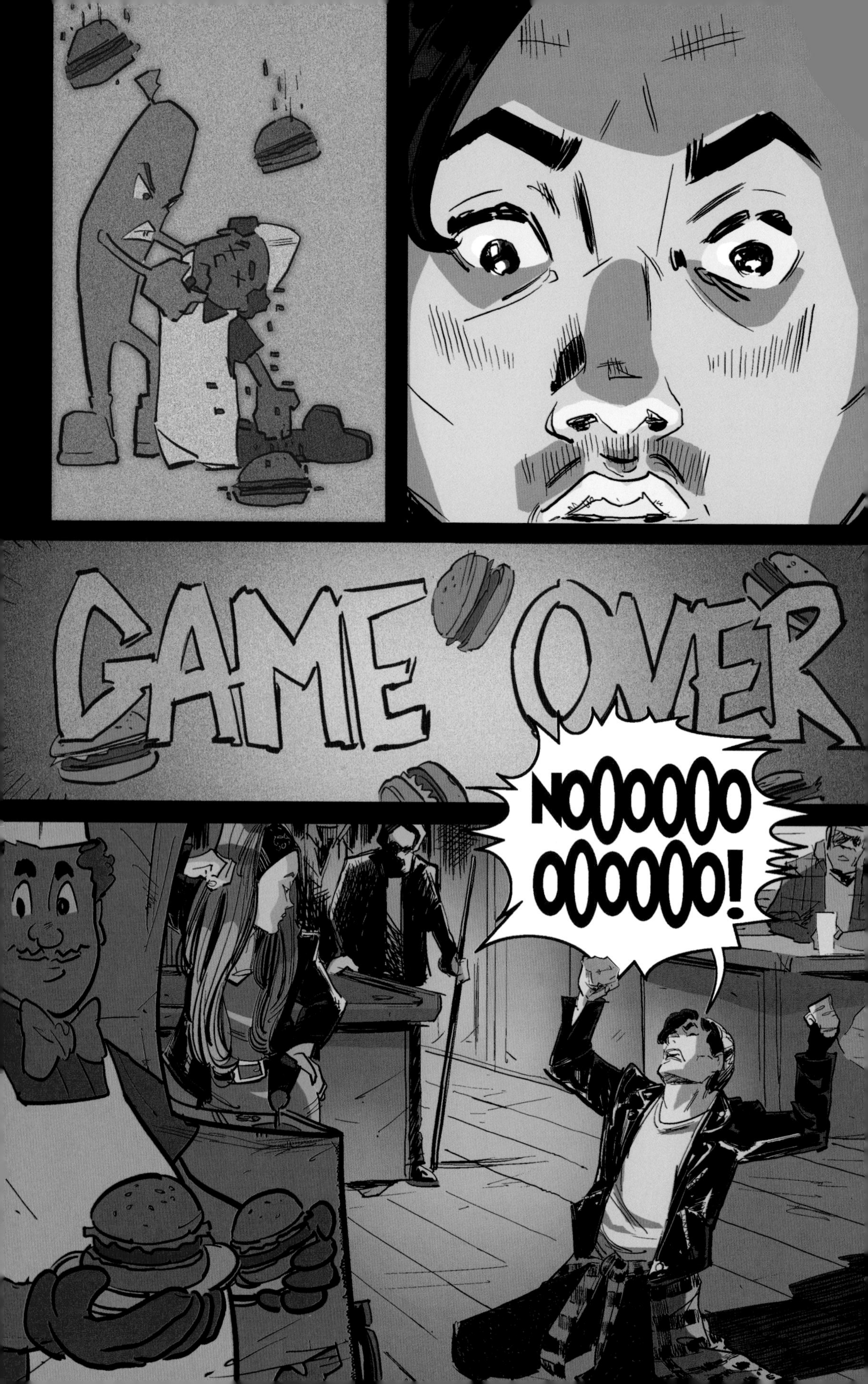
GAME OVER
NOOOOOO
OOOOOO!

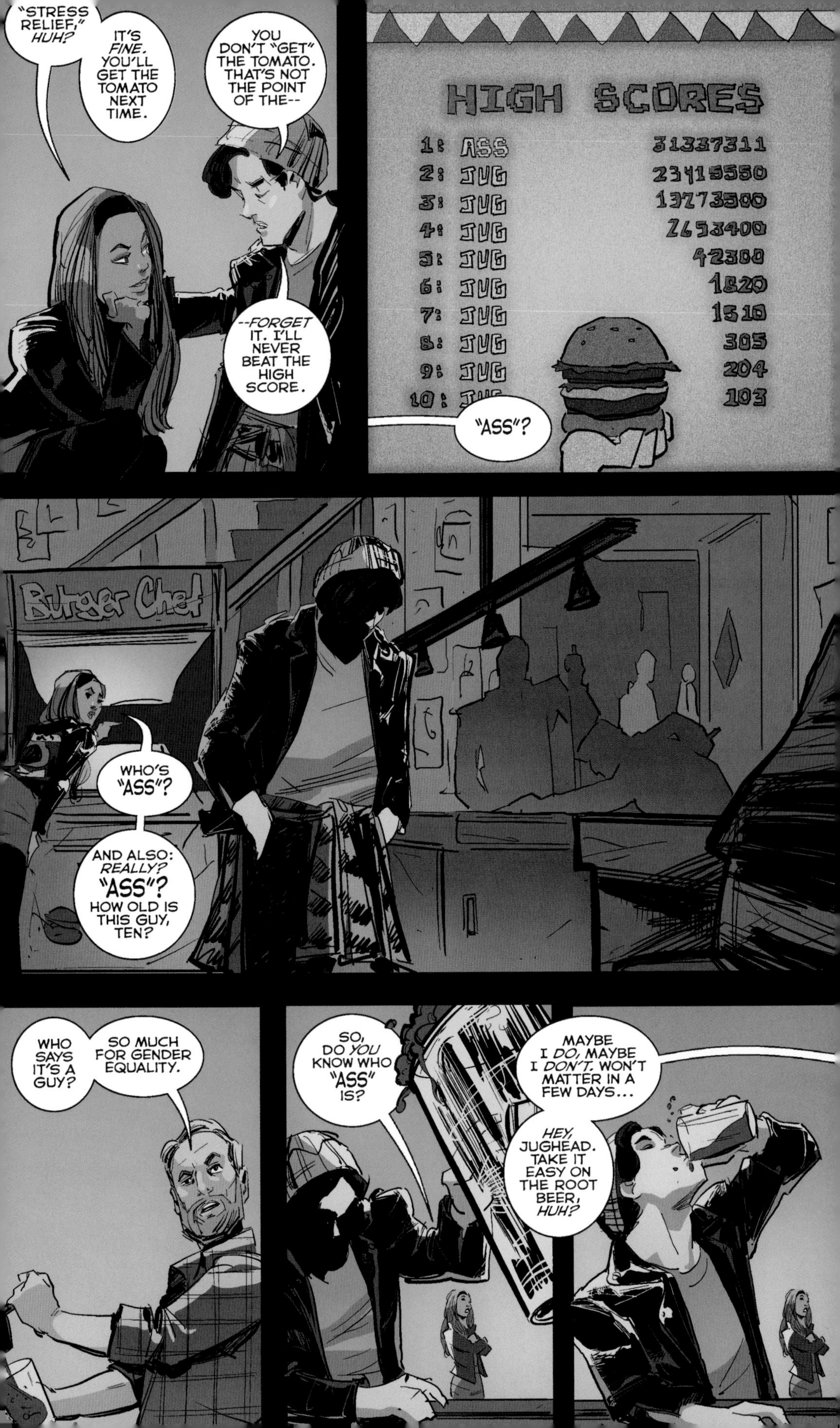
"STRESS RELIEF," HUH?
IT'S FINE. YOU'LL GET THE TOMATO NEXT TIME.
YOU DON'T "GET" THE TOMATO. THAT'S NOT THE POINT OF THE--
--FORGET IT. I'LL NEVER BEAT THE HIGH SCORE.
HIGH SCORES
1: ASS 31337311
2: JUG 23415550
3: JUG 13273500
4: JUG 2653400
5: JUG 42300
6: JUG 1820
7: JUG 1510
8: JUG 305
9: JUG 204
10: 103
"ASS"?
Burger Chef
WHO'S "ASS"?
AND ALSO: REALLY? "ASS"? HOW OLD IS THIS GUY, TEN?
WHO SAYS IT'S A GUY?
SO MUCH FOR GENDER EQUALITY.
SO, DO YOU KNOW WHO "ASS" IS?
MAYBE I DO, MAYBE I DON'T. WON'T MATTER IN A FEW DAYS...
HEY, JUGHEAD. TAKE IT EASY ON THE ROOT BEER, HUH?

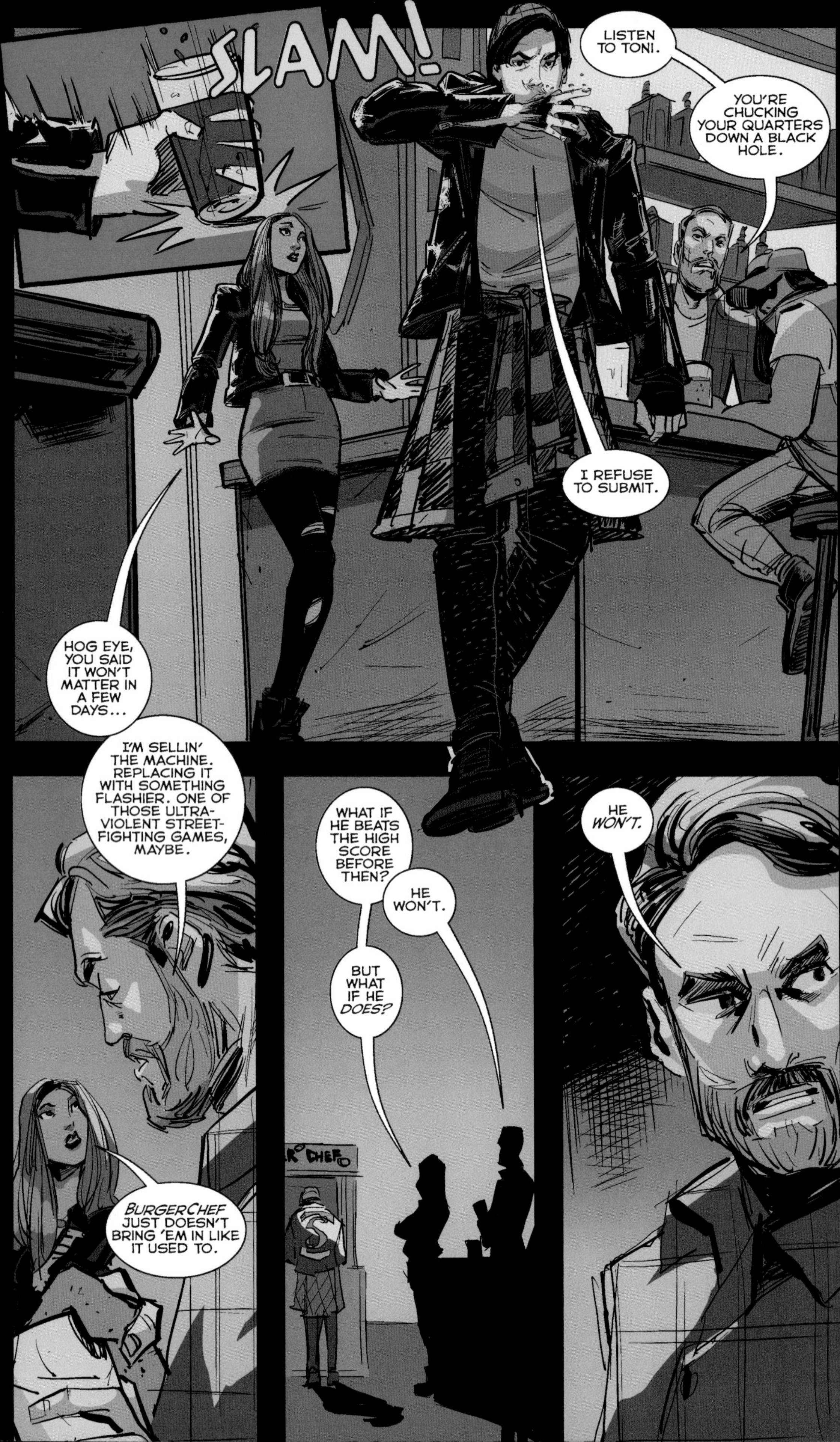
SLAM!
LISTEN TO TONI.
YOU'RE CHUCKING YOUR QUARTERS DOWN A BLACK HOLE.
I REFUSE TO SUBMIT.
HOG EYE, YOU SAID IT WON'T MATTER IN A FEW DAYS...
I'M SELLIN' THE MACHINE. REPLACING IT WITH SOMETHING FLASHIER. ONE OF THOSE ULTRA-VIOLENT STREET-FIGHTING GAMES, MAYBE.
BURGERCHEF JUST DOESN'T BRING 'EM IN LIKE IT USED TO.
WHAT IF HE BEATS THE HIGH SCORE BEFORE THEN?
HE WON'T.
BUT WHAT IF HE *DOES?*
HE *WON'T.*

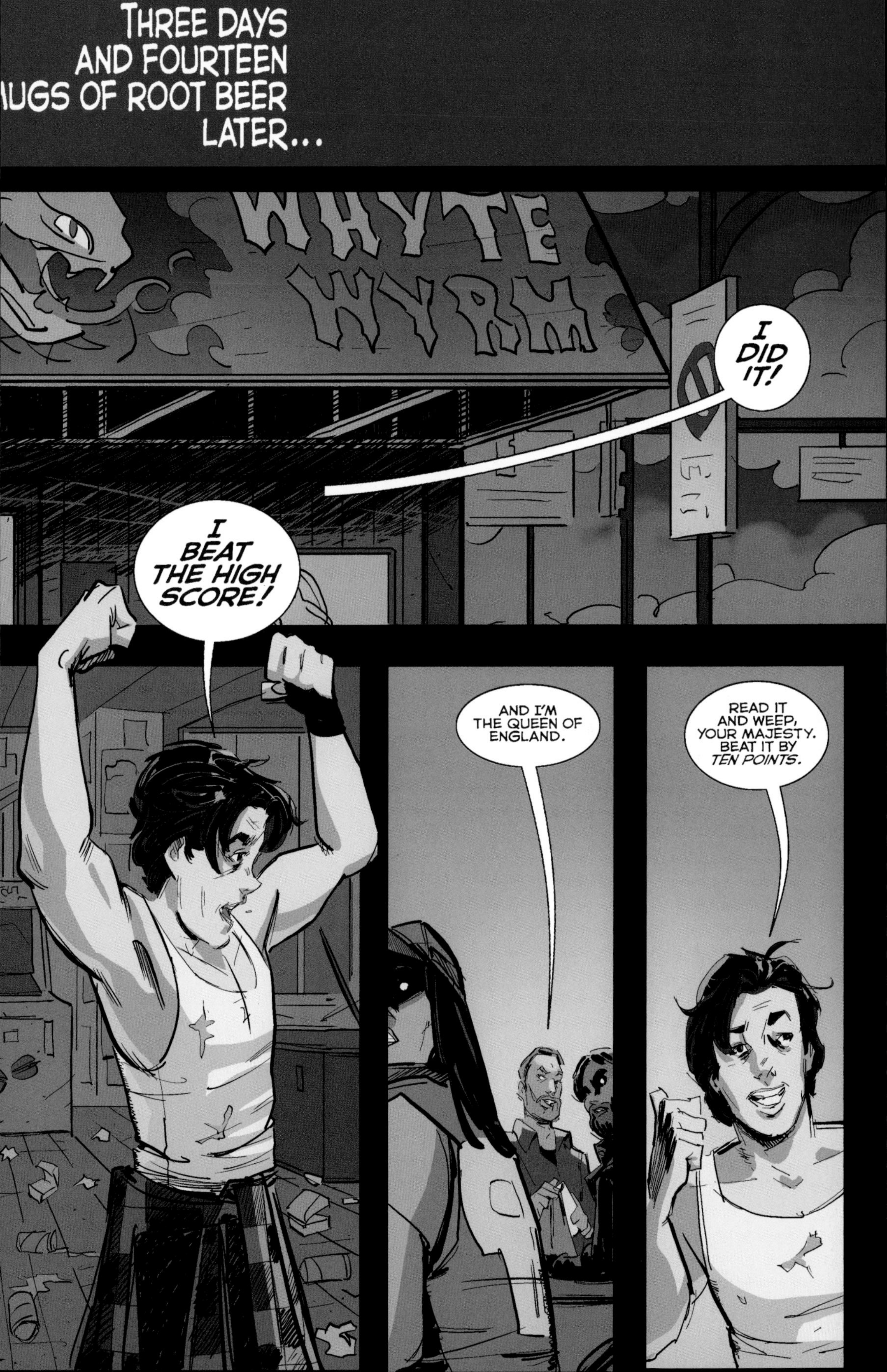
THREE DAYS AND FOURTEEN MUGS OF ROOT BEER LATER...
WHYTE WYRM
I DID IT!
I BEAT THE HIGH SCORE!
AND I'M THE QUEEN OF ENGLAND.
READ IT AND WEEP, YOUR MAJESTY. BEAT IT BY *TEN POINTS*.

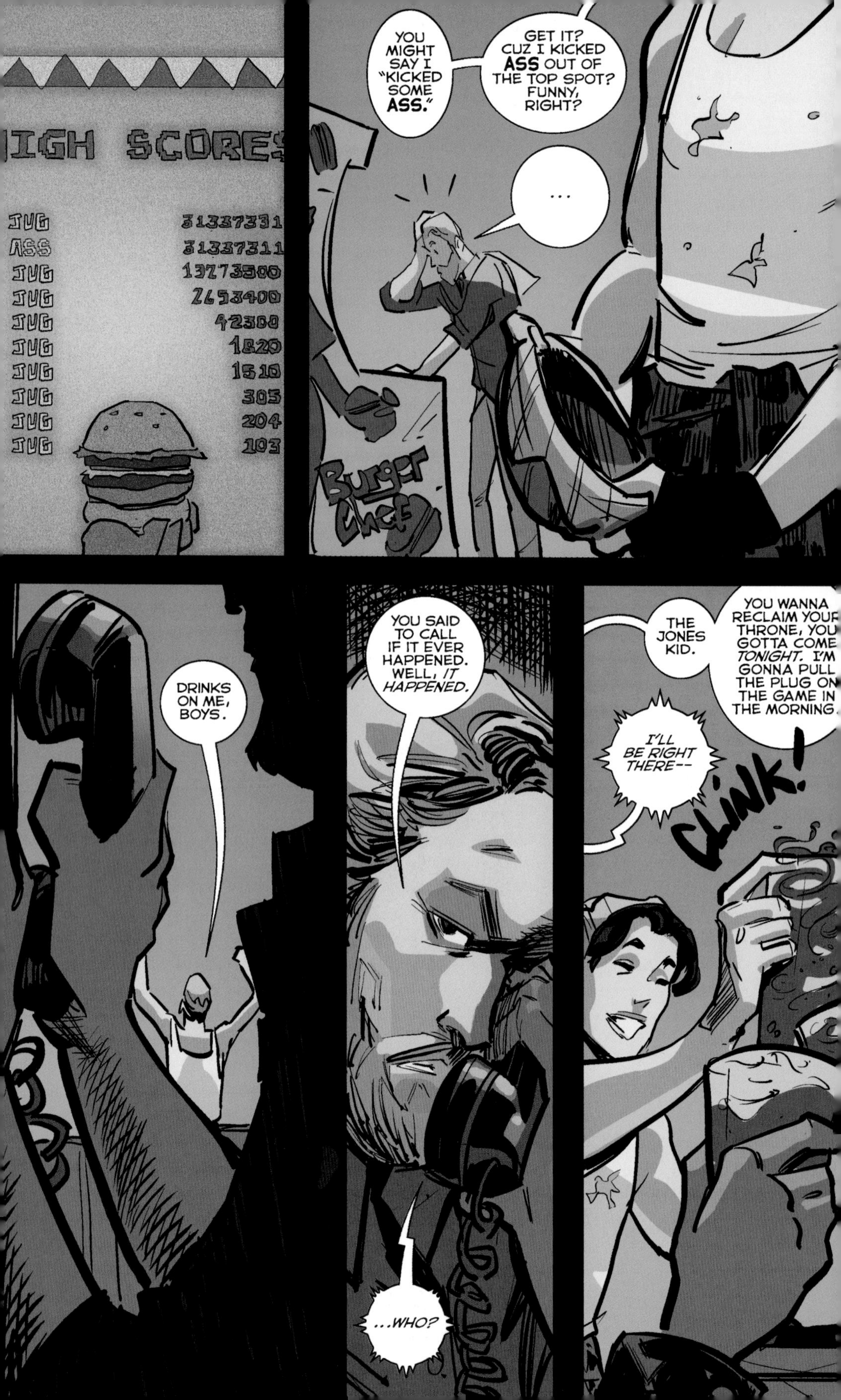
HIGH SCORES
JUG 31337331
ASS 31337311
JUG 13273300
JUG 2653400
JUG 42300
JUG 1820
JUG 1510
JUG 305
JUG 204
JUG 103
YOU MIGHT SAY I "KICKED SOME ASS."
GET IT? CUZ I KICKED ASS OUT OF THE TOP SPOT? FUNNY, RIGHT?
...
Burger Chef
DRINKS ON ME, BOYS.
YOU SAID TO CALL IF IT EVER HAPPENED. WELL, IT HAPPENED.
...WHO?
THE JONES KID.
YOU WANNA RECLAIM YOUR THRONE, YOU GOTTA COME TONIGHT. I'M GONNA PULL THE PLUG ON THE GAME IN THE MORNING.
I'LL BE RIGHT THERE--
CLINK!

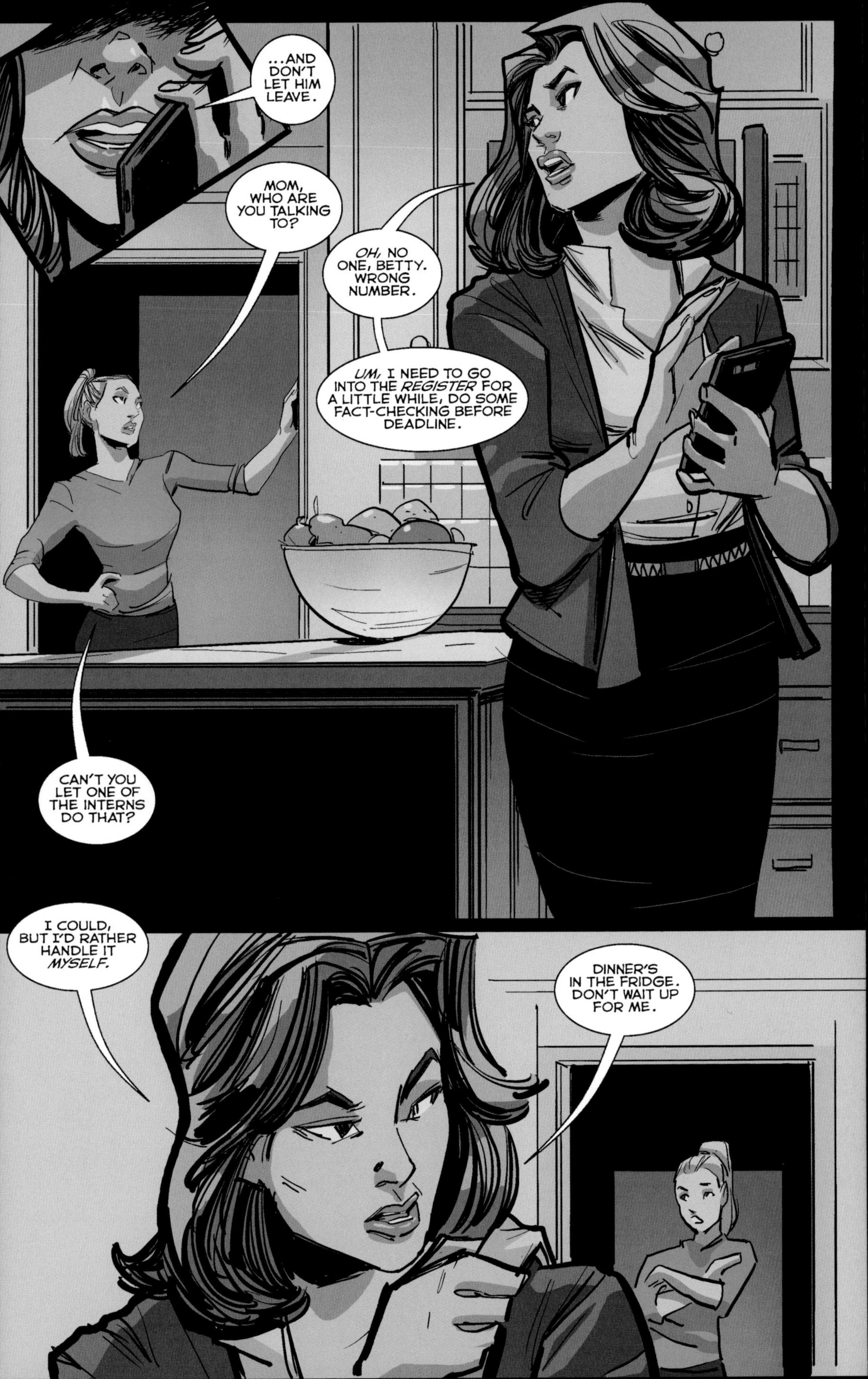
...AND DON'T LET HIM LEAVE.
MOM, WHO ARE YOU TALKING TO?
OH, NO ONE, BETTY. WRONG NUMBER.
UM, I NEED TO GO INTO THE REGISTER FOR A LITTLE WHILE, DO SOME FACT-CHECKING BEFORE DEADLINE.
CAN'T YOU LET ONE OF THE INTERNS DO THAT?
I COULD, BUT I'D RATHER HANDLE IT MYSELF.
DINNER'S IN THE FRIDGE. DON'T WAIT UP FOR ME.

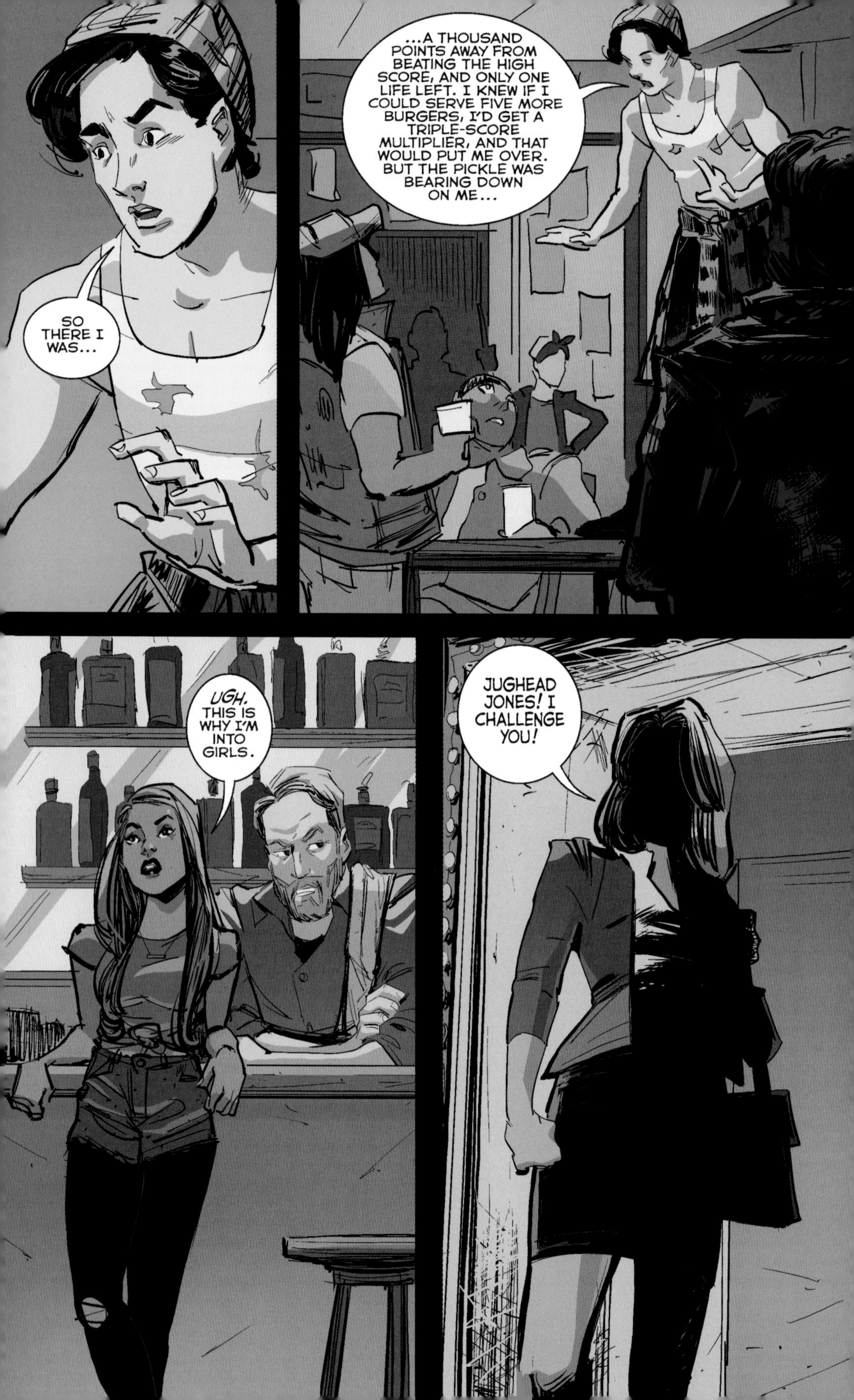
SO THERE I WAS...
...A THOUSAND POINTS AWAY FROM BEATING THE HIGH SCORE, AND ONLY ONE LIFE LEFT. I KNEW IF I COULD SERVE FIVE MORE BURGERS, I'D GET A TRIPLE-SCORE MULTIPLIER, AND THAT WOULD PUT ME OVER. BUT THE PICKLE WAS BEARING DOWN ON ME...
UGH. THIS IS WHY I'M INTO GIRLS.
JUGHEAD JONES! I CHALLENGE YOU!

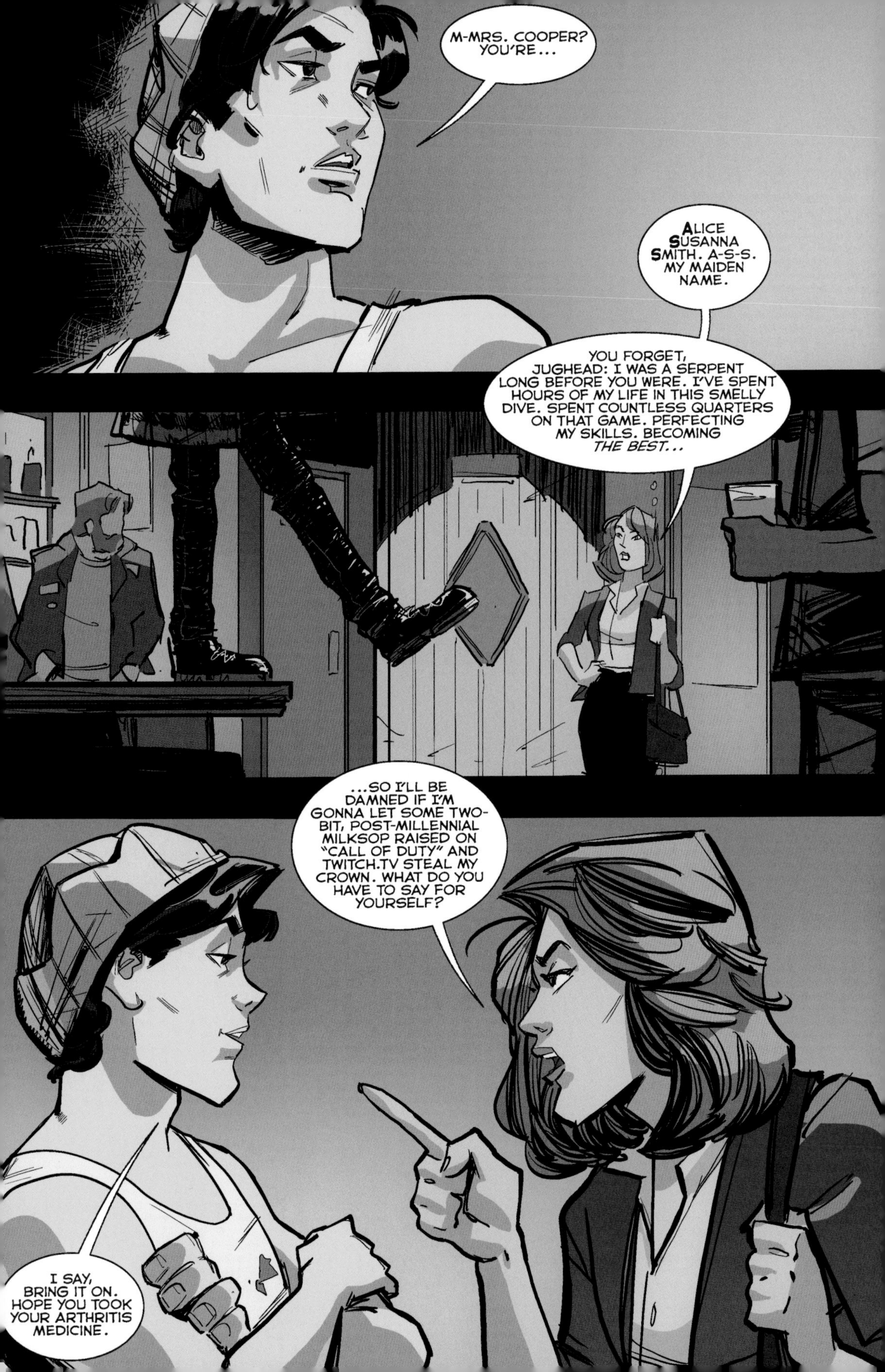
M-MRS. COOPER? YOU'RE...
ALICE SUSANNA SMITH. A-S-S. MY MAIDEN NAME.
YOU FORGET, JUGHEAD: I WAS A SERPENT LONG BEFORE YOU WERE. I'VE SPENT HOURS OF MY LIFE IN THIS SMELLY DIVE. SPENT COUNTLESS QUARTERS ON THAT GAME. PERFECTING MY SKILLS. BECOMING *THE BEST...*
...SO I'LL BE DAMNED IF I'M GONNA LET SOME TWO-BIT, POST-MILLENNIAL MILKSOP RAISED ON "CALL OF DUTY" AND TWITCH.TV STEAL MY CROWN. WHAT DO YOU HAVE TO SAY FOR YOURSELF?
I SAY, BRING IT ON. HOPE YOU TOOK YOUR ARTHRITIS MEDICINE.

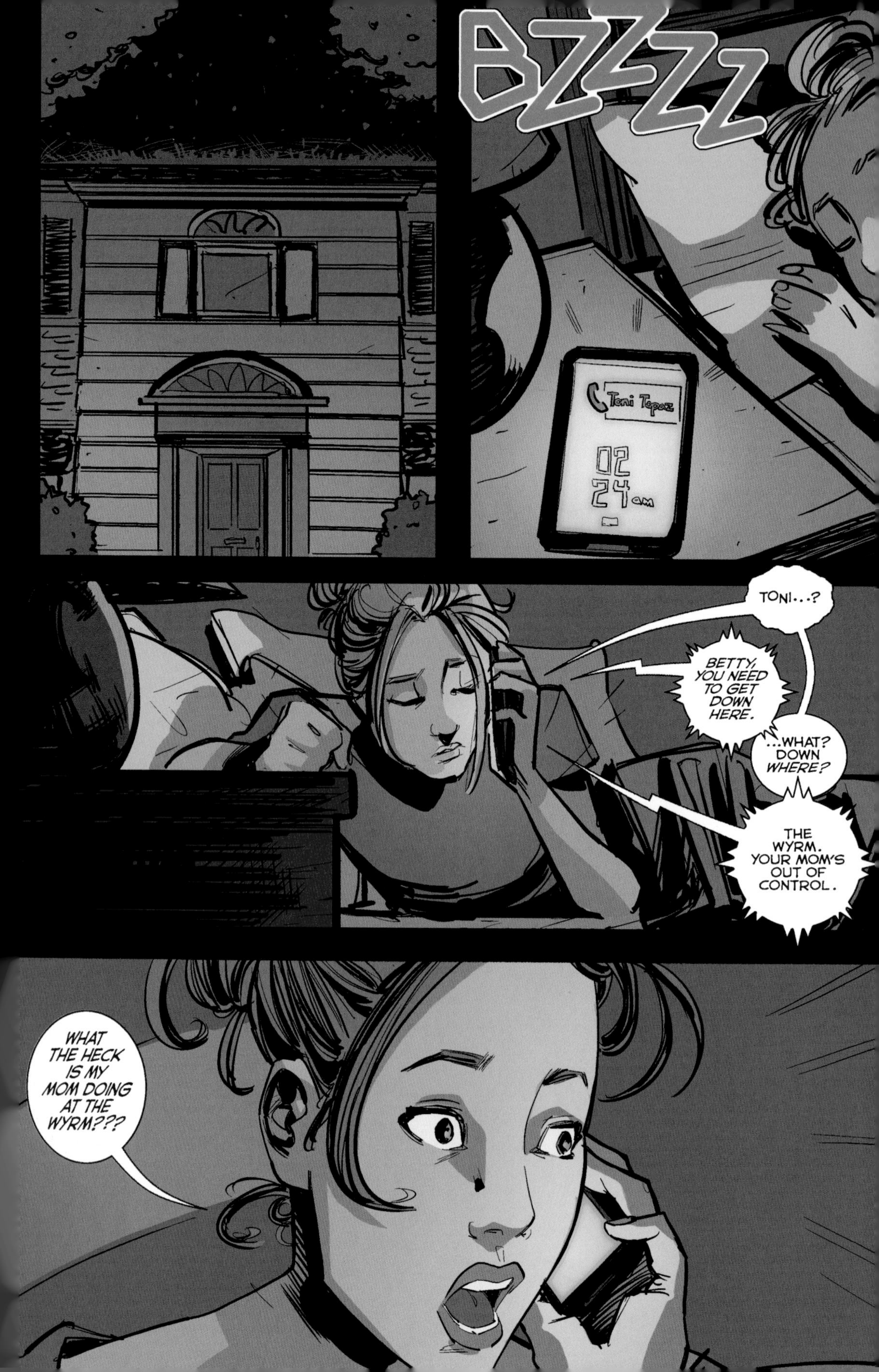
BZZZZ
Toni Topaz
02
24 am
TONI...?
BETTY, YOU NEED TO GET DOWN HERE.
...WHAT? DOWN WHERE?
THE WYRM. YOUR MOM'S OUT OF CONTROL.
WHAT THE HECK IS MY MOM DOING AT THE WYRM???

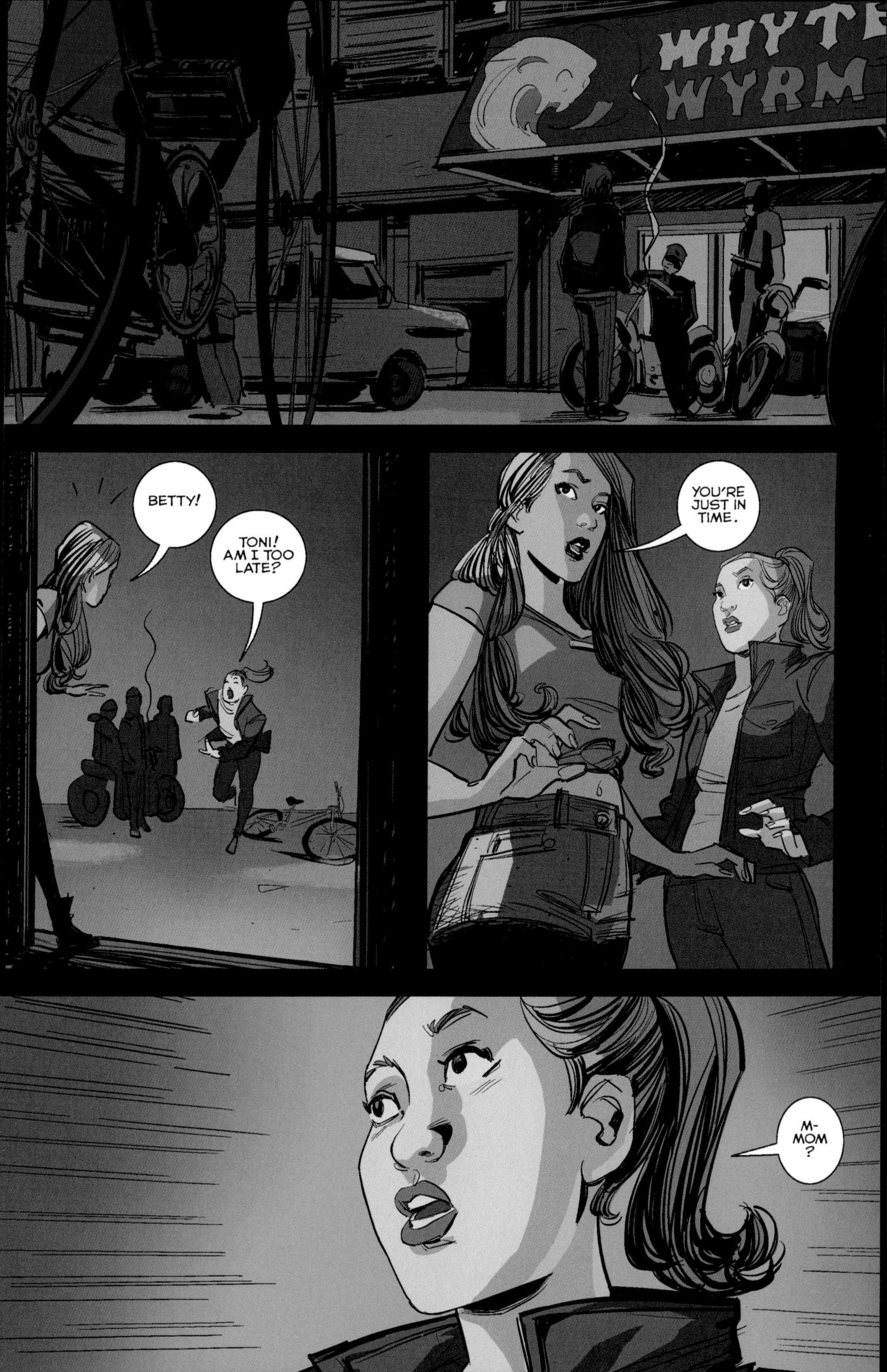
WHYTE WYRM
BETTY!
TONI! AM I TOO LATE?
YOU'RE JUST IN TIME.
M-MOM?

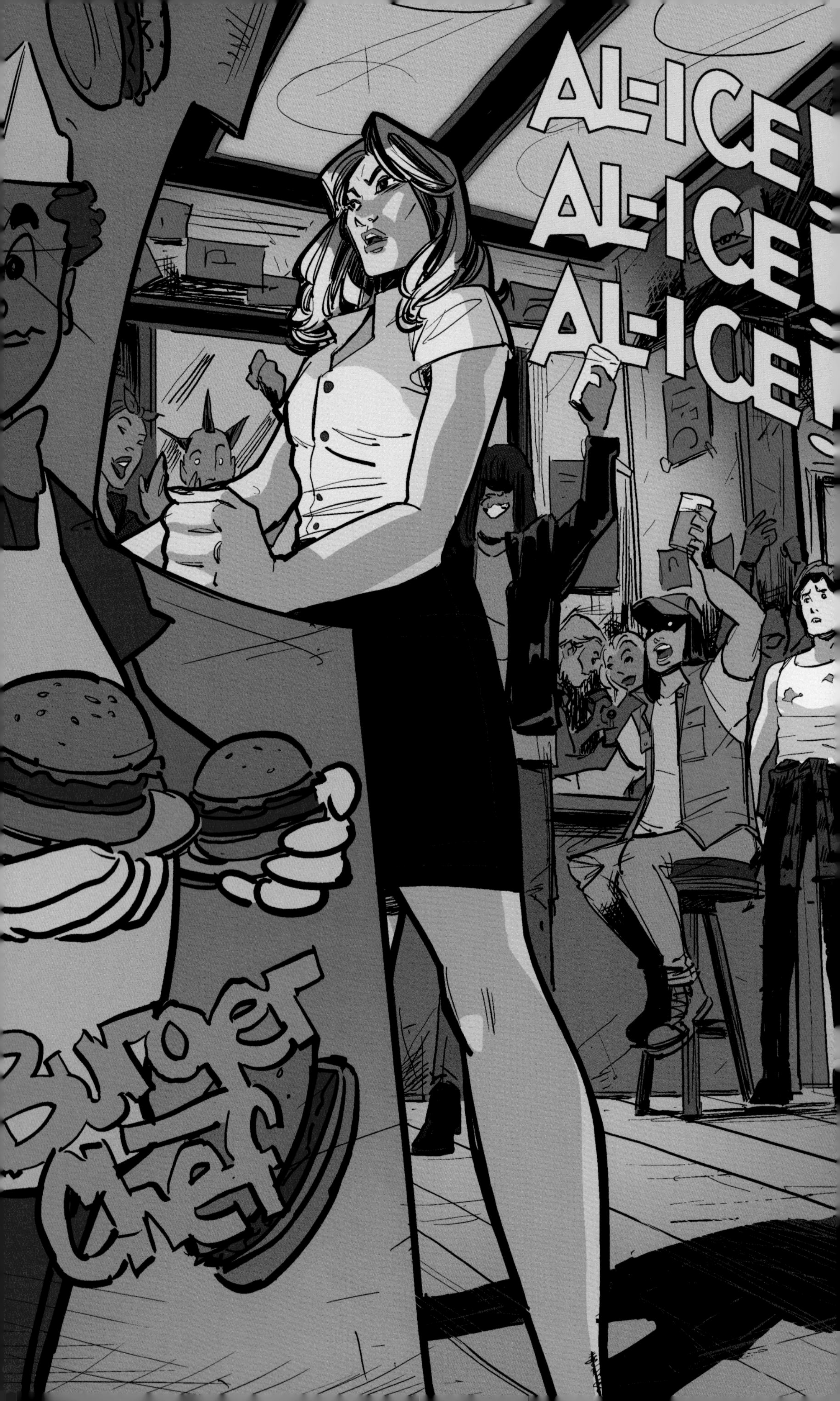
AL-ICE!
AL-ICE!
AL-ICE!
Burger Chef

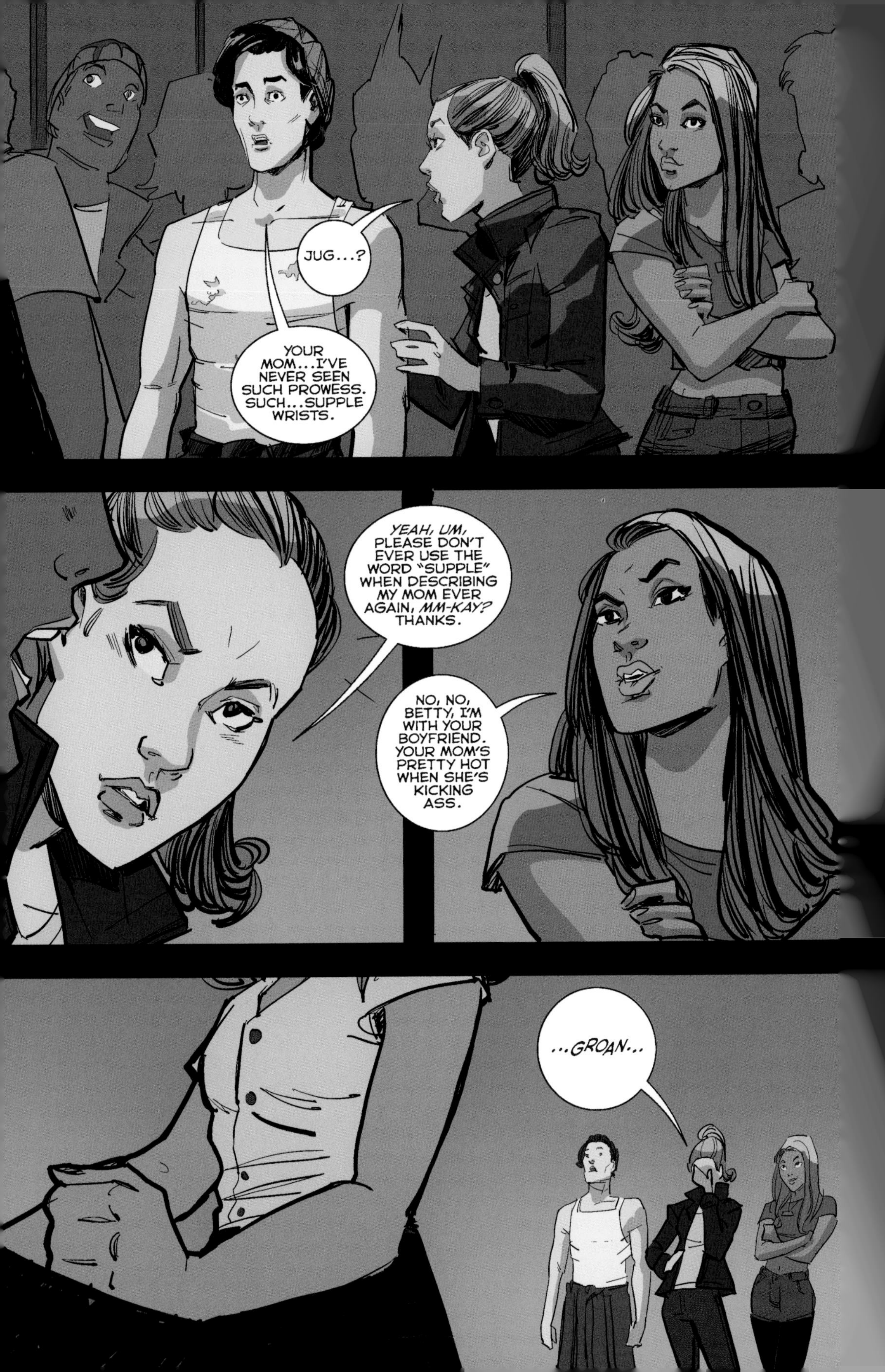
JUG...?
YOUR MOM...I'VE NEVER SEEN SUCH PROWESS. SUCH...SUPPLE WRISTS.
YEAH, UM, PLEASE DON'T EVER USE THE WORD "SUPPLE" WHEN DESCRIBING MY MOM EVER AGAIN, MM-KAY? THANKS.
NO, NO, BETTY, I'M WITH YOUR BOYFRIEND. YOUR MOM'S PRETTY HOT WHEN SHE'S KICKING ASS.
...GROAN...

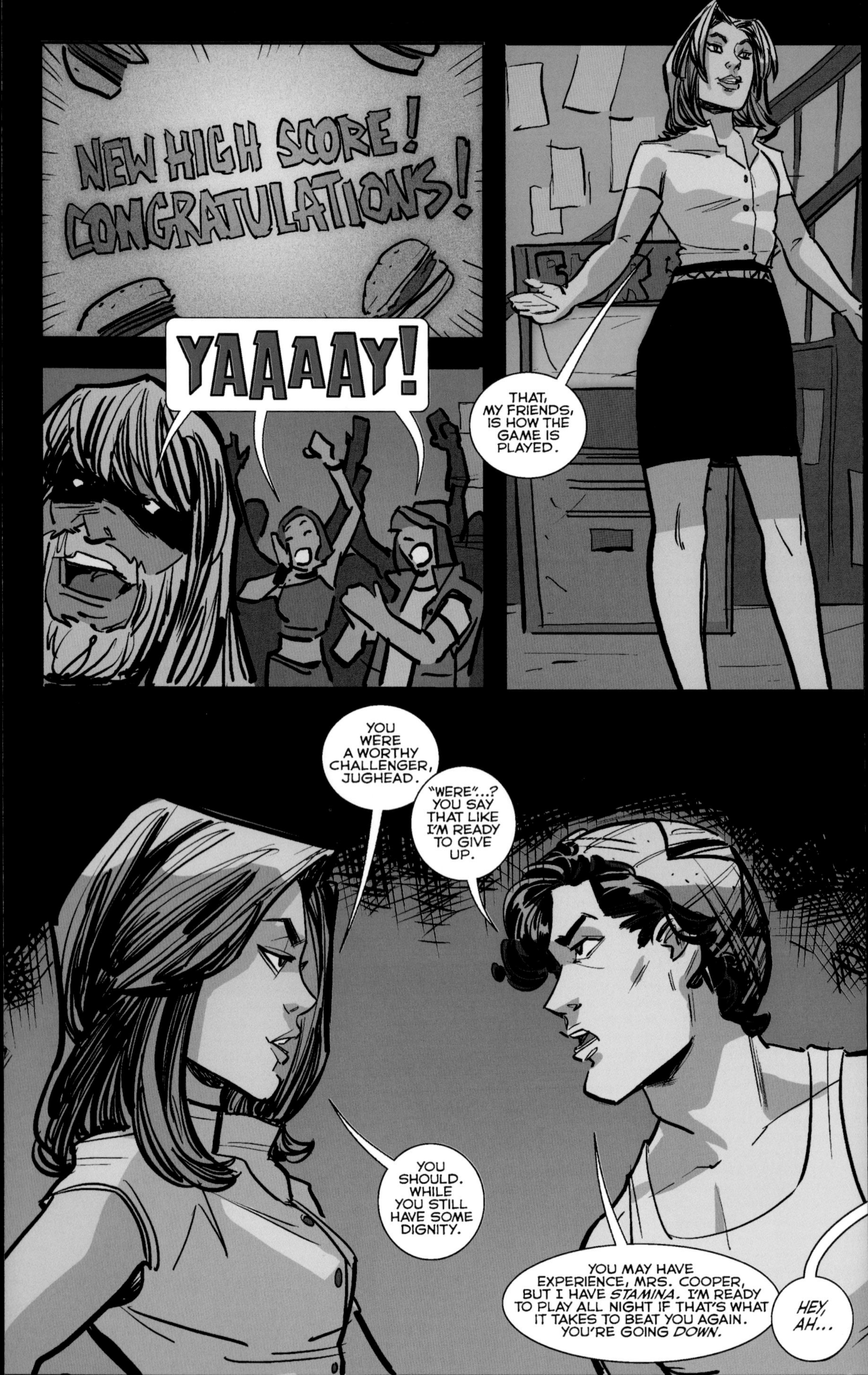
NEW HIGH SCORE!
CONGRATULATIONS!
YAAAAY!
THAT, MY FRIENDS, IS HOW THE GAME IS PLAYED.
YOU WERE A WORTHY CHALLENGER, JUGHEAD.
"WERE"..? YOU SAY THAT LIKE I'M READY TO GIVE UP.
YOU SHOULD. WHILE YOU STILL HAVE SOME DIGNITY.
YOU MAY HAVE EXPERIENCE, MRS. COOPER, BUT I HAVE *STAMINA*. I'M READY TO PLAY ALL NIGHT IF THAT'S WHAT IT TAKES TO BEAT YOU AGAIN. YOU'RE GOING *DOWN*.
HEY, AH...

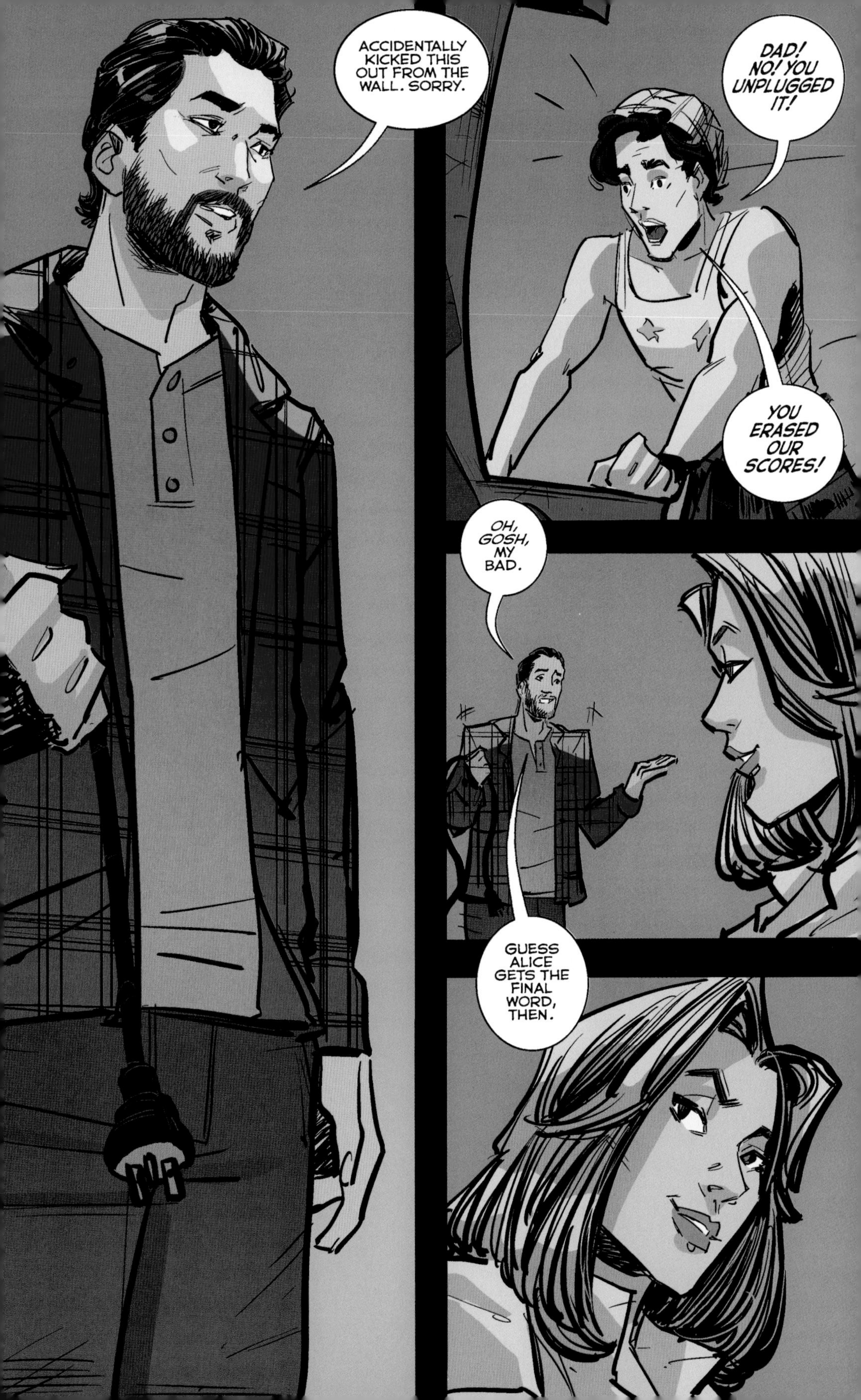
ACCIDENTALLY KICKED THIS OUT FROM THE WALL. SORRY.
DAD! NO! YOU UNPLUGGED IT!
YOU ERASED OUR SCORES!
OH, GOSH, MY BAD.
GUESS ALICE GETS THE FINAL WORD, THEN.

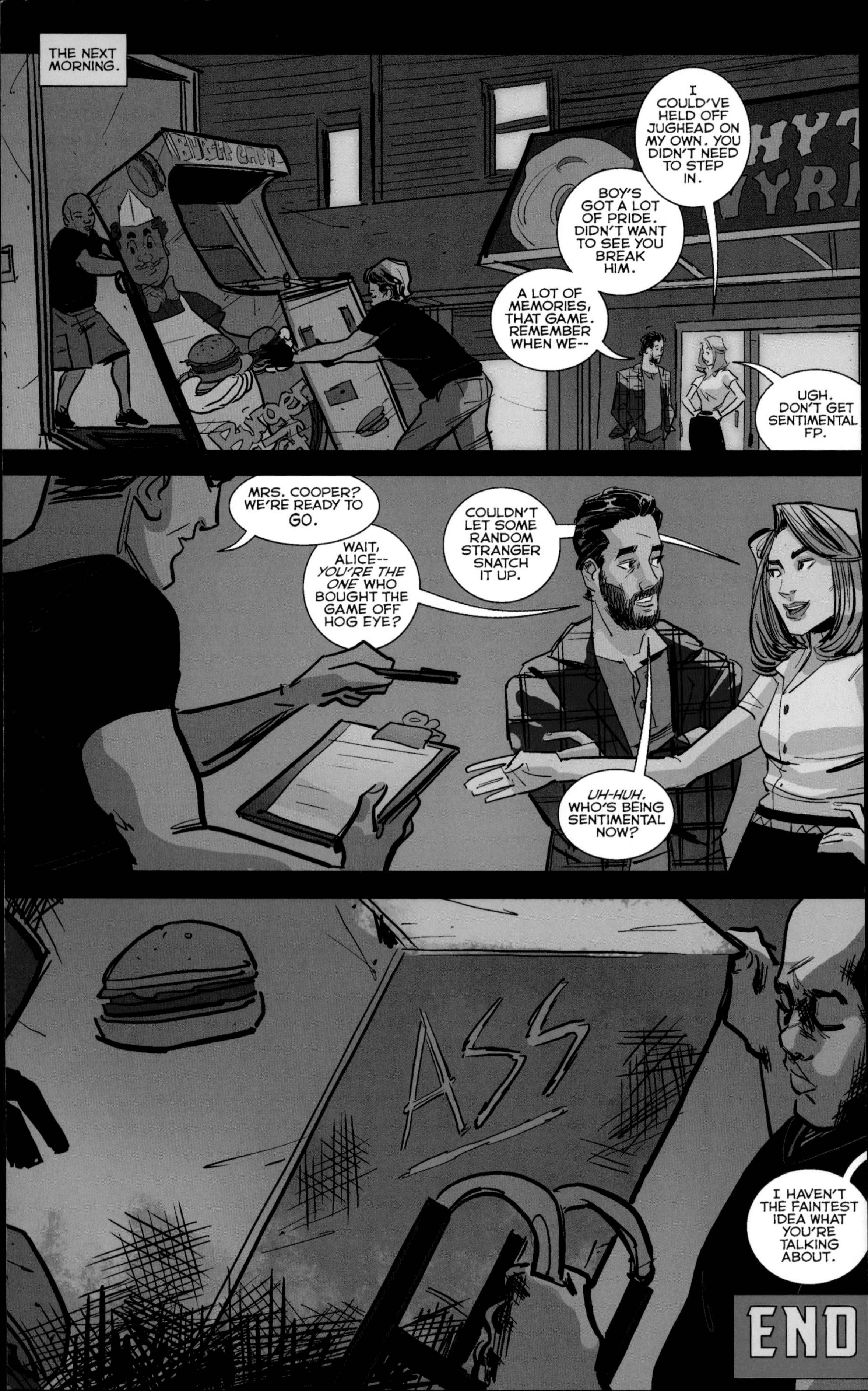
THE NEXT MORNING.
I COULD'VE HELD OFF JUGHEAD ON MY OWN. YOU DIDN'T NEED TO STEP IN.
BOY'S GOT A LOT OF PRIDE. DIDN'T WANT TO SEE YOU BREAK HIM.
A LOT OF MEMORIES, THAT GAME. REMEMBER WHEN WE--
UGH. DON'T GET SENTIMENTAL FP.
MRS. COOPER? WE'RE READY TO GO.
WAIT, ALICE-- *YOU'RE THE ONE* WHO BOUGHT THE GAME OFF HOG EYE?
COULDN'T LET SOME RANDOM STRANGER SNATCH IT UP.
UH-HUH. WHO'S BEING SENTIMENTAL NOW?
ASS
I HAVEN'T THE FAINTEST IDEA WHAT YOU'RE TALKING ABOUT.
END

RIVERDALE®

SPECIAL FEATURES

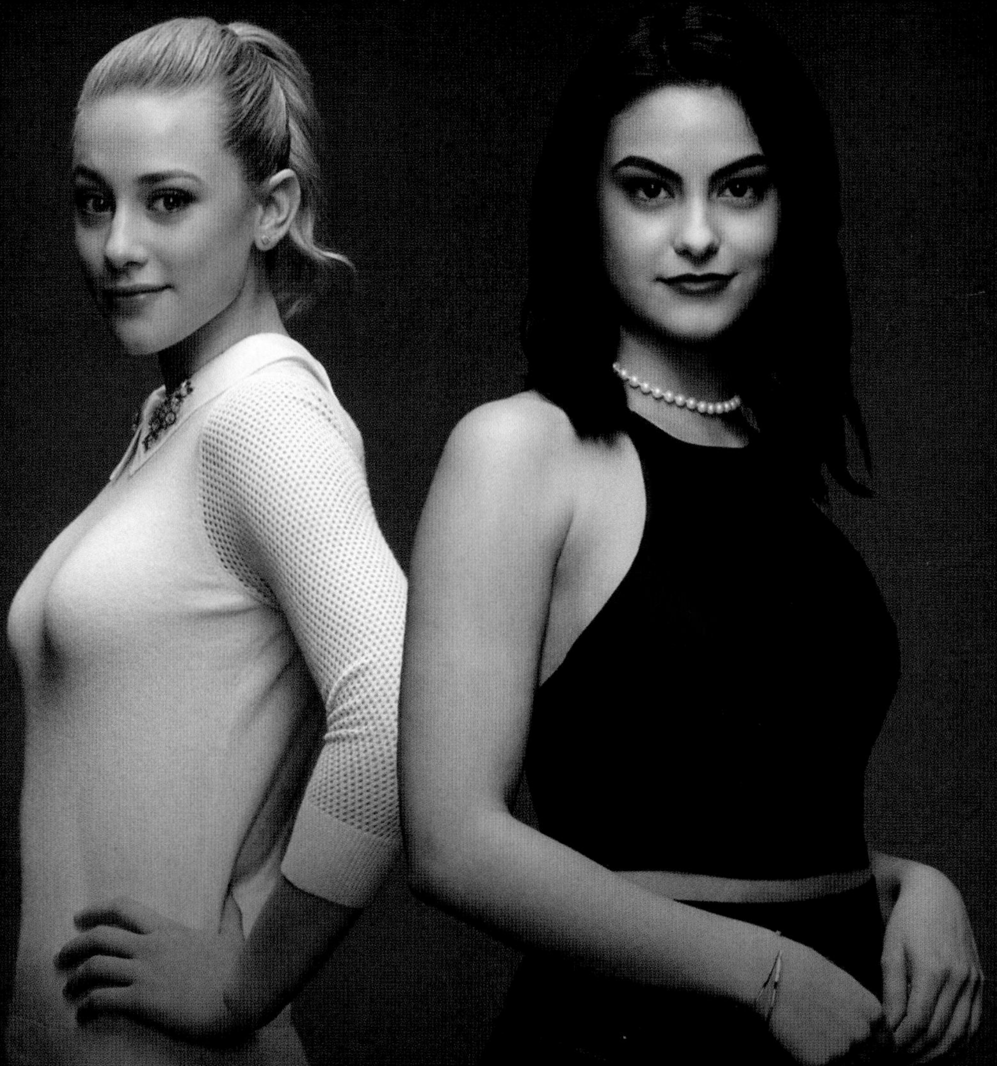

RIVERDALE®

COVER GALLERY

Take a look at our eye-catching main and variant covers for the four issues included in this graphic novel collection. These are comprised of high quality promotional photos of the The CW's *Riverdale* cast courtesy of The CW/Warner Bros.

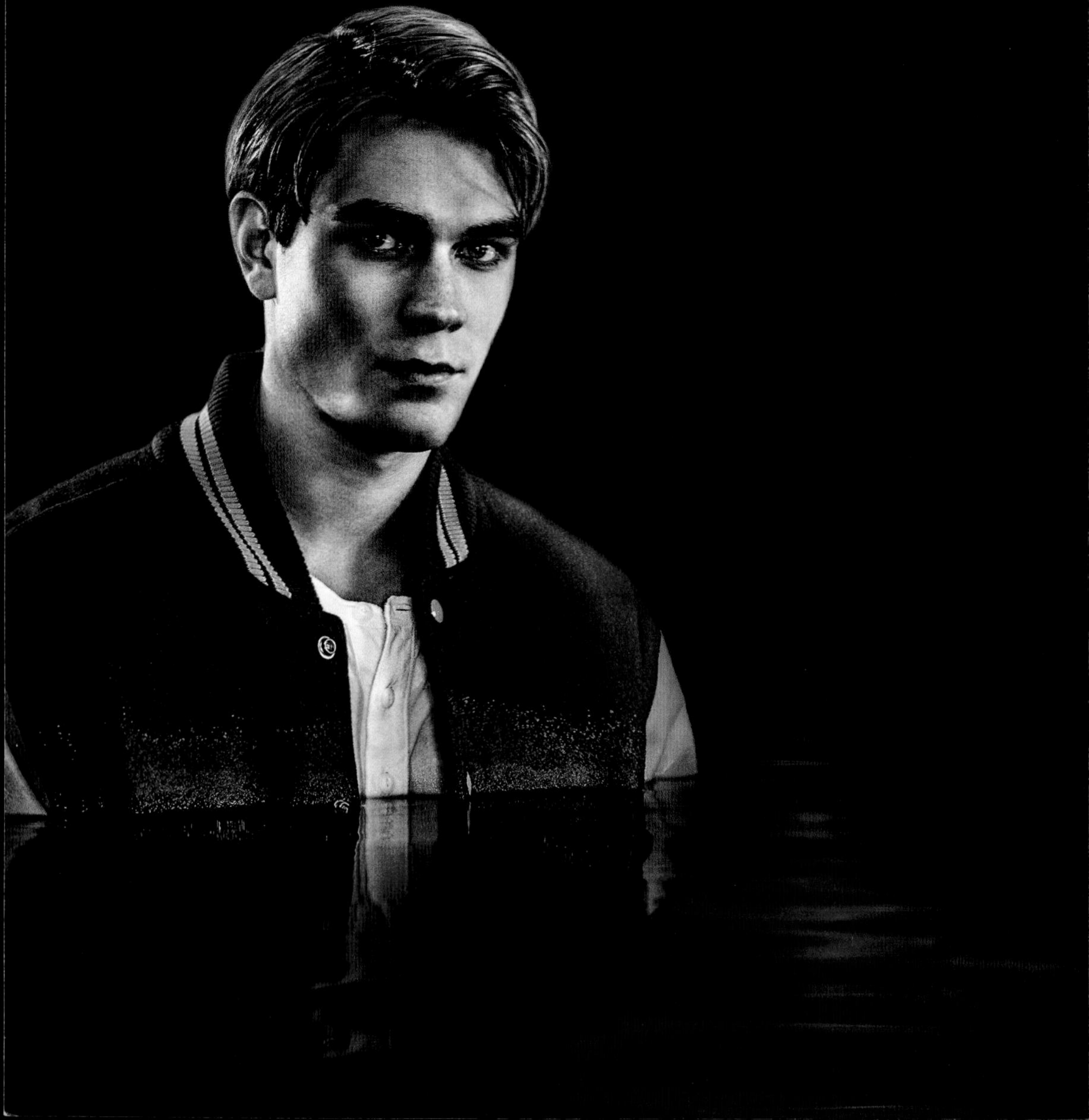

ISSUE
TEN

1

PHOTO COVER
JOSIE:
ASHLEIGH
MURRAY

2

PHOTO COVER
BETTY &
VERONICA:
LILI REINHART
& CAMILA
MENDES

ISSUE ELEVEN

1

PHOTO COVER
ARCHIE: KJ APA

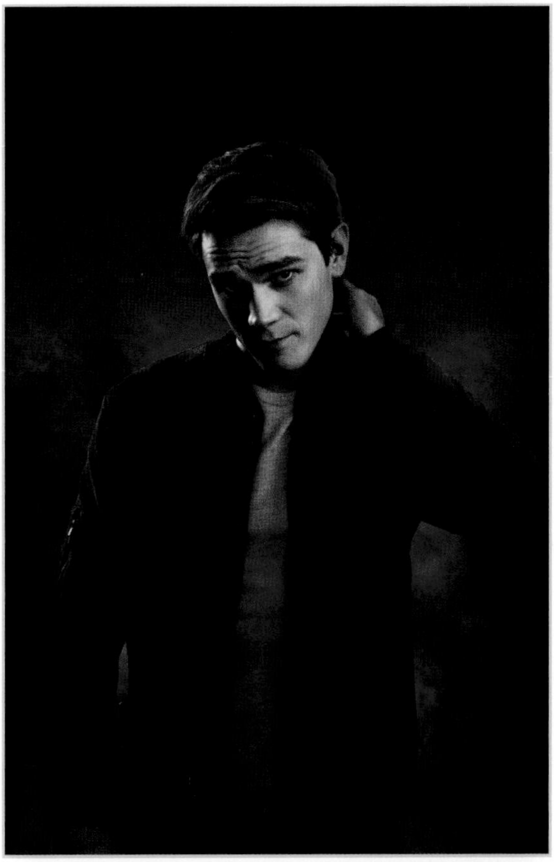

2

PHOTO COVER
JUGHEAD:
COLE SPROUSE

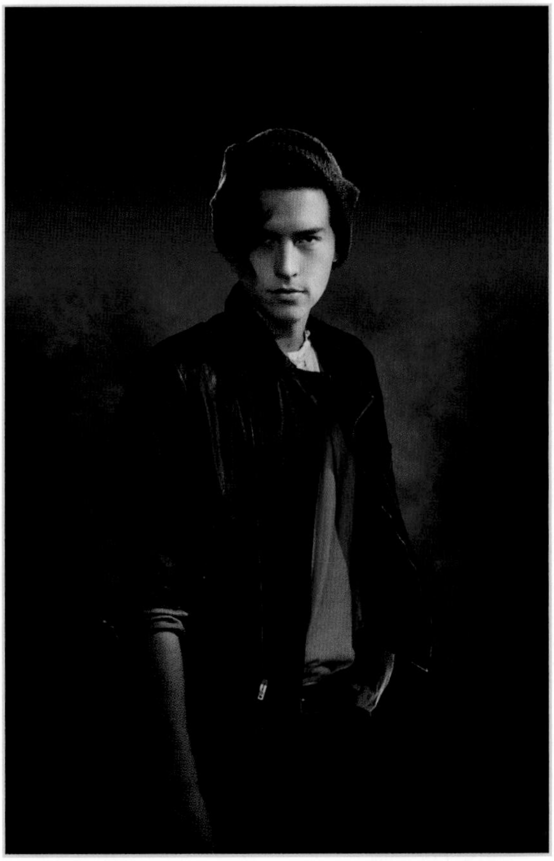

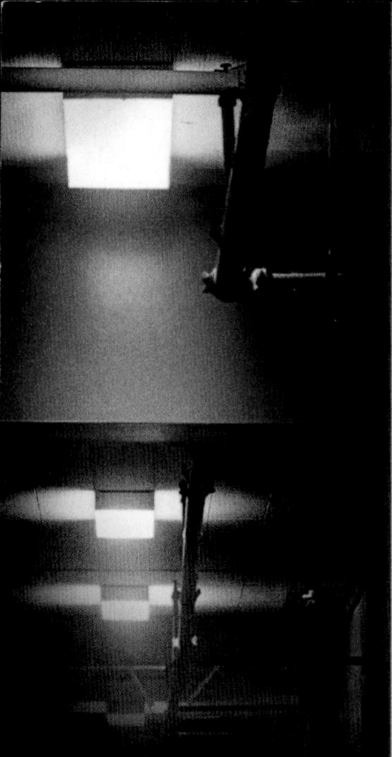

ISSUE
TWELVE

1

PHOTO COVER
JOSIE:
ASHLEIGH
MURRAY

2

PHOTO COVER
BETTY &
JUGHEAD:
LILI REINHART &
COLE SPROUSE

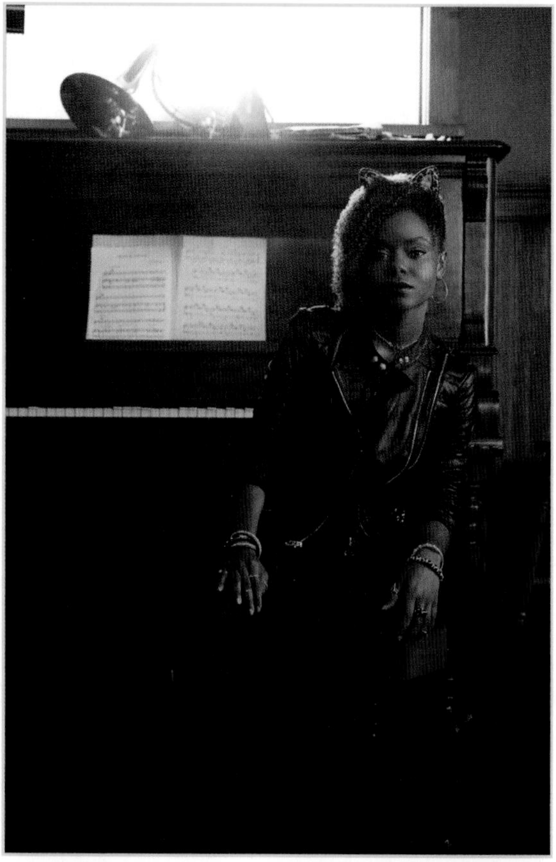

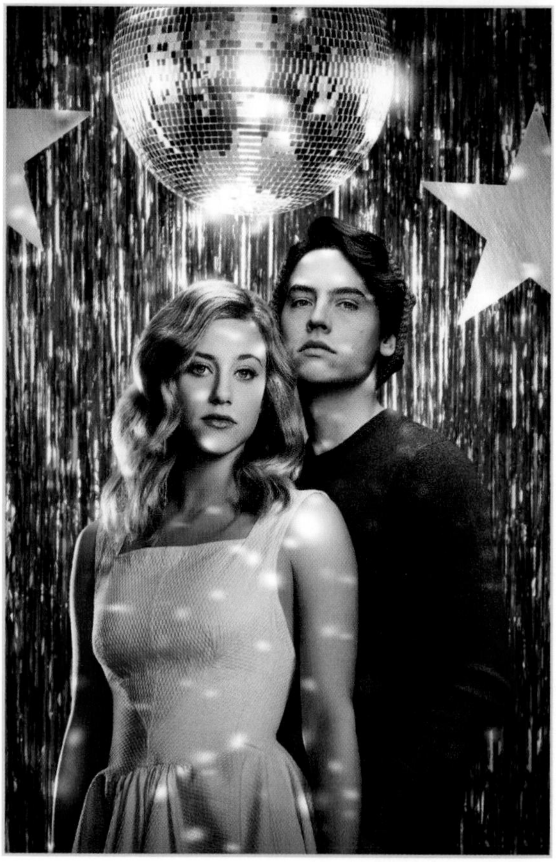

RIVERDALE®

ART PROCESS

Take an inside look at our amazing artist THOMAS PITILLI's process for creating the beautiful pages that make up *Riverdale Volume 3*. Check out how the artwork for issue 10 of *Riverdale* goes from the initial sketch phase to the black and white inked pages and then the final art complete with vibrant colors by ANDRE SZYMANOWICZ and lettering by JOHN WORKMAN.

ISSUE 10 PAGE 1

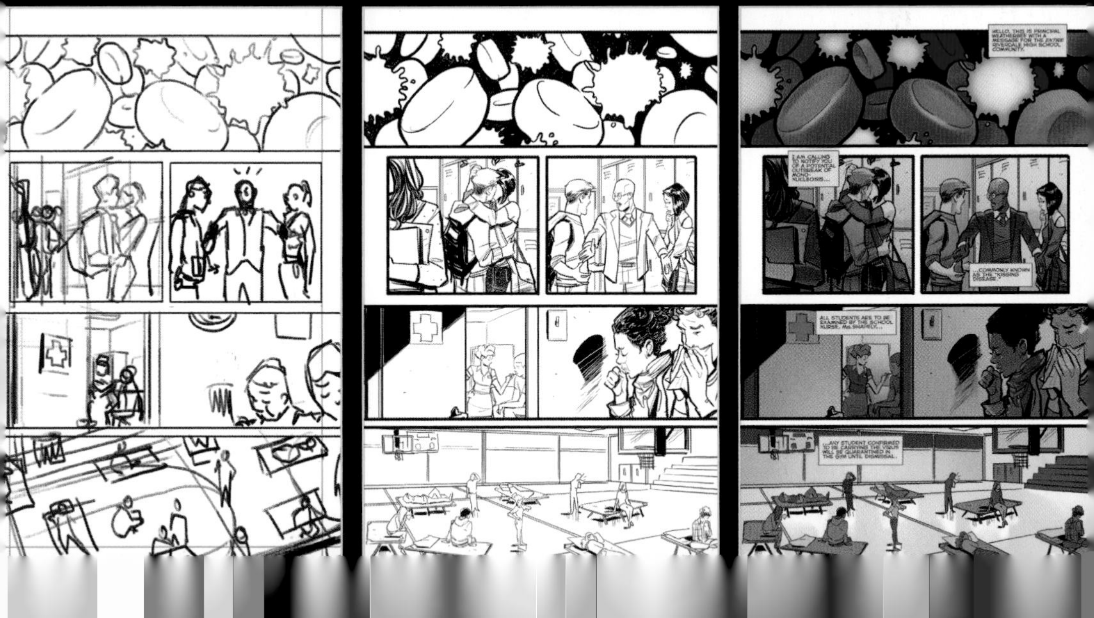
HELLO, THIS IS PRINCIPAL WEATHERBEE WITH A MESSAGE FOR THE *ENTIRE* RIVERDALE HIGH SCHOOL COMMUNITY.
I AM CALLING TO NOTIFY YOU OF A POTENTIAL OUTBREAK OF MONO-NUCLEOSIS...
...COMMONLY KNOWN AS THE "KISSING DISEASE."
ALL STUDENTS ARE TO BE EXAMINED BY THE SCHOOL NURSE, Ms. SHAPELY...
...ANY STUDENT CONFIRMED TO BE CARRYING THE VIRUS WILL BE QUARANTINED IN THE GYM UNTIL DISMISSAL.

ISSUE 10 PAGE 2

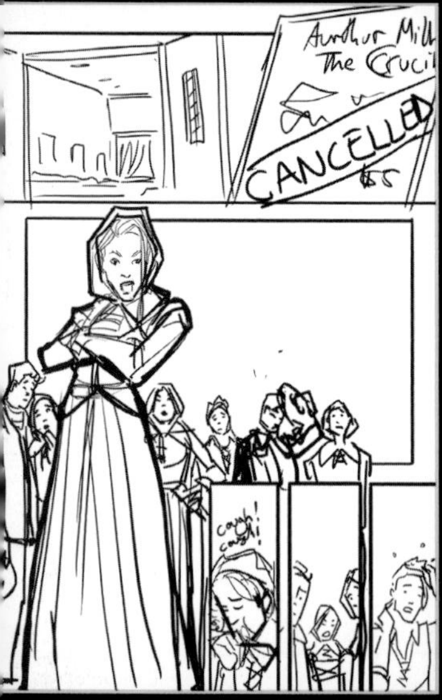

CANCELLED

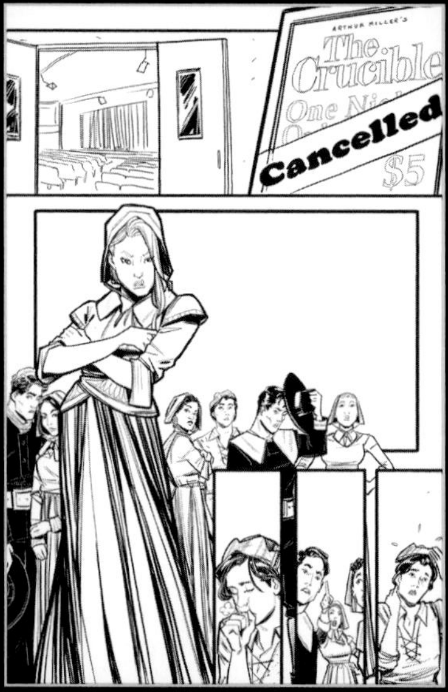

The Crucible
Cancelled
$5

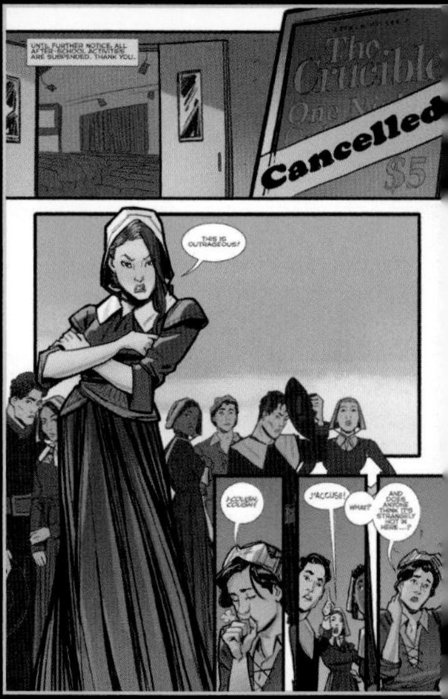

UNTIL FURTHER NOTICE, ALL AFTER-SCHOOL ACTIVITIES ARE SUSPENDED. THANK YOU.
The Crucible
Cancelled
$5
THIS IS OUTRAGEOUS!
J'ACCUSE!
WHAT?
AND DOES ANYONE THINK IT'S STRANGELY HOT IN HERE...?

LAYOUTS INKS FINAL

ISSUE 10 PAGE 3

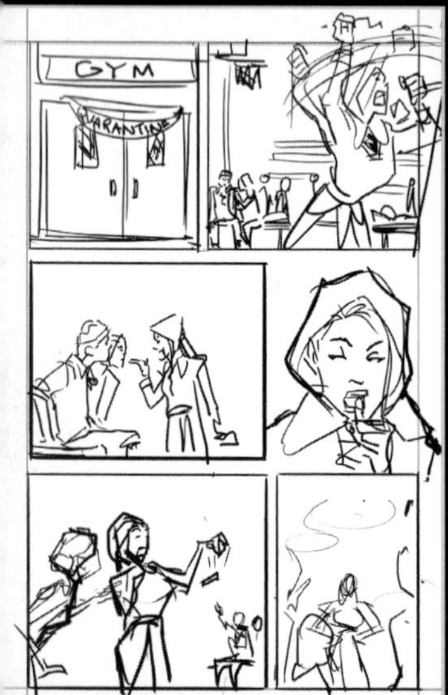

GYM
QUARANTINE

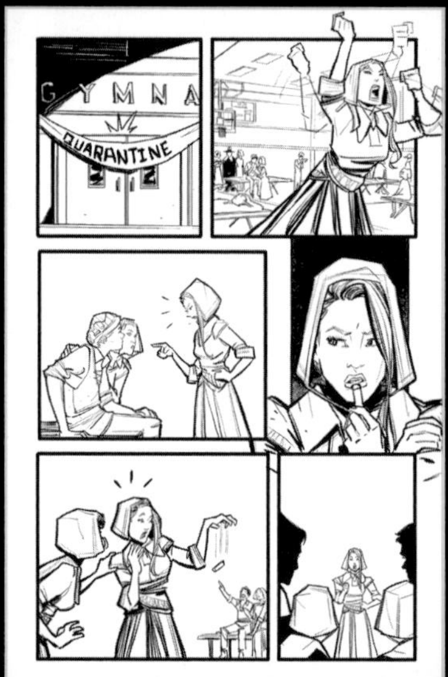

QUARANTINE

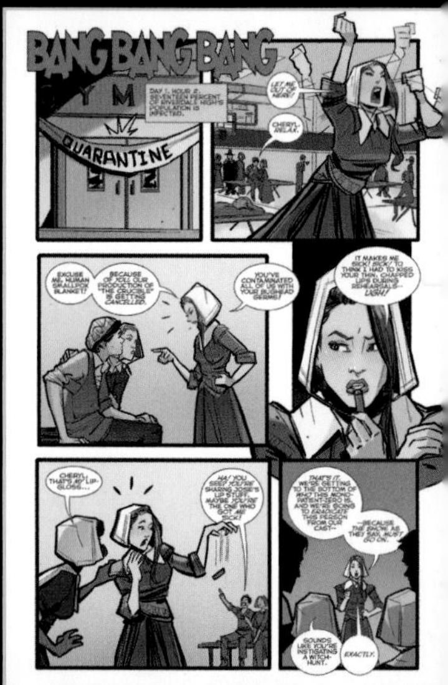

BANG BANG BANG
DAY 1, HOUR 2. SEVENTEEN PERCENT OF RIVERDALE HIGH'S POPULATION IS INFECTED.
QUARANTINE
LET ME OUT OF HERE!
CHERYL, RELAX.
EXCUSE ME, HUMAN SMALLPOX BLANKET!
BECAUSE OF YOU, OUR PRODUCTION OF "THE CRUCIBLE" IS GETTING CANCELLED.
YOU'VE CONTAMINATED ALL OF US WITH YOUR BUGHEAD GERMS!
IT MAKES ME SICK! SICK! TO THINK I HAD TO KISS YOUR THIN, CHAPPED LIPS DURING REHEARSALS-- UGH!
CHERYL, THAT'S MY LIP-GLOSS...
HA! YOU SEE? YOU'RE SHARING JOSIE'S LIP STUFF. MAYBE YOU'RE THE ONE WHO GOT ME SICK!
THAT'S IT. WE'RE GETTING TO THE BOTTOM OF WHO THIS MONO-PATIENT-ZERO IS, AND WE'RE GOING TO ERADICATE THIS PERSON FROM OUR CAST--
--BECAUSE THE SHOW, AS THEY SAY, MUST GO ON.
SOUNDS LIKE YOU'RE INSTIGATING A WITCH-HUNT.
EXACTLY.

BONUS ISSUE

ARCHIE®

If you like *Riverdale* then you'll love the *Archie* comic series! Here's a preview of the upcoming *Archie Vol. 6* graphic novel from the writing team of Mark Waid and Ian Flynn and rising star artist Audrey Mok.

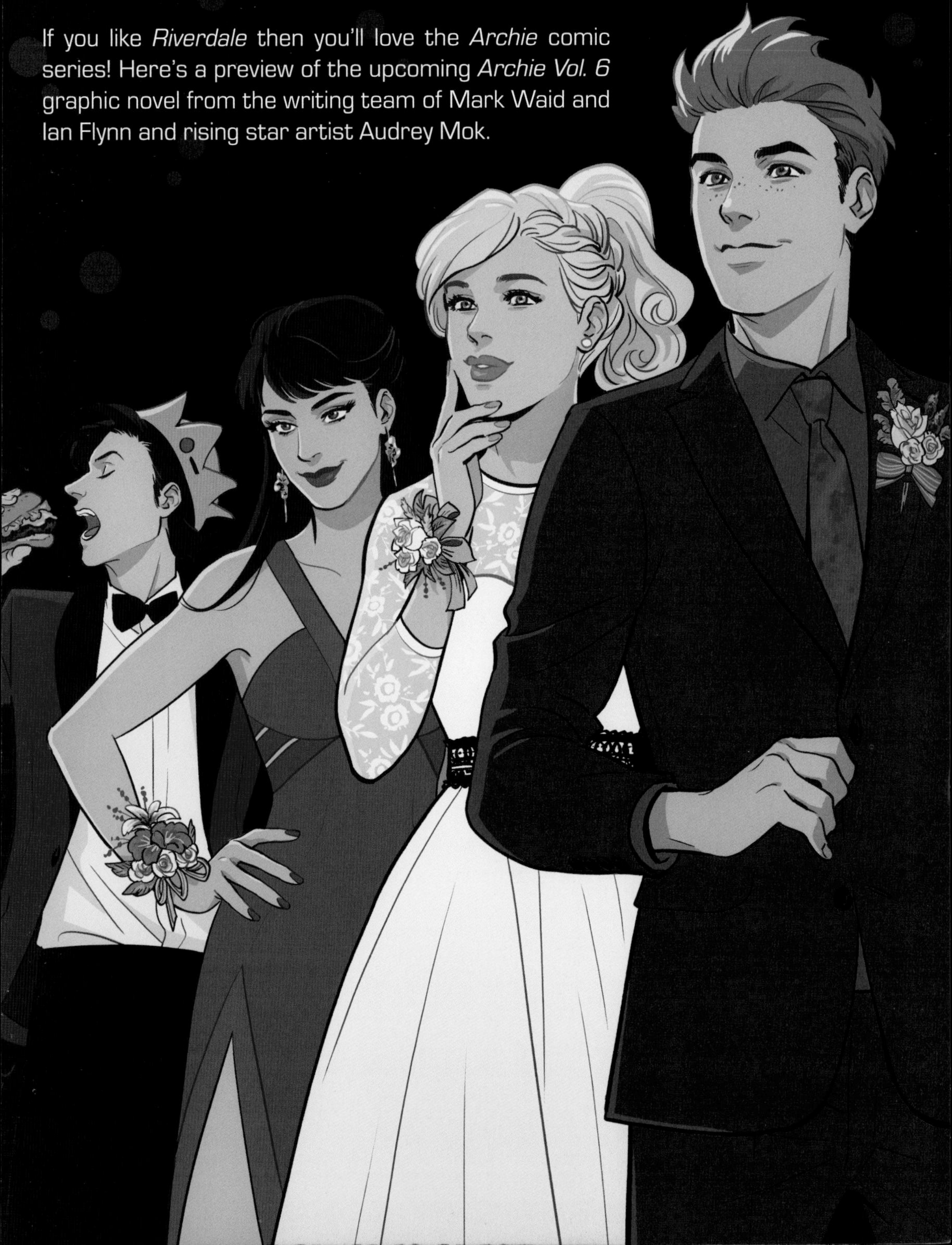

ISSUE TWENTY EIGHT

WRITERS:
MARK WAID & IAN FLYNN

ART:
AUDREY MOK

COLORS:
KELLY FITZPATRICK

LETTERS:
JACK MORELLI

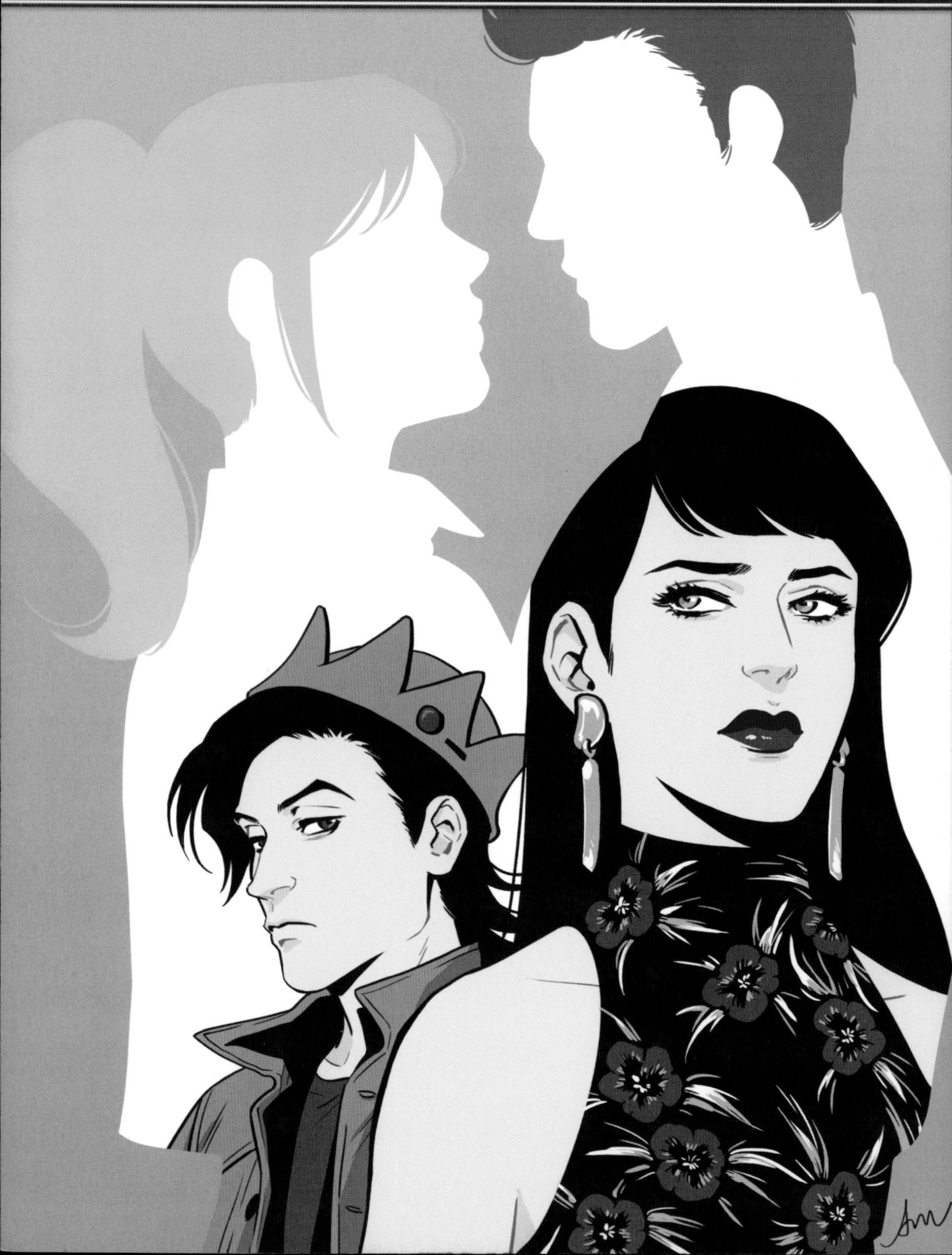

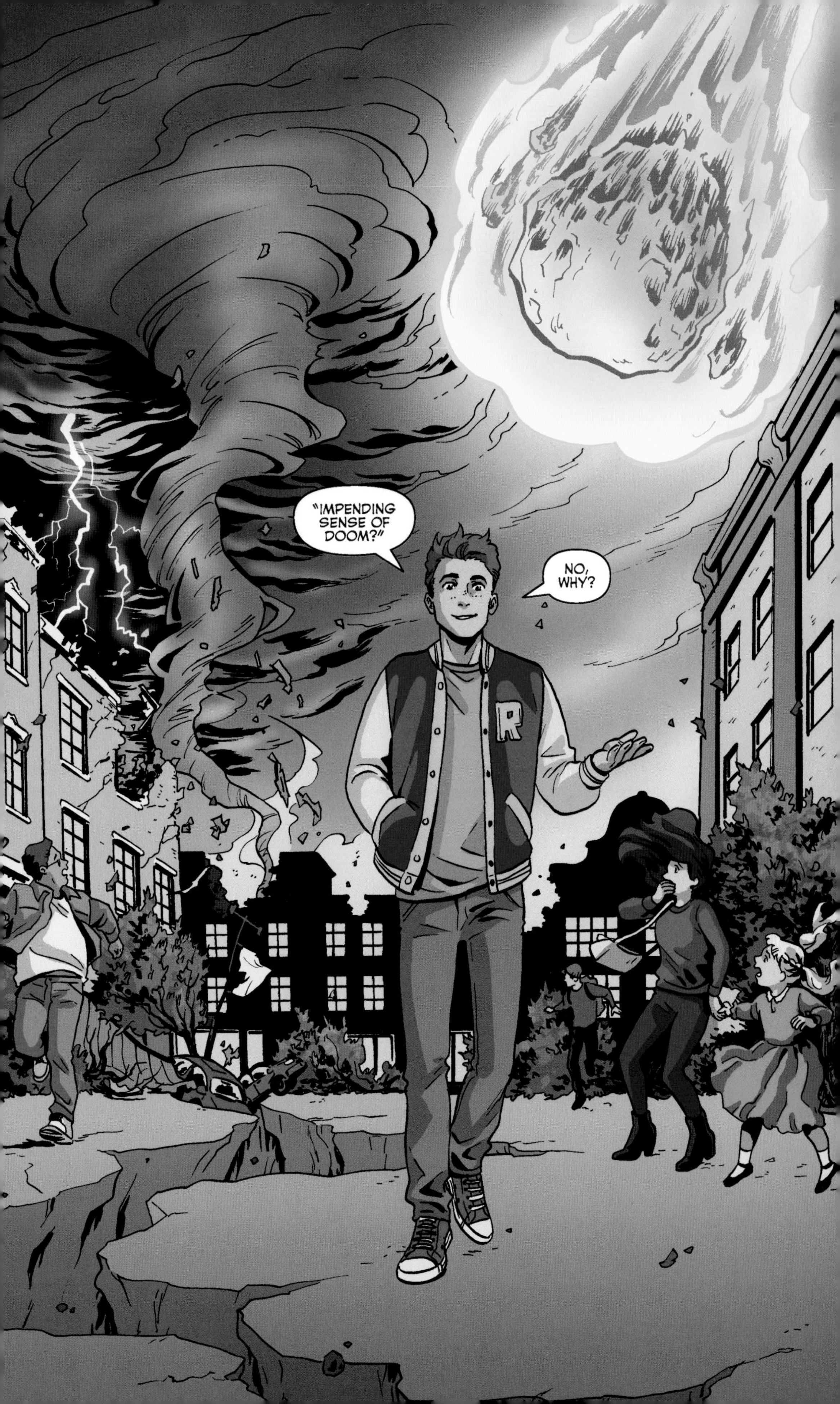
"IMPENDING SENSE OF DOOM?"
NO, WHY?

CHAPTER ONE: RIVERDALE'S The BACHELOR

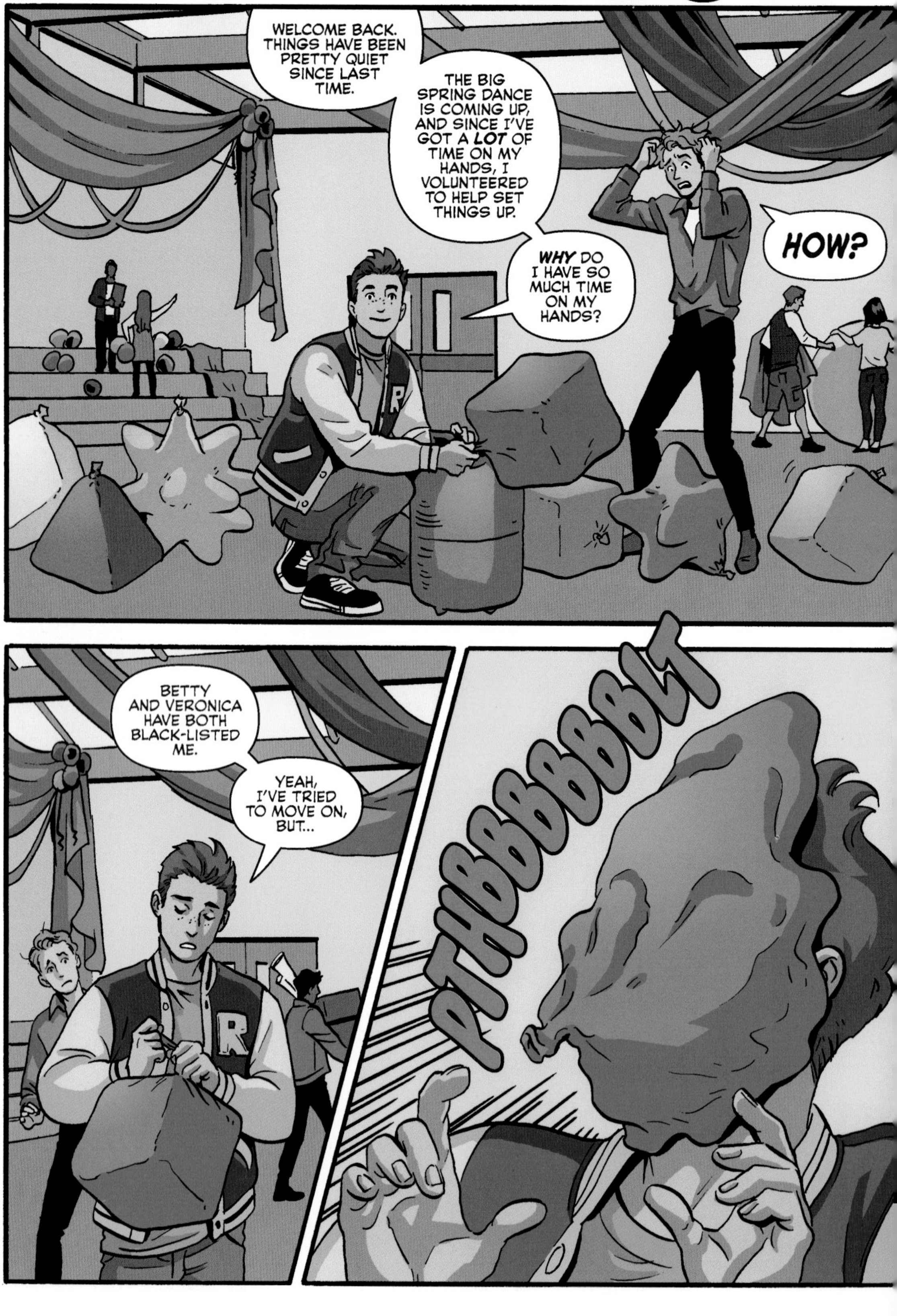
WELCOME BACK. THINGS HAVE BEEN PRETTY QUIET SINCE LAST TIME.
THE BIG SPRING DANCE IS COMING UP, AND SINCE I'VE GOT A LOT OF TIME ON MY HANDS, I VOLUNTEERED TO HELP SET THINGS UP.
WHY DO I HAVE SO MUCH TIME ON MY HANDS?
HOW?
BETTY AND VERONICA HAVE BOTH BLACK-LISTED ME.
YEAH, I'VE TRIED TO MOVE ON, BUT...
PTHBBBBBBLT

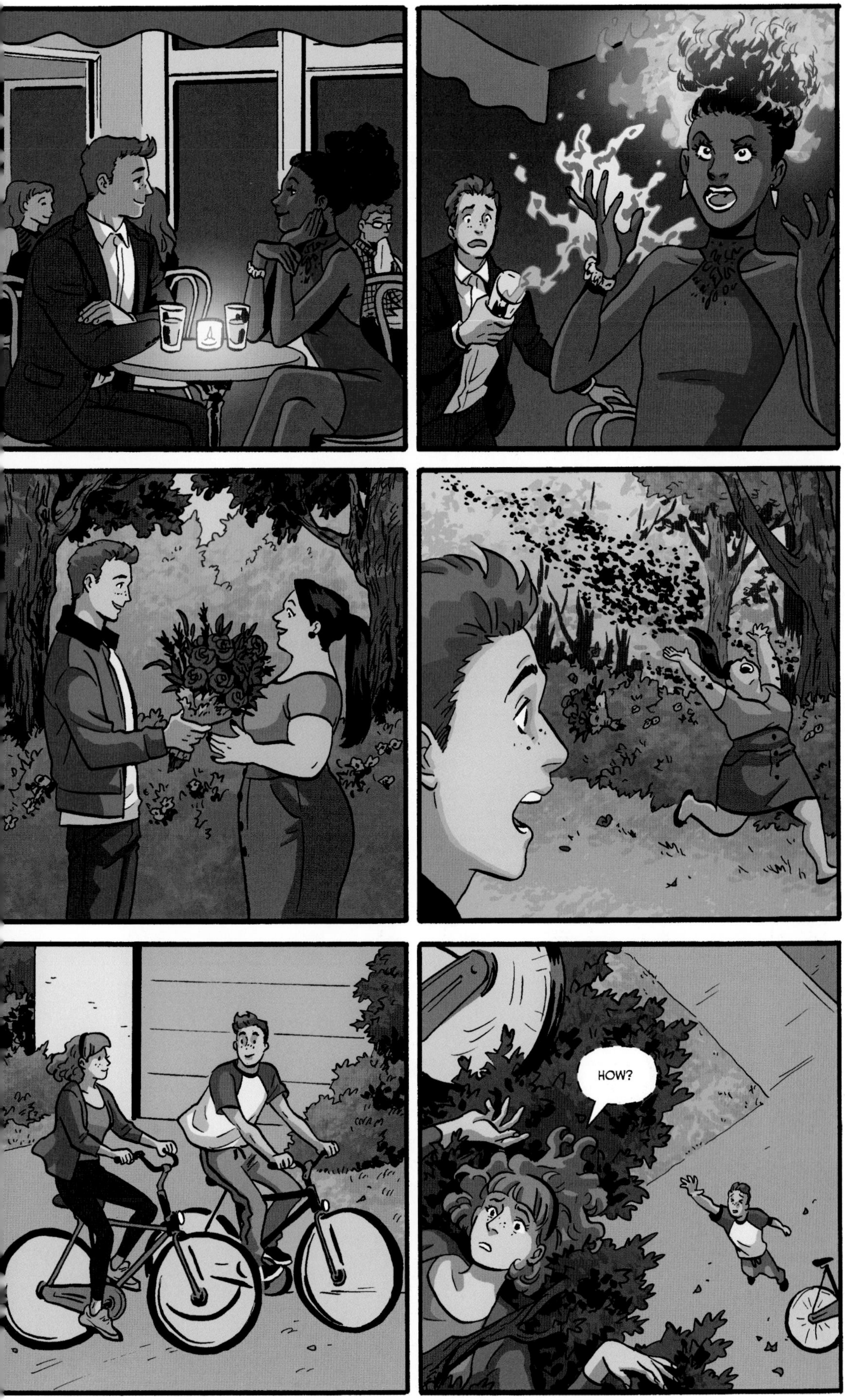
HOW?

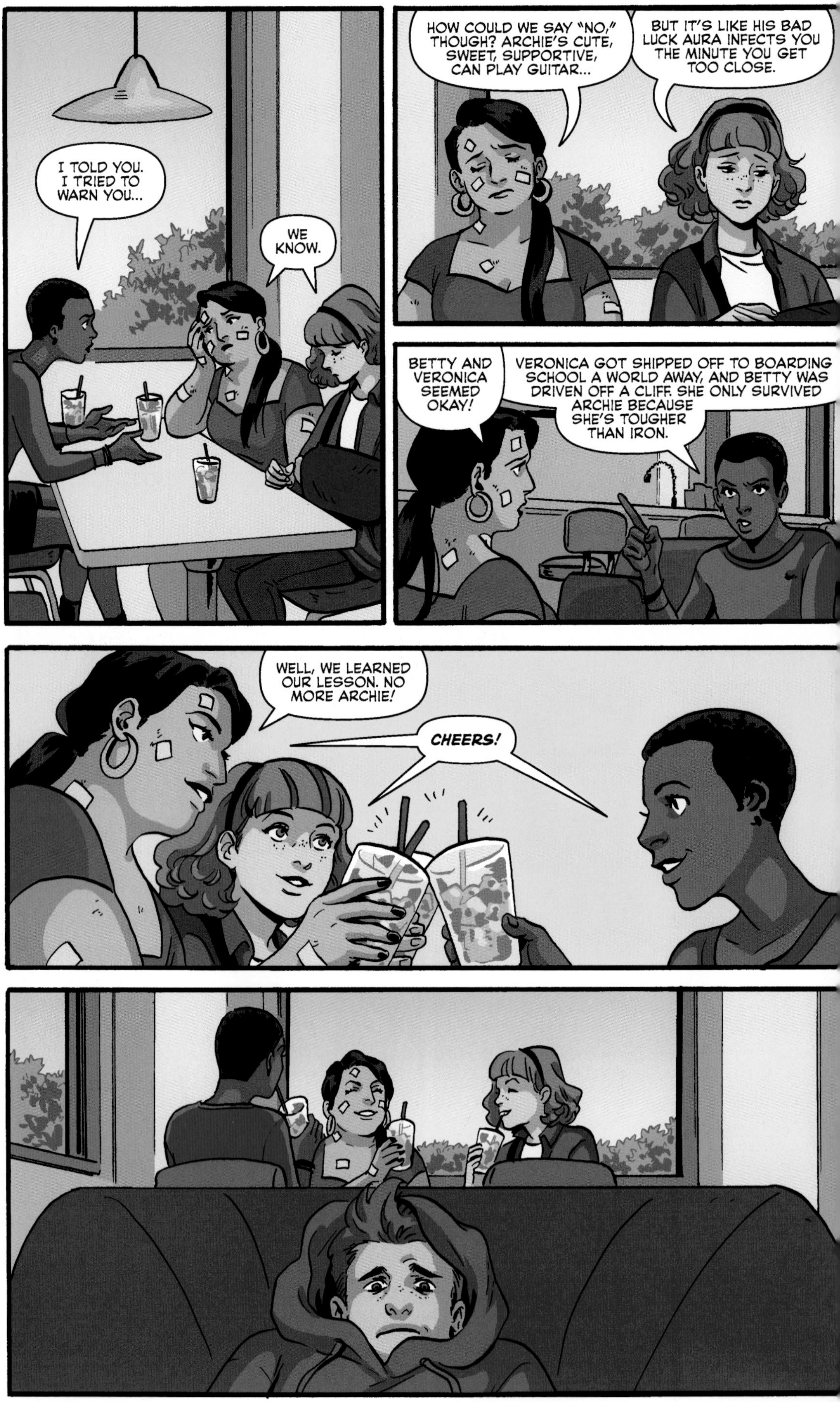

I TOLD YOU. I TRIED TO WARN YOU...
WE KNOW.
HOW COULD WE SAY "NO," THOUGH? ARCHIE'S CUTE, SWEET, SUPPORTIVE, CAN PLAY GUITAR...
BUT IT'S LIKE HIS BAD LUCK AURA INFECTS YOU THE MINUTE YOU GET TOO CLOSE.
BETTY AND VERONICA SEEMED OKAY!
VERONICA GOT SHIPPED OFF TO BOARDING SCHOOL A WORLD AWAY, AND BETTY WAS DRIVEN OFF A CLIFF. SHE ONLY SURVIVED ARCHIE BECAUSE SHE'S TOUGHER THAN IRON.
WELL, WE LEARNED OUR LESSON. NO MORE ARCHIE!
CHEERS!

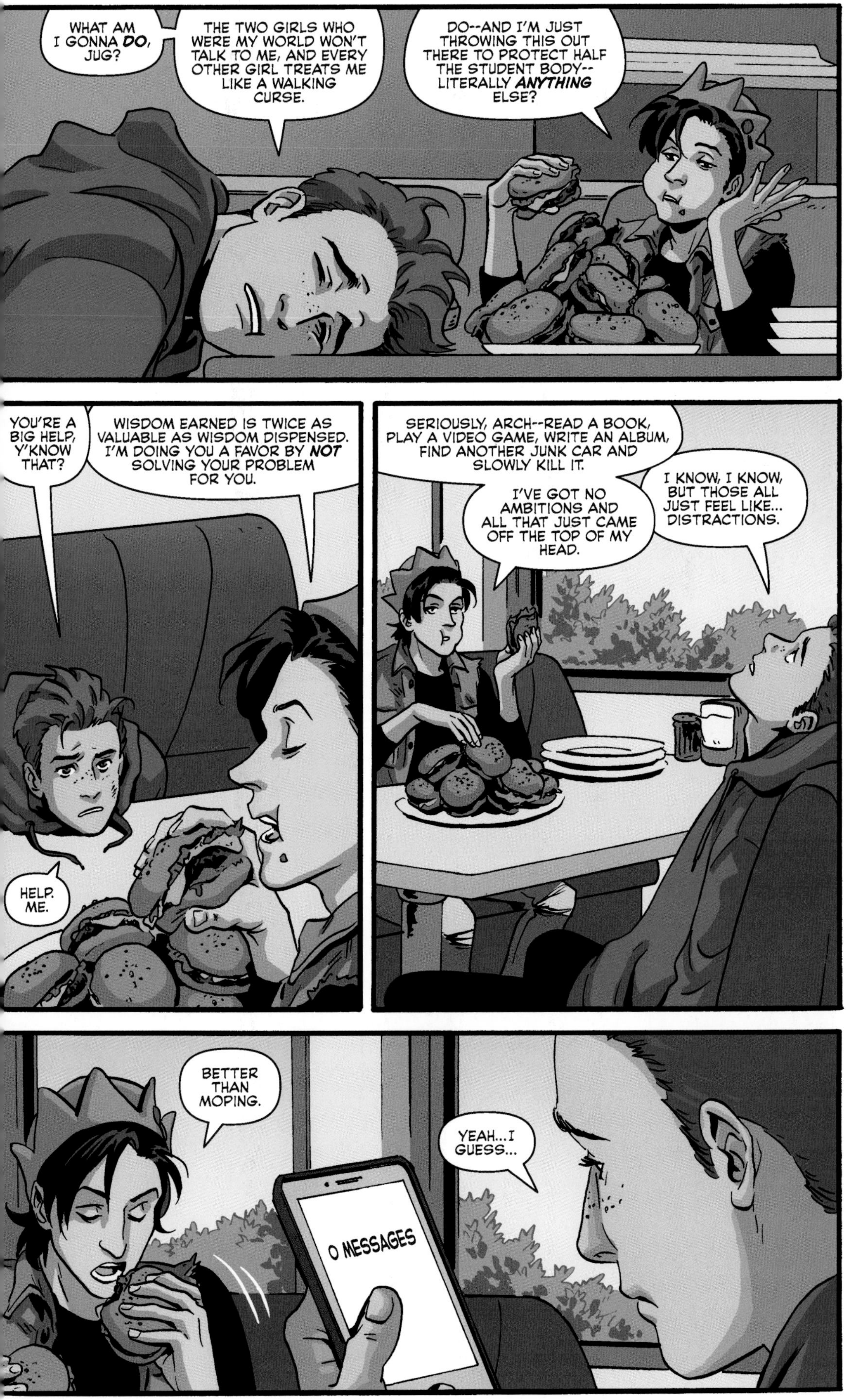
WHAT AM I GONNA *DO*, JUG?
THE TWO GIRLS WHO WERE MY WORLD WON'T TALK TO ME, AND EVERY OTHER GIRL TREATS ME LIKE A WALKING CURSE.
DO--AND I'M JUST THROWING THIS OUT THERE TO PROTECT HALF THE STUDENT BODY--LITERALLY *ANYTHING* ELSE?
YOU'RE A BIG HELP, Y'KNOW THAT?
WISDOM EARNED IS TWICE AS VALUABLE AS WISDOM DISPENSED. I'M DOING YOU A FAVOR BY *NOT* SOLVING YOUR PROBLEM FOR YOU.
HELP. ME.
SERIOUSLY, ARCH--READ A BOOK, PLAY A VIDEO GAME, WRITE AN ALBUM, FIND ANOTHER JUNK CAR AND SLOWLY KILL IT.
I'VE GOT NO AMBITIONS AND ALL THAT JUST CAME OFF THE TOP OF MY HEAD.
I KNOW, I KNOW, BUT THOSE ALL JUST FEEL LIKE... DISTRACTIONS.
BETTER THAN MOPING.
YEAH...I GUESS...
0 MESSAGES

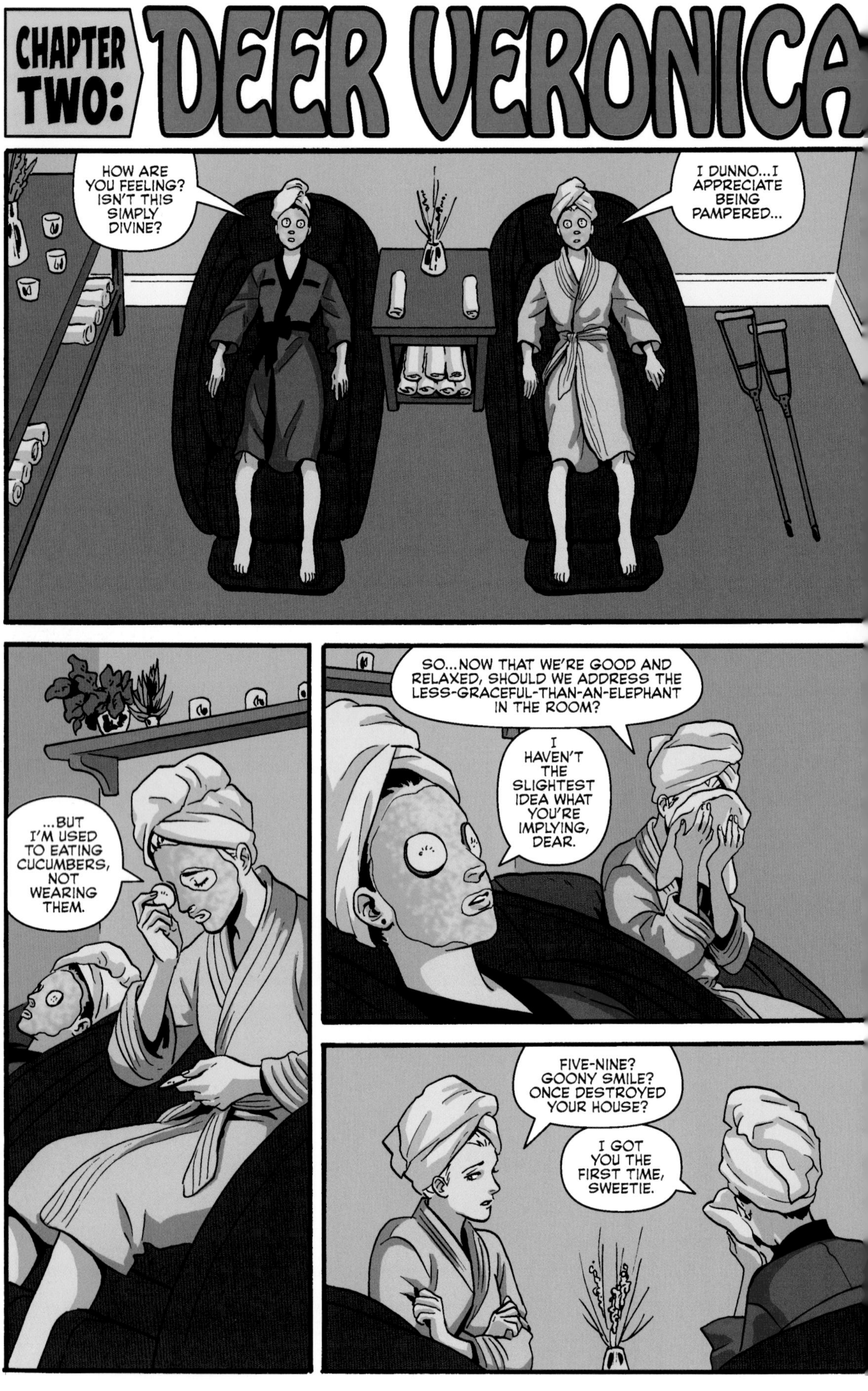
CHAPTER TWO:
DEER VERONICA
HOW ARE YOU FEELING? ISN'T THIS SIMPLY DIVINE?
I DUNNO...I APPRECIATE BEING PAMPERED...
...BUT I'M USED TO EATING CUCUMBERS, NOT WEARING THEM.
SO...NOW THAT WE'RE GOOD AND RELAXED, SHOULD WE ADDRESS THE LESS-GRACEFUL-THAN-AN-ELEPHANT IN THE ROOM?
I HAVEN'T THE SLIGHTEST IDEA WHAT YOU'RE IMPLYING, DEAR.
FIVE-NINE? GOONY SMILE? ONCE DESTROYED YOUR HOUSE?
I GOT YOU THE FIRST TIME, SWEETIE.

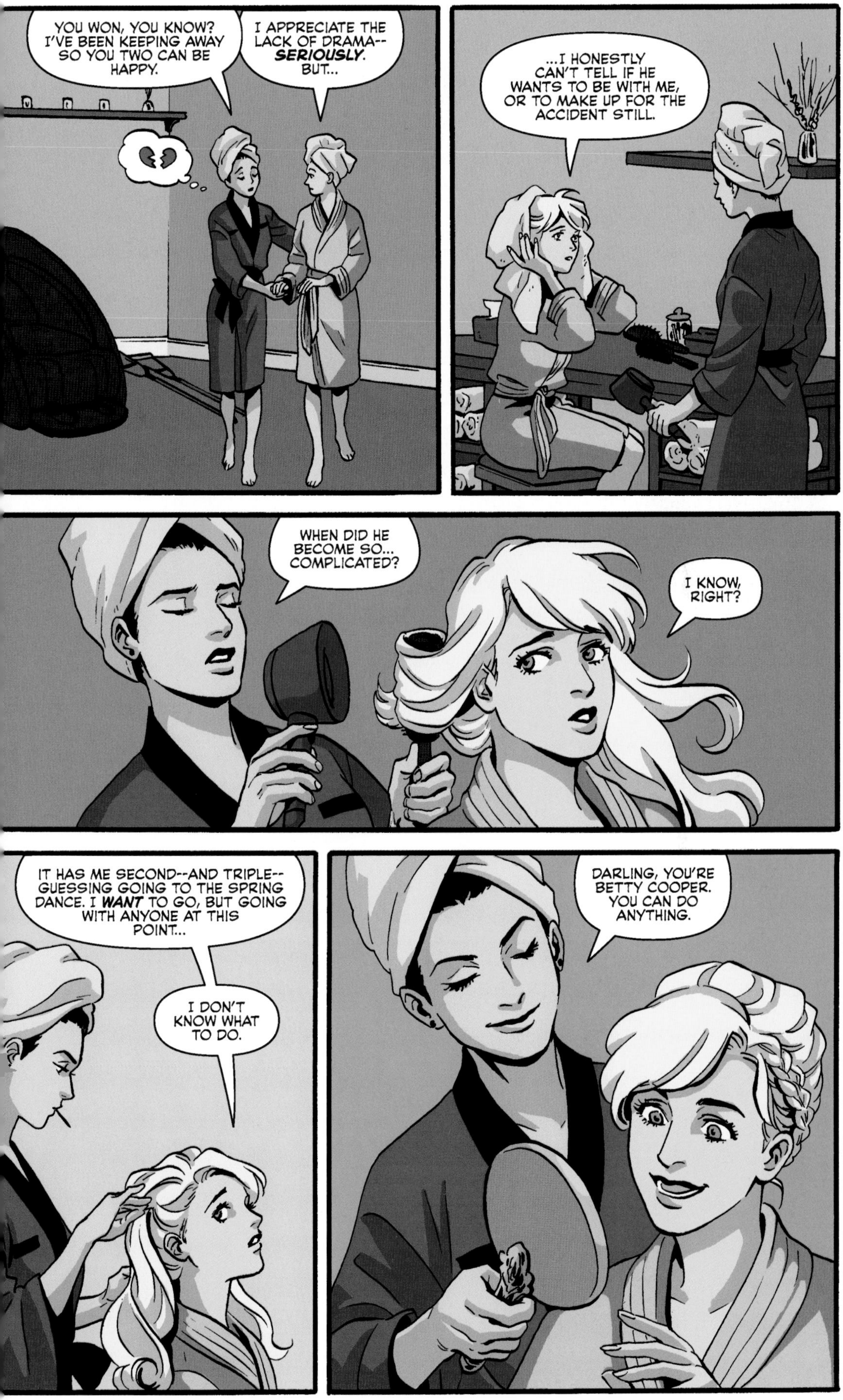
YOU WON, YOU KNOW? I'VE BEEN KEEPING AWAY SO YOU TWO CAN BE HAPPY.
I APPRECIATE THE LACK OF DRAMA-- ***SERIOUSLY***. BUT...
...I HONESTLY CAN'T TELL IF HE WANTS TO BE WITH ME, OR TO MAKE UP FOR THE ACCIDENT STILL.
WHEN DID HE BECOME SO... COMPLICATED?
I KNOW, RIGHT?
IT HAS ME SECOND--AND TRIPLE--GUESSING GOING TO THE SPRING DANCE. I ***WANT*** TO GO, BUT GOING WITH ANYONE AT THIS POINT...
I DON'T KNOW WHAT TO DO.
DARLING, YOU'RE BETTY COOPER. YOU CAN DO ANYTHING.

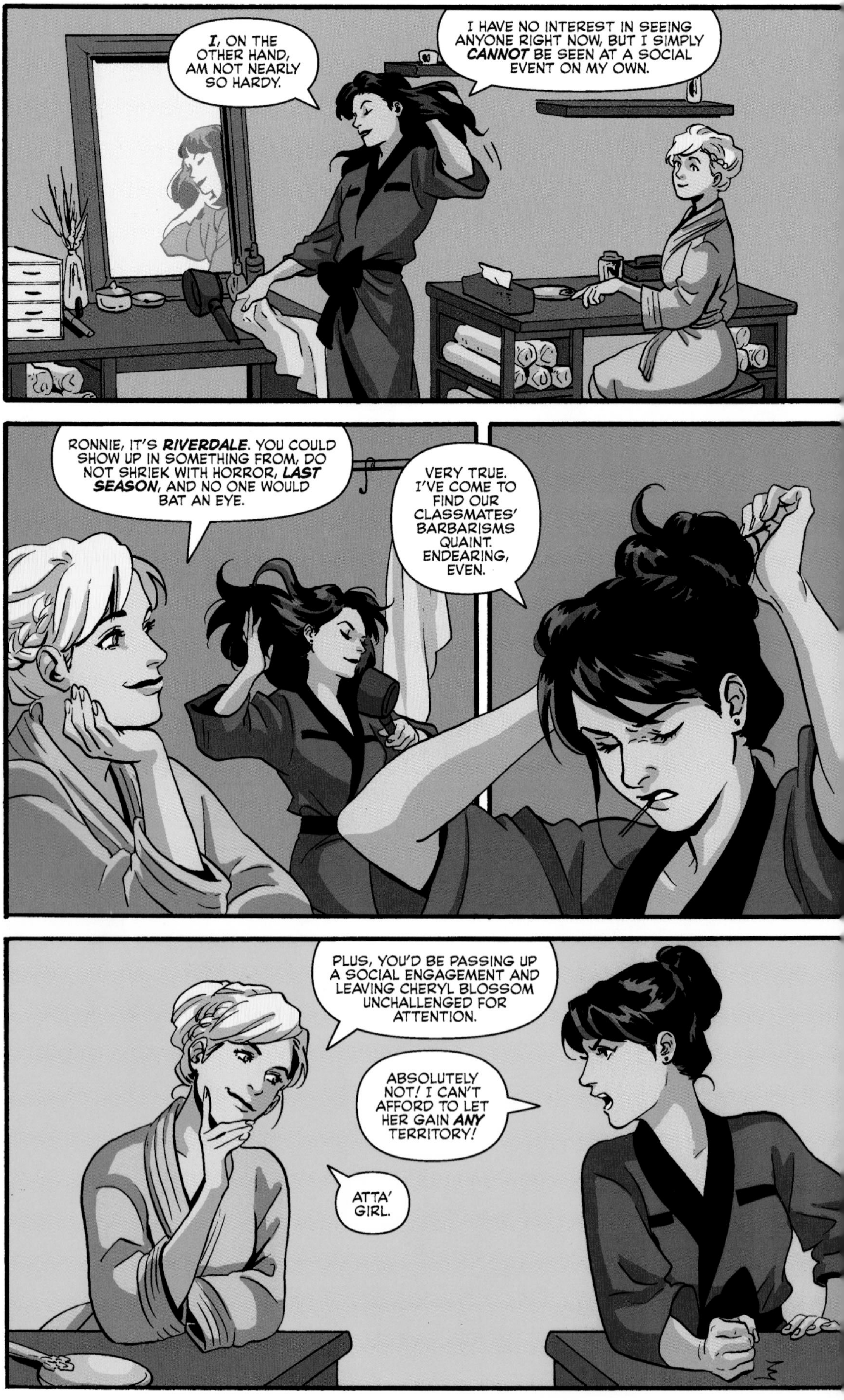

I, ON THE OTHER HAND, AM NOT NEARLY SO HARDY.
I HAVE NO INTEREST IN SEEING ANYONE RIGHT NOW, BUT I SIMPLY ***CANNOT*** BE SEEN AT A SOCIAL EVENT ON MY OWN.
RONNIE, IT'S ***RIVERDALE***. YOU COULD SHOW UP IN SOMETHING FROM, DO NOT SHRIEK WITH HORROR, ***LAST SEASON***, AND NO ONE WOULD BAT AN EYE.
VERY TRUE. I'VE COME TO FIND OUR CLASSMATES' BARBARISMS QUAINT. ENDEARING, EVEN.
PLUS, YOU'D BE PASSING UP A SOCIAL ENGAGEMENT AND LEAVING CHERYL BLOSSOM UNCHALLENGED FOR ATTENTION.
ABSOLUTELY NOT! I CAN'T AFFORD TO LET HER GAIN ***ANY*** TERRITORY!
ATTA' GIRL.

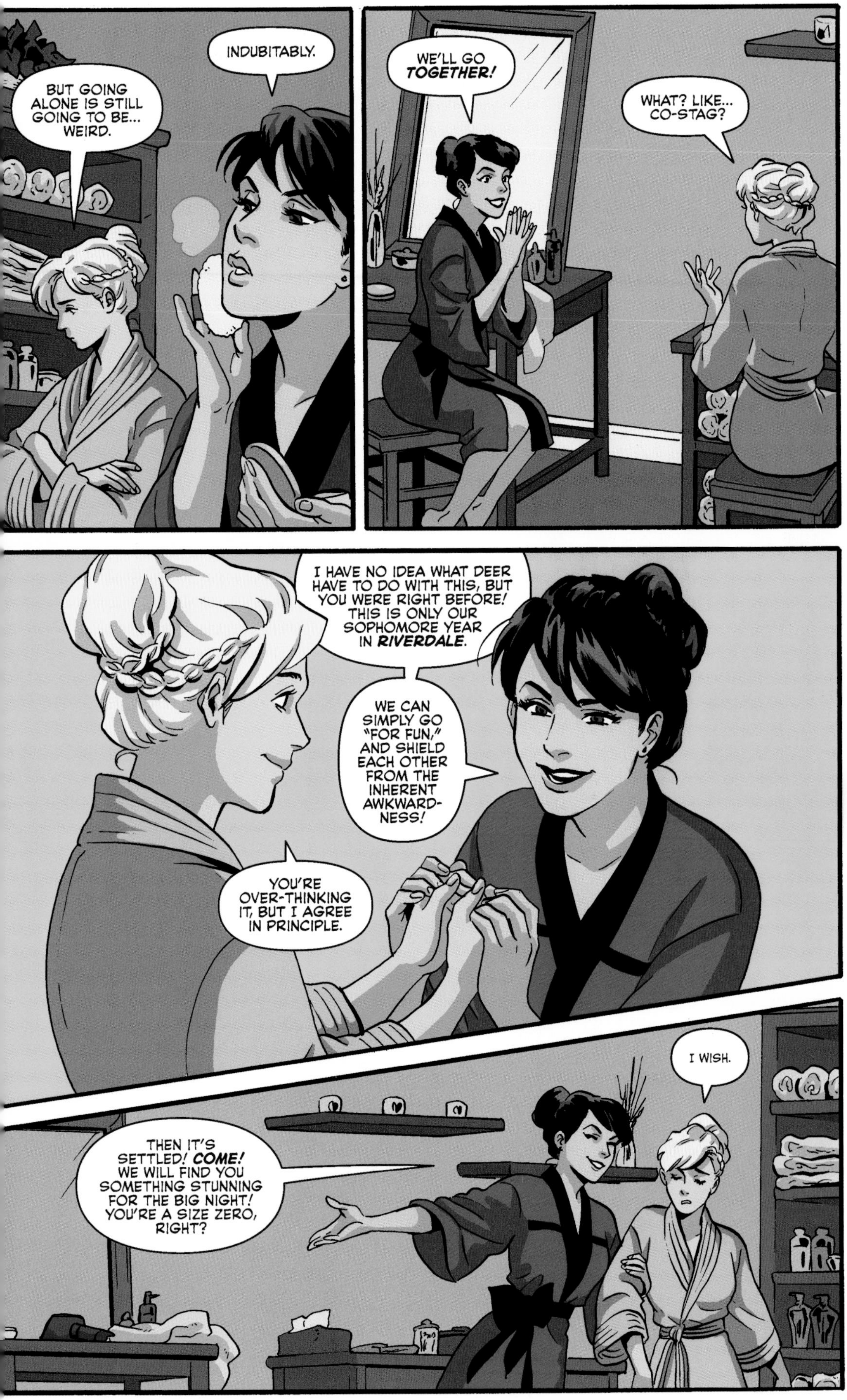
INDUBITABLY.
BUT GOING ALONE IS STILL GOING TO BE... WEIRD.
WE'LL GO *TOGETHER!*
WHAT? LIKE... CO-STAG?
I HAVE NO IDEA WHAT DEER HAVE TO DO WITH THIS, BUT YOU WERE RIGHT BEFORE! THIS IS ONLY OUR SOPHOMORE YEAR IN *RIVERDALE*.
WE CAN SIMPLY GO "FOR FUN," AND SHIELD EACH OTHER FROM THE INHERENT AWKWARD-NESS!
YOU'RE OVER-THINKING IT, BUT I AGREE IN PRINCIPLE.
THEN IT'S SETTLED! *COME!* WE WILL FIND YOU SOMETHING STUNNING FOR THE BIG NIGHT! YOU'RE A SIZE ZERO, RIGHT?
I WISH.

CHAPTER THREE: PLIGHT OF THE WEATHERBEE

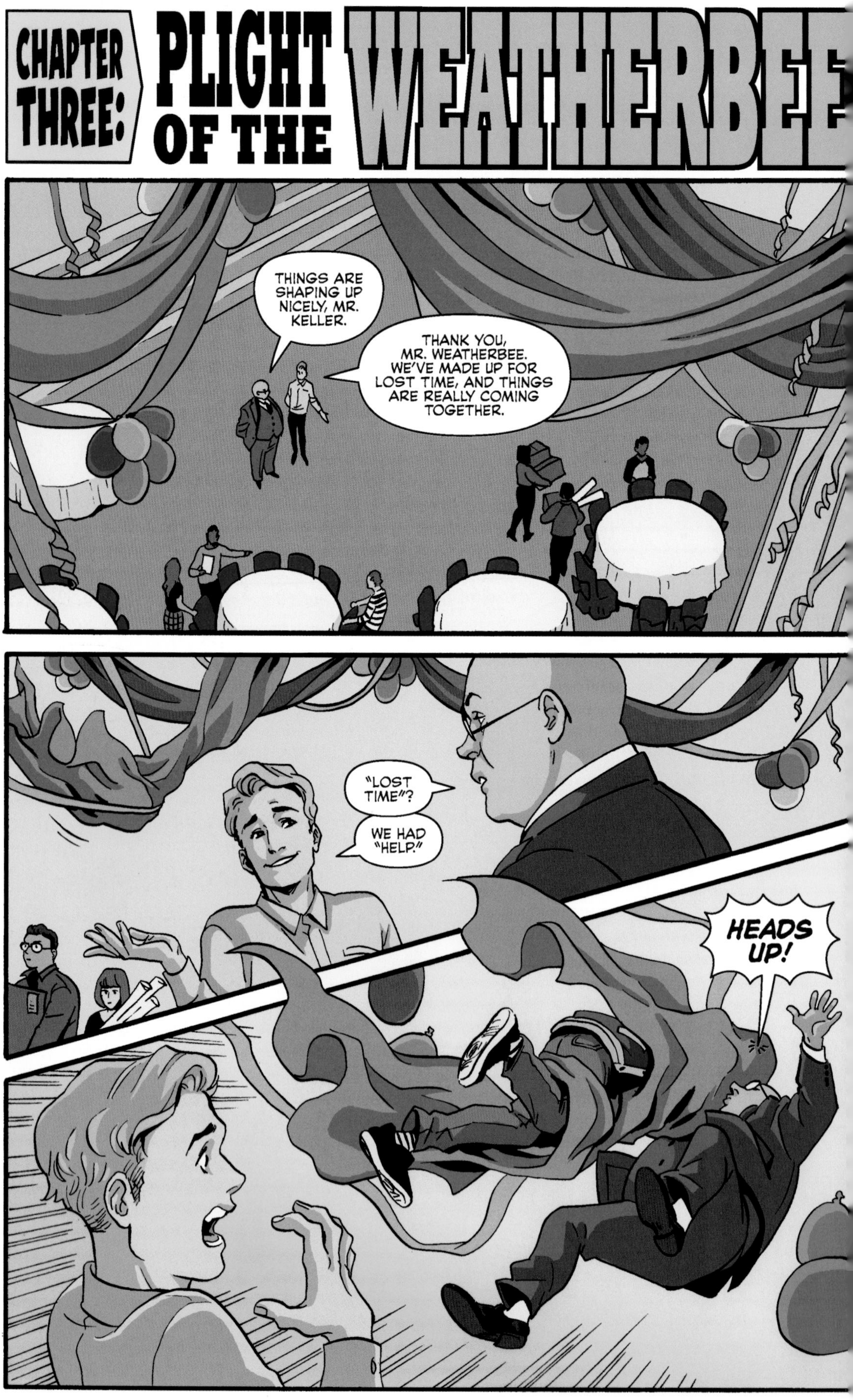
THINGS ARE SHAPING UP NICELY, MR. KELLER.
THANK YOU, MR. WEATHERBEE. WE'VE MADE UP FOR LOST TIME, AND THINGS ARE REALLY COMING TOGETHER.
"LOST TIME"?
WE HAD "HELP."
HEADS UP!

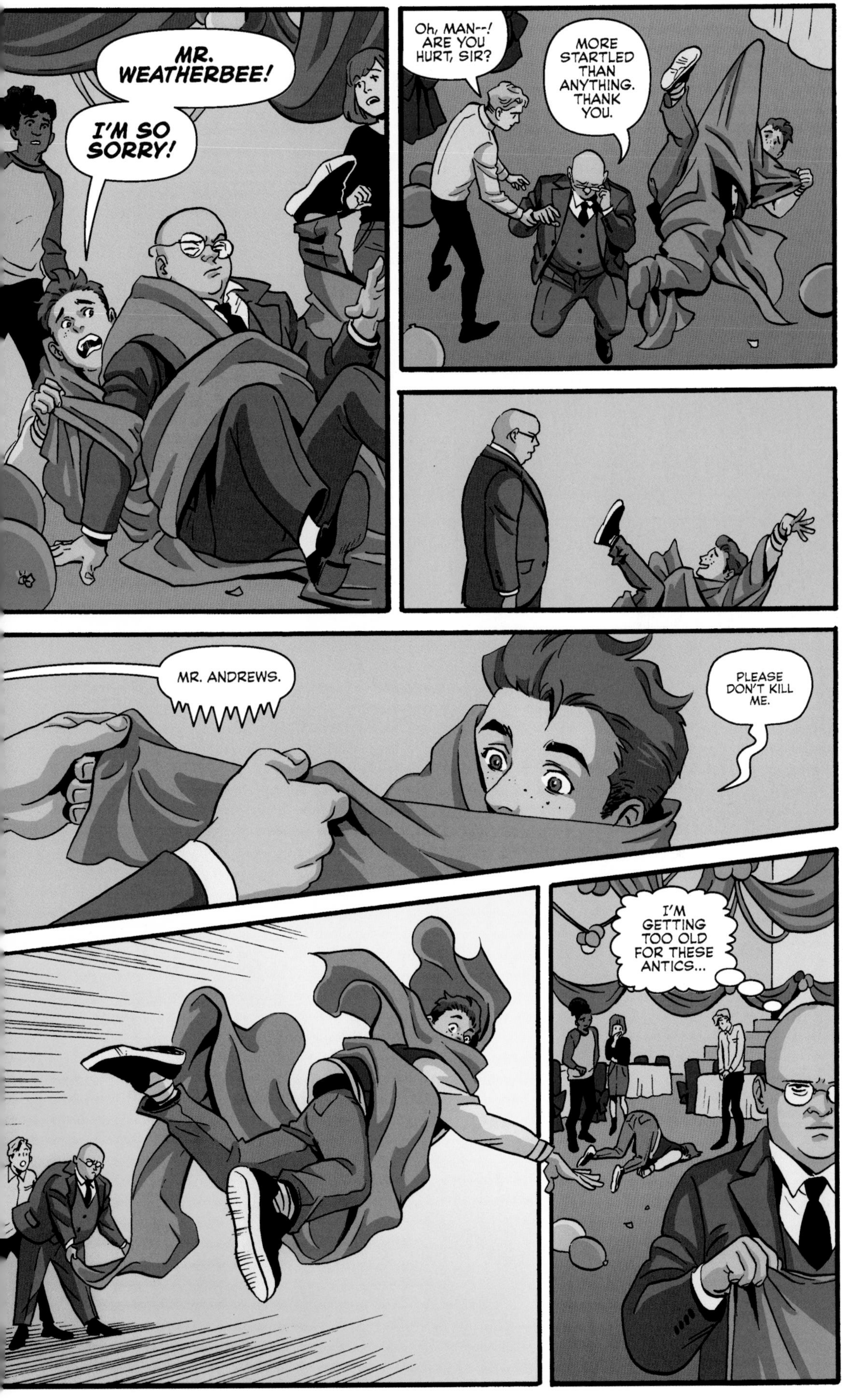
MR. WEATHERBEE!
I'M SO SORRY!
Oh, MAN--! ARE YOU HURT, SIR?
MORE STARTLED THAN ANYTHING. THANK YOU.
MR. ANDREWS.
PLEASE DON'T KILL ME.
I'M GETTING TOO OLD FOR THESE ANTICS...

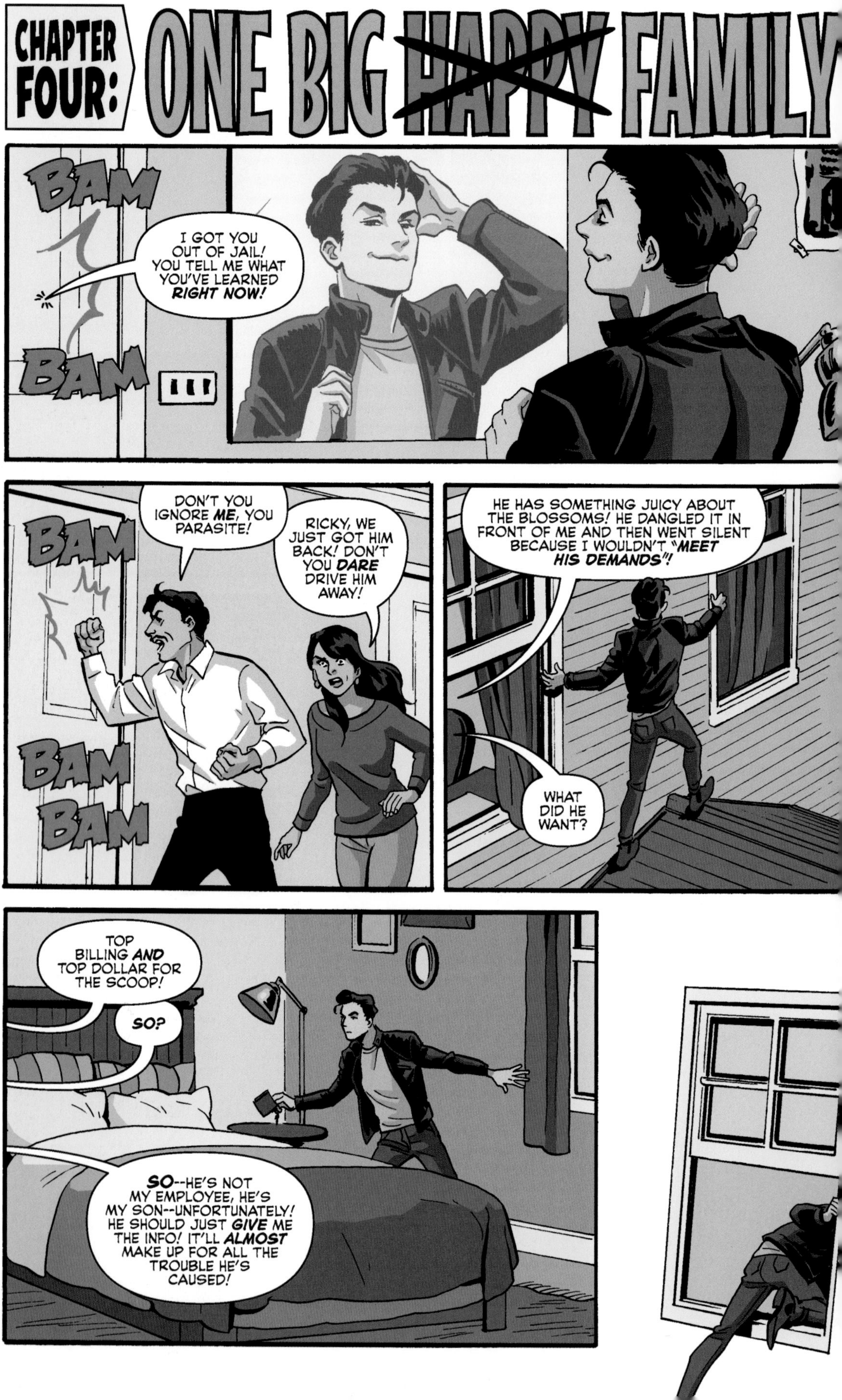
CHAPTER FOUR: ONE BIG HAPPY FAMILY
BAM
I GOT YOU OUT OF JAIL! YOU TELL ME WHAT YOU'VE LEARNED RIGHT NOW!
BAM
BAM
DON'T YOU IGNORE ME, YOU PARASITE!
RICKY, WE JUST GOT HIM BACK! DON'T YOU DARE DRIVE HIM AWAY!
BAM
BAM
HE HAS SOMETHING JUICY ABOUT THE BLOSSOMS! HE DANGLED IT IN FRONT OF ME AND THEN WENT SILENT BECAUSE I WOULDN'T "MEET HIS DEMANDS"!
WHAT DID HE WANT?
TOP BILLING AND TOP DOLLAR FOR THE SCOOP!
SO?
SO--HE'S NOT MY EMPLOYEE, HE'S MY SON--UNFORTUNATELY! HE SHOULD JUST GIVE ME THE INFO! IT'LL ALMOST MAKE UP FOR ALL THE TROUBLE HE'S CAUSED!

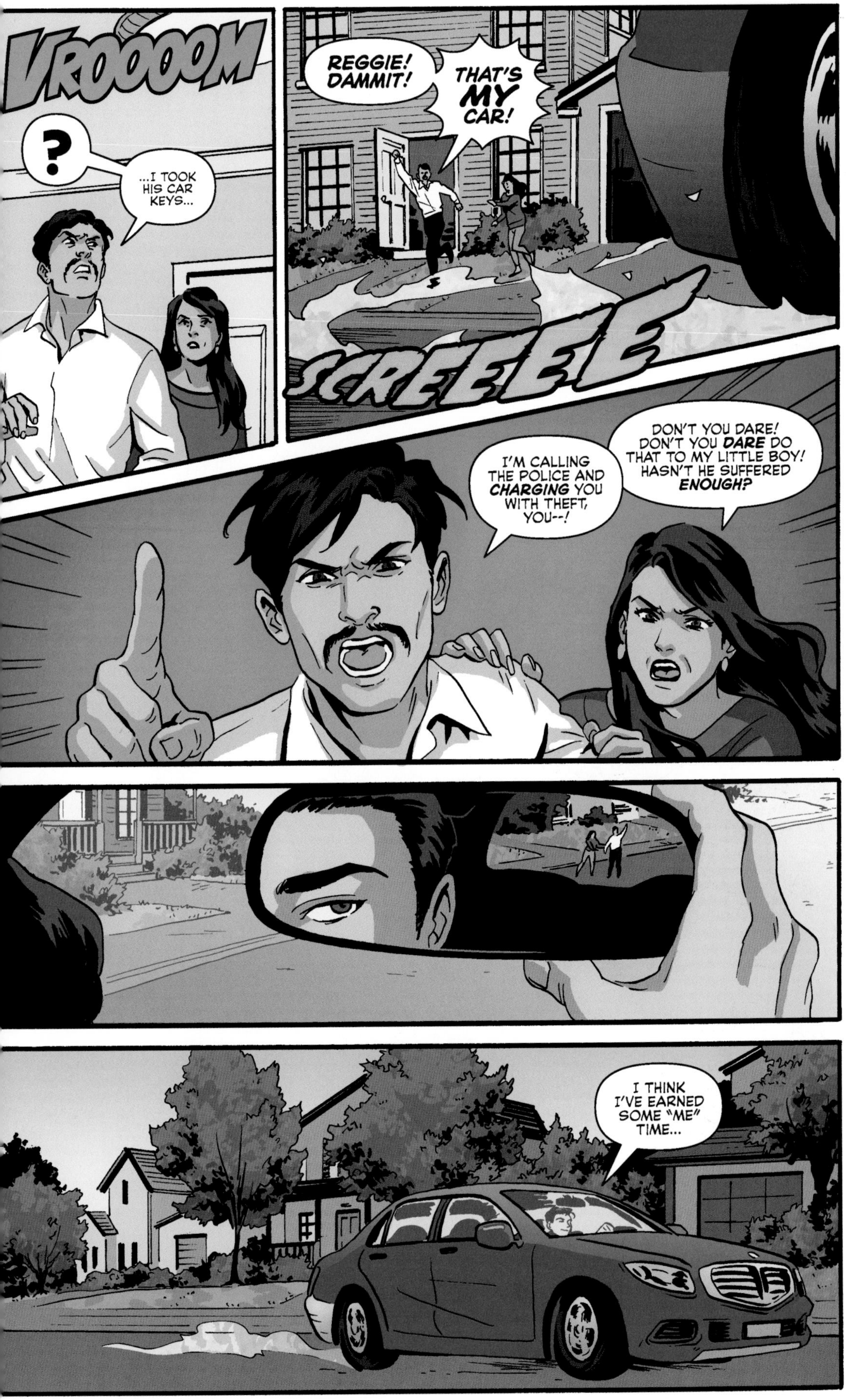
VROOOOM
?
...I TOOK HIS CAR KEYS...
REGGIE! DAMMIT!
THAT'S MY CAR!
SCREEEEE
I'M CALLING THE POLICE AND CHARGING YOU WITH THEFT, YOU--!
DON'T YOU DARE! DON'T YOU DARE DO THAT TO MY LITTLE BOY! HASN'T HE SUFFERED ENOUGH?
I THINK I'VE EARNED SOME "ME" TIME...

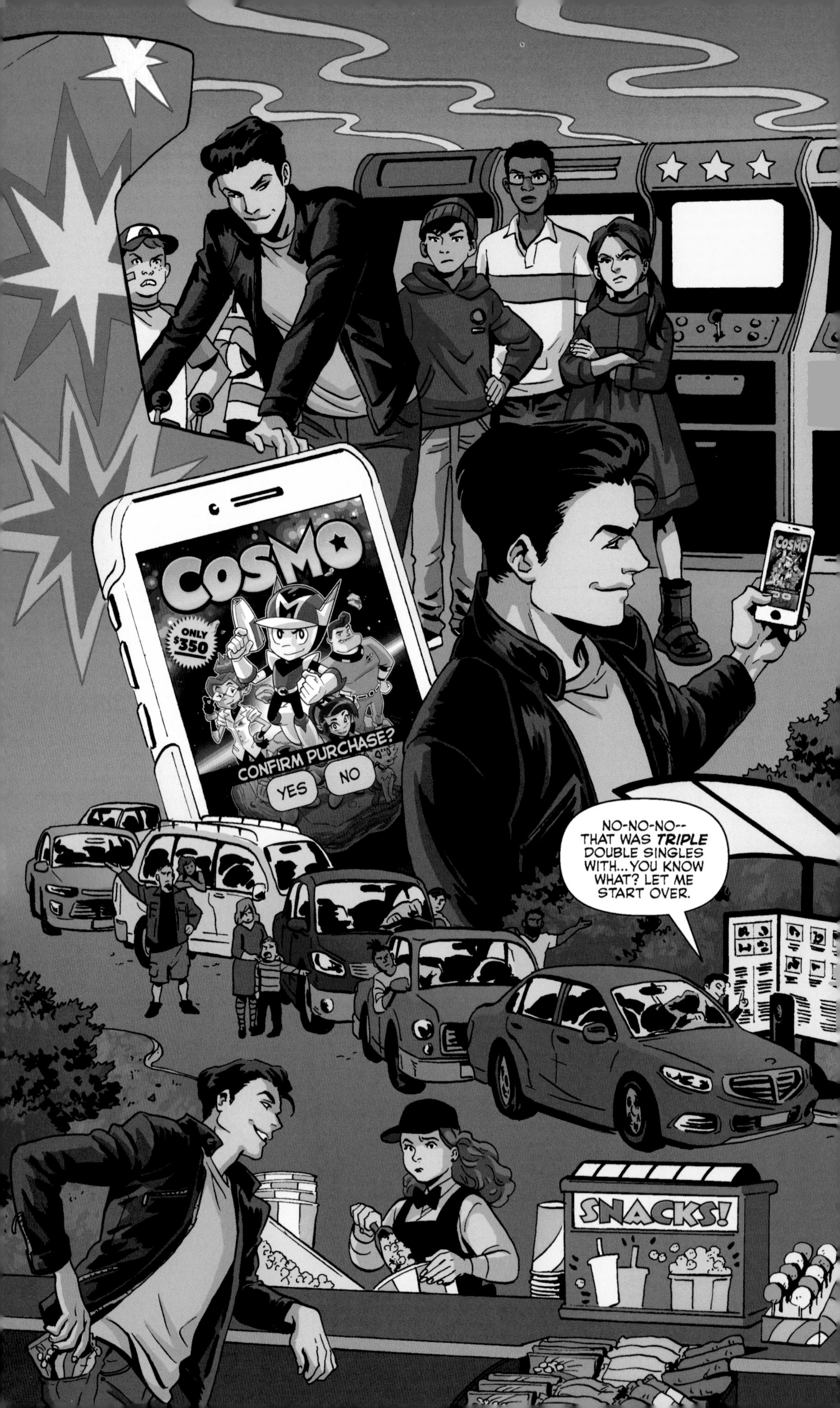
COSMO
ONLY $350
CONFIRM PURCHASE?
YES
NO
NO-NO-NO-- THAT WAS TRIPLE DOUBLE SINGLES WITH...YOU KNOW WHAT? LET ME START OVER.
SNACKS!

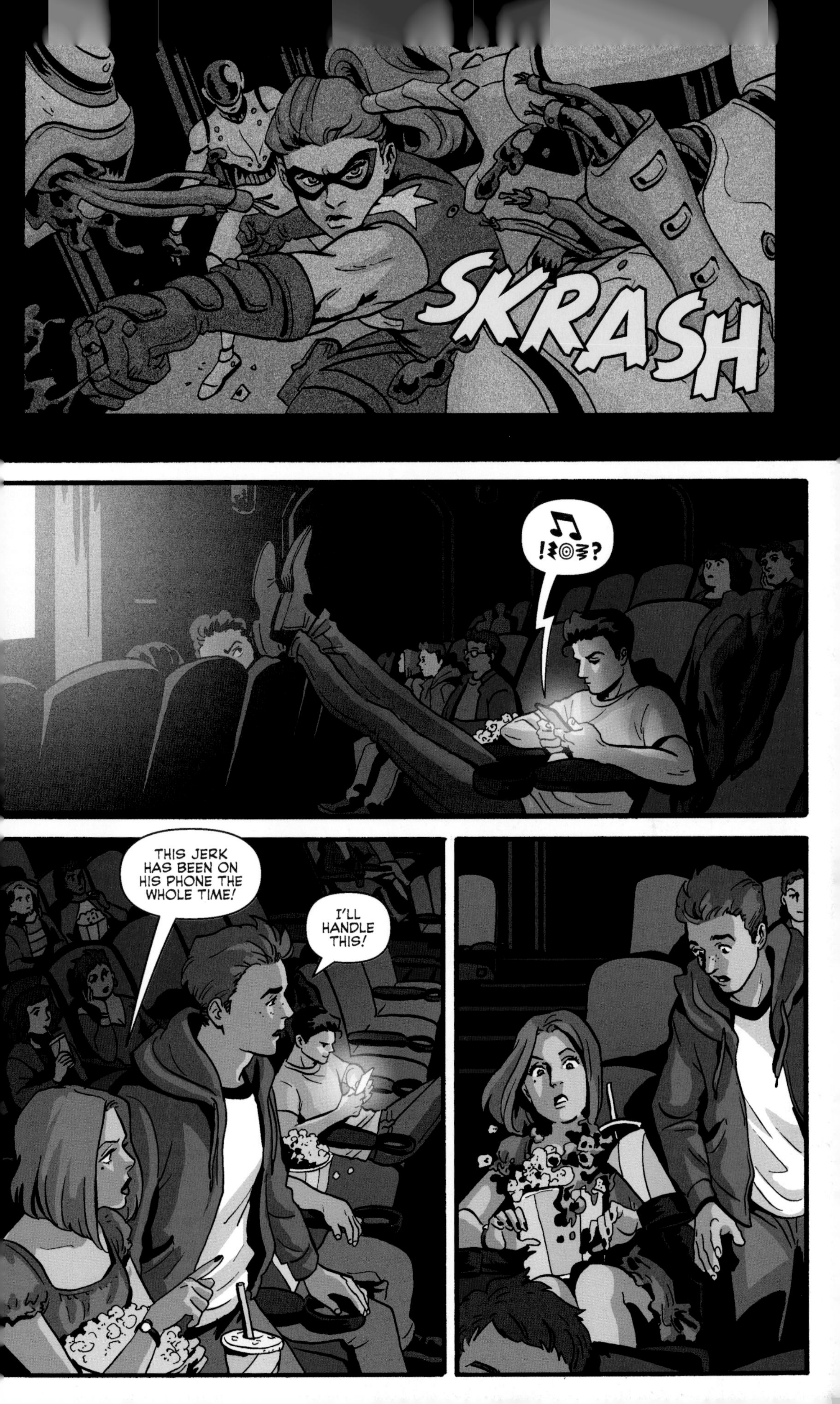
SKRASH
THIS JERK HAS BEEN ON HIS PHONE THE WHOLE TIME!
I'LL HANDLE THIS!

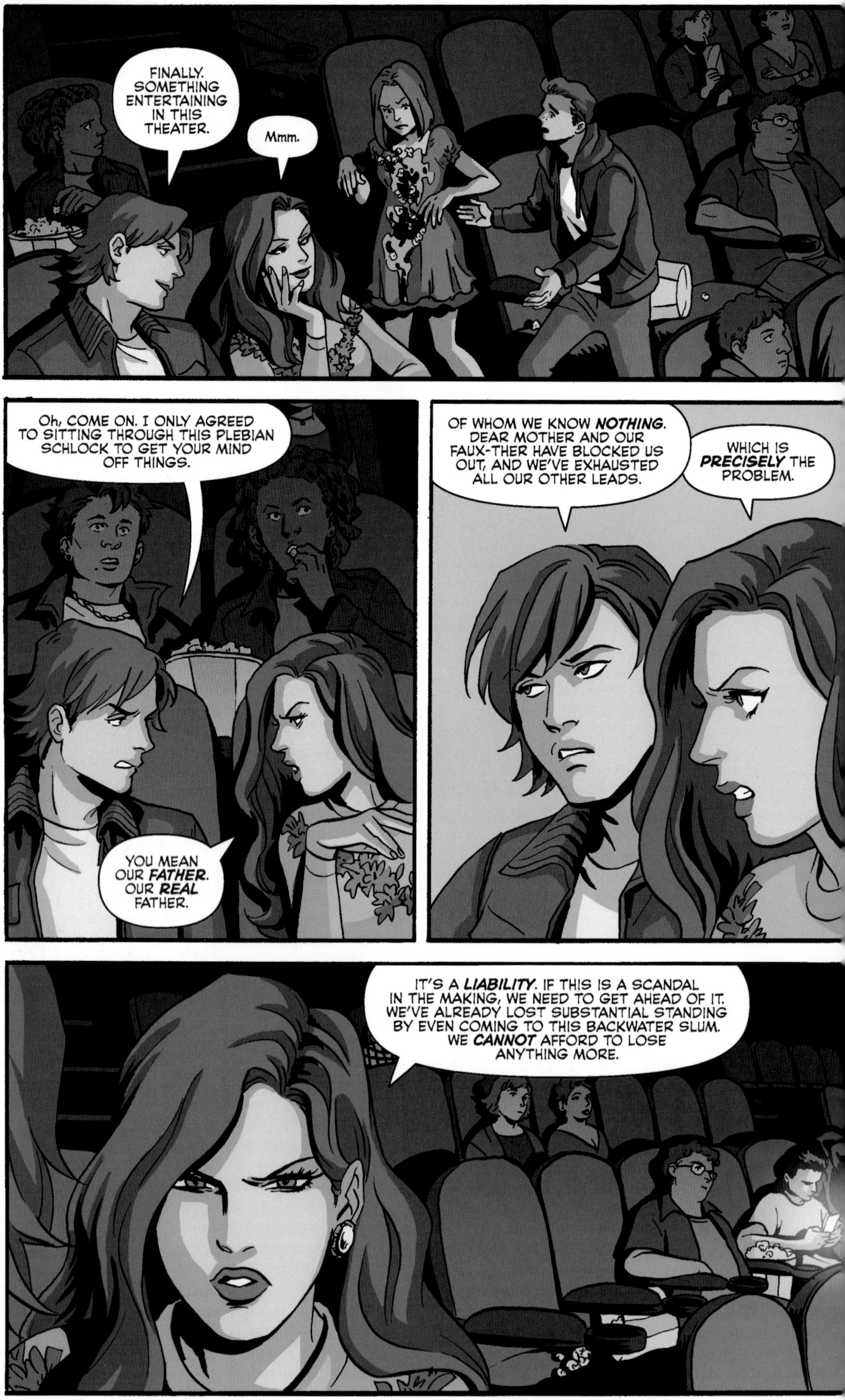
FINALLY. SOMETHING ENTERTAINING IN THIS THEATER.
Mmm.
Oh, COME ON. I ONLY AGREED TO SITTING THROUGH THIS PLEBIAN SCHLOCK TO GET YOUR MIND OFF THINGS.
YOU MEAN OUR **FATHER**. OUR **REAL** FATHER.
OF WHOM WE KNOW **NOTHING**. DEAR MOTHER AND OUR FAUX-THER HAVE BLOCKED US OUT, AND WE'VE EXHAUSTED ALL OUR OTHER LEADS.
WHICH IS **PRECISELY** THE PROBLEM.
IT'S A **LIABILITY**. IF THIS IS A SCANDAL IN THE MAKING, WE NEED TO GET AHEAD OF IT. WE'VE ALREADY LOST SUBSTANTIAL STANDING BY EVEN COMING TO THIS BACKWATER SLUM. WE **CANNOT** AFFORD TO LOSE ANYTHING MORE.

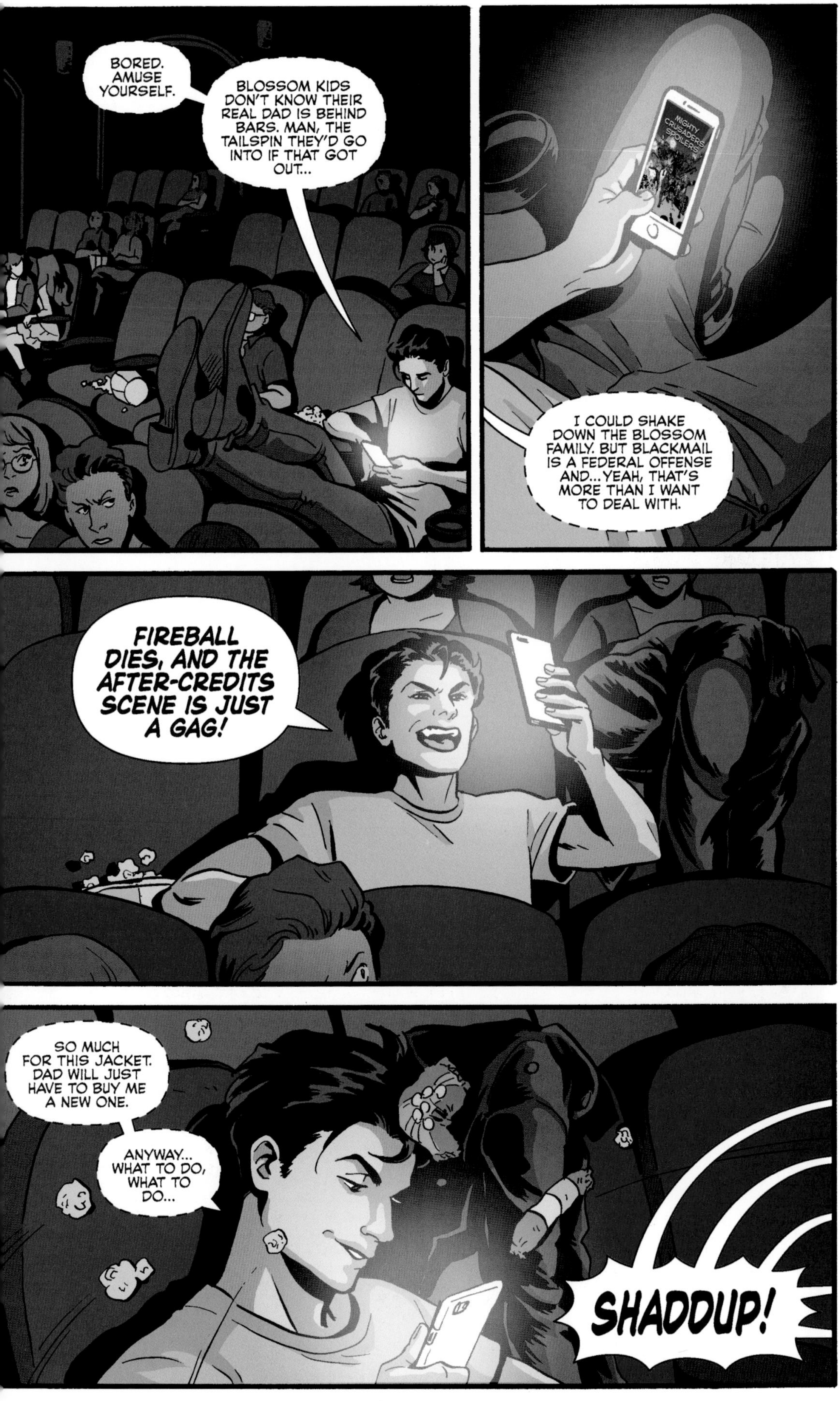
BORED. AMUSE YOURSELF.
BLOSSOM KIDS DON'T KNOW THEIR REAL DAD IS BEHIND BARS. MAN, THE TAILSPIN THEY'D GO INTO IF THAT GOT OUT...
MIGHTY CRUSADERS SPOILERS
I COULD SHAKE DOWN THE BLOSSOM FAMILY. BUT BLACKMAIL IS A FEDERAL OFFENSE AND...YEAH, THAT'S MORE THAN I WANT TO DEAL WITH.
FIREBALL DIES, AND THE AFTER-CREDITS SCENE IS JUST A GAG!
SO MUCH FOR THIS JACKET. DAD WILL JUST HAVE TO BUY ME A NEW ONE.
ANYWAY... WHAT TO DO, WHAT TO DO...
SHADDUP!

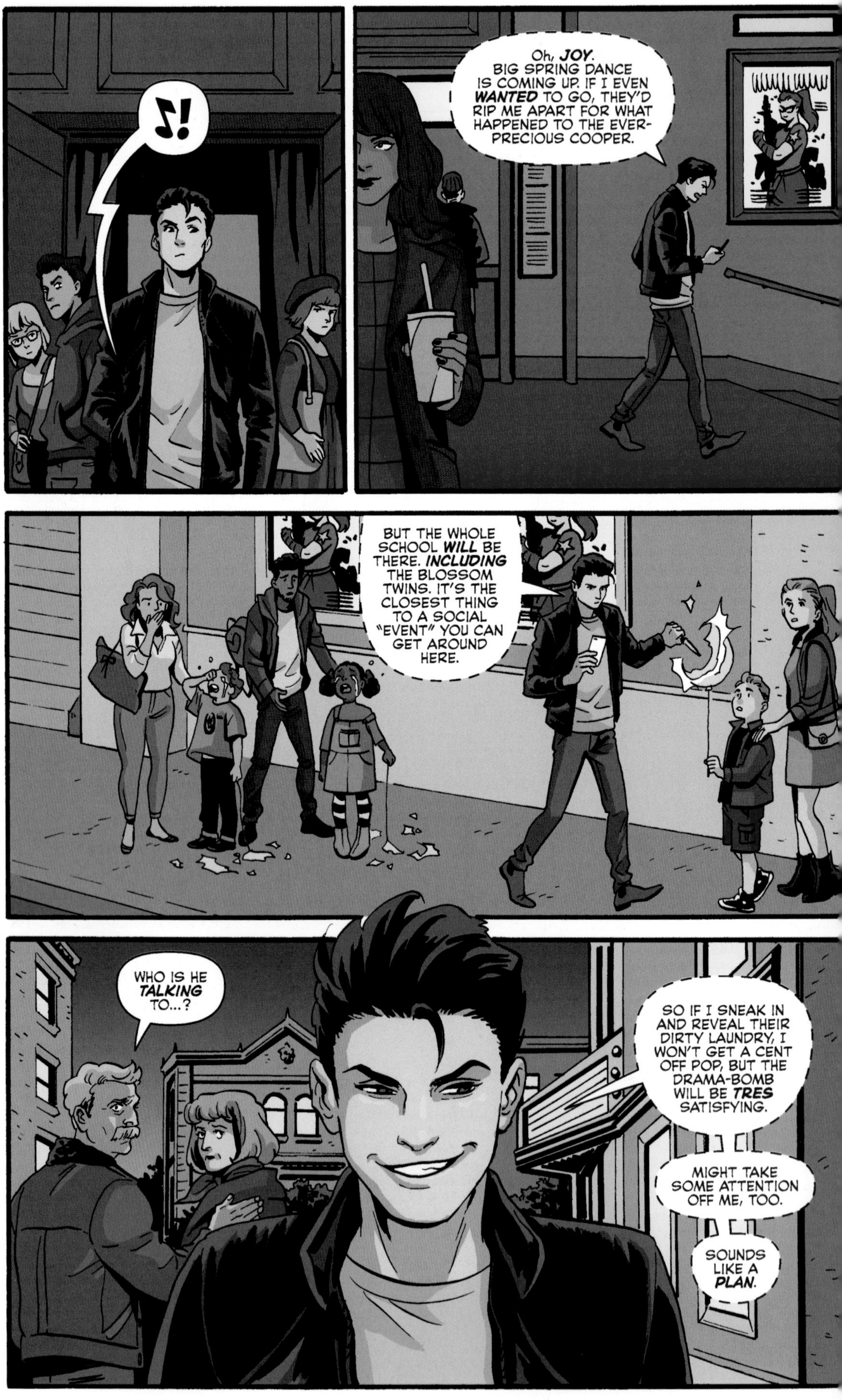
♪!
Oh, JOY. BIG SPRING DANCE IS COMING UP. IF I EVEN WANTED TO GO, THEY'D RIP ME APART FOR WHAT HAPPENED TO THE EVER-PRECIOUS COOPER.
BUT THE WHOLE SCHOOL WILL BE THERE. INCLUDING THE BLOSSOM TWINS. IT'S THE CLOSEST THING TO A SOCIAL "EVENT" YOU CAN GET AROUND HERE.
WHO IS HE TALKING TO...?
SO IF I SNEAK IN AND REVEAL THEIR DIRTY LAUNDRY, I WON'T GET A CENT OFF POP, BUT THE DRAMA-BOMB WILL BE TRES SATISFYING.
MIGHT TAKE SOME ATTENTION OFF ME, TOO.
SOUNDS LIKE A PLAN.

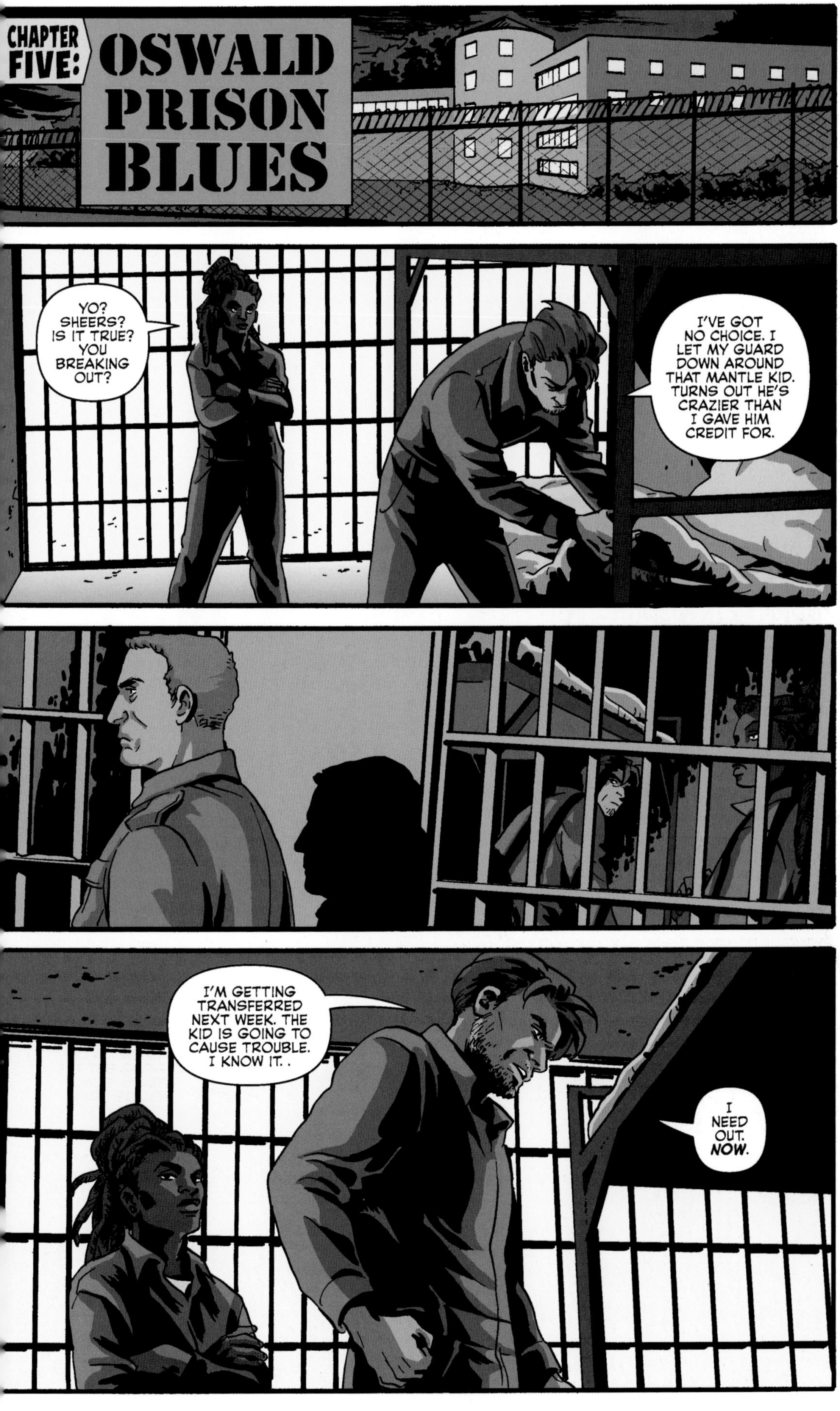

CHAPTER FIVE: OSWALD PRISON BLUES
YO? SHEERS? IS IT TRUE? YOU BREAKING OUT?
I'VE GOT NO CHOICE. I LET MY GUARD DOWN AROUND THAT MANTLE KID. TURNS OUT HE'S CRAZIER THAN I GAVE HIM CREDIT FOR.
I'M GETTING TRANSFERRED NEXT WEEK. THE KID IS GOING TO CAUSE TROUBLE. I KNOW IT. .
I NEED OUT. NOW.

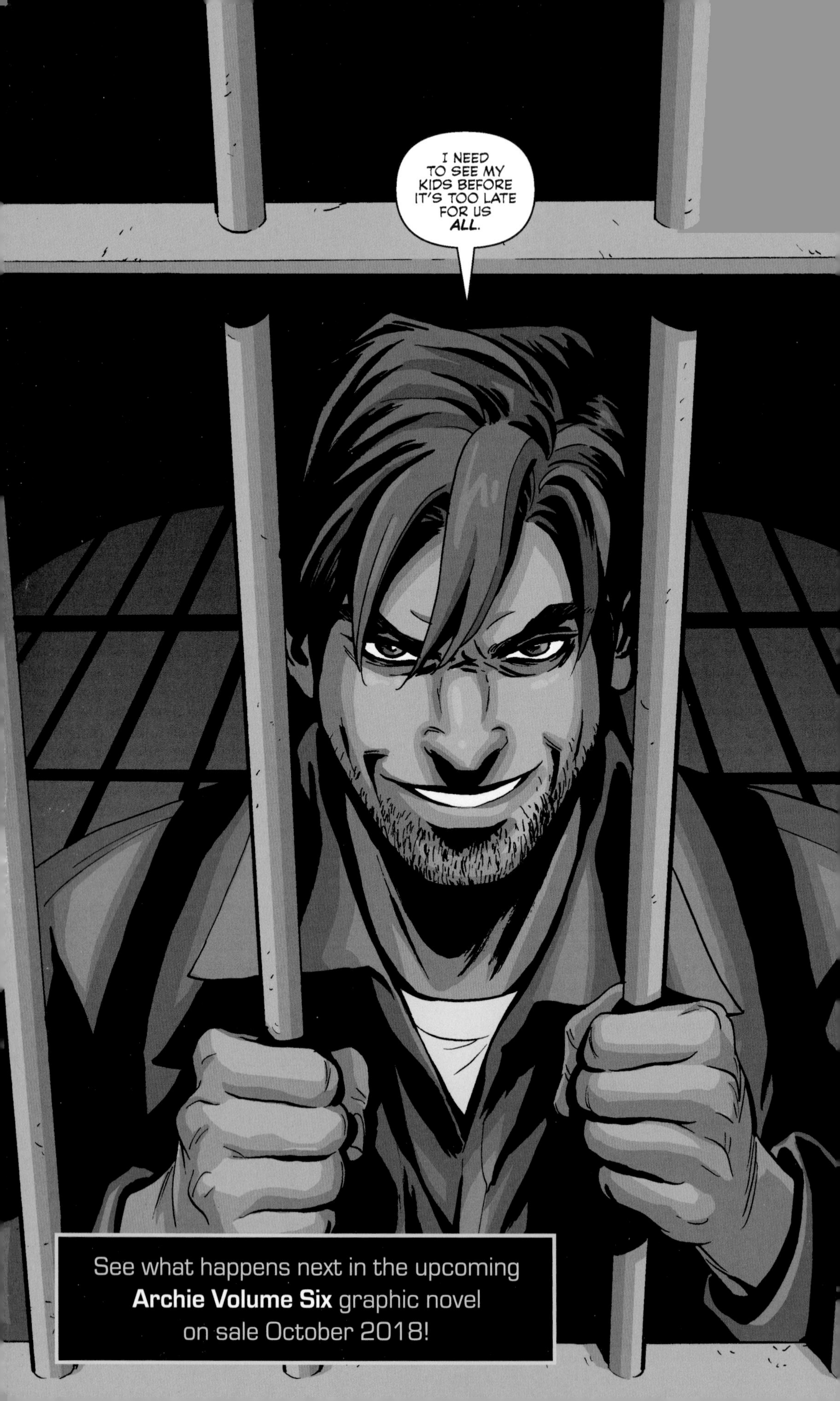

I NEED TO SEE MY KIDS BEFORE IT'S TOO LATE FOR US *ALL*.
See what happens next in the upcoming **Archie Volume Six** graphic novel on sale October 2018!